Municipal disorder policing

MUNICIPAL DISORDER POLICING

Dealing with annoyances in public places

Teun Eikenaar

eleven
international publishing

Published, sold and distributed by Eleven International Publishing
P.O. Box 85576
2508 CG The Hague
The Netherlands
Tel.: +31 70 33 070 33
Fax: +31 70 33 070 30
e-mail: sales@elevenpub.nl
www.elevenpub.com

Sold and distributed in USA and Canada
International Specialized Book Services
920 NE 58th Avenue, Suite 300
Portland, OR 97213-3786, USA
Tel: 1-800-944-6190 (toll-free)
Fax: +1-503-280-8832
orders@isbs.com
www.isbs.com

Eleven International Publishing is an imprint of Boom uitgevers Den Haag.

ISBN 978-94-6236-786-9
ISBN 978-94-6274-759-3 (E-book)

Printed in The Netherlands

FOREWORD

This study is about *municipal disorder policing*, a relatively new form of surveillance and law enforcement by Dutch local government officers. As 'non-police policing providers' these officers fulfil vital policing tasks while not being part of the police itself. They share in policing responsibilities.

Such sharing of responsibilities raises questions, for instance about how and why these new officers evolved, who decides on their work, and what kind of work they do. By addressing these questions, this book not only sheds light on the issues of a newly evolving policing occupation, but also on the way in which local governments try to deal with issues of public safety and citizens' concerns about disorder.

Getting involved with municipal disorder policing

In the spring of 2012 I was first introduced to the subject of this study when I was asked to undertake a two-year research project of municipal disorder policing in six large Dutch cities. It was to be my first experience with the study of police and policing.

During this first experience being largely unacquainted with police and police work appeared to be something of an asset. It gave me the opportunity to study this occupation with an open mind, to be amazed by a new professional world and to approach these municipal officers as a new occupational group of which I was hitherto largely unaware. This first two-year timespan resulted in a first publication, in Dutch: *Van Stadswacht naar nieuwe gemeentepolitie?* ('From city warden to new municipal police?').

Yet, it was not until the second part of this research that the subject of municipal disorder policing grew on me. In 2015 and 2016 I was given the opportunity to extend the first publication into a dissertation. I was able to study municipal disorder policing in depth during this second half of the research, to develop a more thorough understanding of the various ideas, meanings and discourses that shape the policies and practices of this occupation.

This meant I had to find my way into a large body of texts yet unknown to me. I had to re-compose a theoretical framework with which to approach previous findings and with which to collect new material. Moreover, a large part of the initial publication did not fit with this new approach and new research questions *and* I had to invest a considerable amount of time in re-entering the field and collecting new material. Writing itself sometimes felt like wrestling with an amorphous body of findings, interview material, notes, theoretical reflections and preliminary conclusions. At times I had the idea that I managed to direct this monster towards a proper dissertation, with a clear mark of my own perspective. At other times, it felt the monster was taking over, and it would take several days before I could force myself back on top of it.

Limitations

My particular perspective on municipal disorder policing implies several aspects are not addressed here. Some of these are mentioned briefly in chapter 1, but I also name a few here. Hence, my research is limited, both in scope and time frame and with this book I do not pretend to present a definite image of this profession, but merely an impression that is limited to a specific time span and defined by my own academic point of view.

First of all, this is not an evaluative research. Efficiency and effectivity of municipal disorder policing are not taken into account. Secondly, some readers may be interested in my point of view on an expansion of powers and equipment. My approach, however, does not provide sufficient ground for such considerations, nor does this study consider what elements of municipal officers' approach would 'work best'. Thirdly, municipal disorder policing appears to be quickly changing. Structures, policy perspectives and relations with other organisations sometimes seemed to have changed as soon as I left a specific research site. For one part, this seems typical for a new profession that is looking for new concepts and trying out new policies. For another part, municipalities appear to be particularly prone to reorganisations and a reframing of recurrent ideas in changing terms. Any reference to local policies, numbers and particular points of view are therefore restricted to the period the fieldwork for this book was done: 2012-2015.

Acknowledgements

This book would not have been possible without the support of several people.

First of all, I want to thank various people for various parts of this study. The first part of this research is made possible with the financial support of the *Politie & Wetenschap* programme. I would like to thank them for their support and trust.

Next, at the very heart of this research are the respondents that opened up their professional lives to me. During various periods, respondents welcomed me with open arms, showed me around and responded to my questions. This particularly applied to several 'gate-keepers' in this research: the people who introduced me and helped me along in the puzzling matrixes of large Dutch municipalities and assisted me in shaping my research.

For the last phase of the study, I would like to thank Jill Bradley for her corrections and helpful comments on the manuscript.

Overall I am deeply indebted to my supervisors, Jan Terpstra and Bas van Stokkom. Without their patience with my unruliness on the one hand, and my somewhat overwrought ideas on the other hand, this whole project would never have happened. Bas, thank you for introducing me to this subject in the first place, for your continued willingness to read my writings in all stages, your good humour and for all the nice talks, both on- and off-topic. Jan, for all the efforts to enable my position, for your detailed comments on the draft texts of my dissertation, and for making the section of criminology a hospitable environment for very different, yet like-minded people.

I also want to thank my direct colleagues at the Criminal Justice and Criminology department. I know I wasn't much of a colleague myself sometimes, glued to my screen and skipping pretty much every lunch. Thank you for dragging me from behind my desk for a coffee, for sharing your thoughts with me, and for your willingness to listen to my thoughts, ideas, plans and frustrations so characteristic for anyone in our position. You know who you are.

My family and friends have also been witnesses to my academic highs and lows. Mom and dad, thank you for your trust, your support and for providing me with the self-confidence to get to this point. Thanks to all friends (too many to mention here), for all the much needed distraction, in music, talk, alcohol or otherwise. And last but certainly not least, Michelle and Sam. Mies, this was the third time you had to go through this; witnessing someone very near to you being held hostage by a PhD dissertation. I am immensely grateful for all your patience and support. And you, Sam, of course, you are the best piece of disorder I could have wished for.

TABLE OF CONTENTS

1 | INTRODUCTION

1 CONCERNS ABOUT DISORDER

In the past thirty years the Netherlands has faced a growth of new concerns about disorder in public places. This comprises a large range of issues as diverse as illegally dumped household waste, dog fouling, cars parked on the pavement, cyclists in pedestrian areas, loitering youths, drunks and junks.

Although these issues might not all be novel, many interventions to deal with them are, new forms of surveillance and law enforcement being among the most obvious. In addition to regular police forces, new officers are given the responsibility of dealing with allegedly neglected incivilities, addressing improper behaviour and trying to take mounting concerns about disorder seriously. In this book one of these new forms of policing in the Netherlands is discussed – municipal disorder policing.

In recent years many countries have witnessed changes in policing and the advent of new forms of disorder policing in particular. As such, Dutch municipal disorder policing should be seen as part of a more general trend of an ever growing body of services providing 'policing', such as surveillance, patrols, law enforcement and criminal investigation. This evolving and expanding group of officers has been named the police extended family (Crawford & Lister, 2006; Johnston, 2003), or the police's junior partners (Button, 2002), but is mostly referred to as 'plural police' (Jones & Newburn, 2007; Jones, Van Steden & Boutellier, 2009; Loader, 2000).

In this introductory chapter several general developments are addressed before the goals and scope of this study are presented. In section 2 the backgrounds of municipal disorder policing are sketched briefly. This is done by addressing how changes in crime and disorder, the urban environment and policing responsibilities have resulted in the advent of municipal disorder policing. Section 3 introduces some of the most important changes in Dutch public safety policies over the past thirty years. Next, section 4 presents some relevant findings on the present practice of disorder policing – the officers' daily work, professionalisation and collaboration with the police. In the fifth section of this chapter the scope of this study and the research questions are introduced. An outline of the book is presented in the final section.

2   BACKGROUNDS OF NEW FORMS OF DISORDER POLICING

In recent years the policing landscape of various Western countries shows corresponding changes that can be associated with similar social and cultural developments. At least three of these developments are relevant to explain the rise of disorder policing.[1]

First of all, new forms of disorder policing are related to factual changes in crime and disorder on the one hand, and to the idea that *fear* of crime is rising on the other. Many Western nations have witnessed a steep rise in crime and disorder during much of the 1980s and 1990s (Terpstra, 2010b: 16). This growth in crime figures was such that police and criminal justice were increasingly confronted with their inability to address these high numbers and started to outsource some of their initial responsibilities (Garland, 2001; cf. chapter 3). In addition, feelings of fear and insecurity grew among the general public.[2] These initially increased parallel to rising crime rates, but remained on a high level or rose further, even when crime rates started declining (Crawford, 2006; Van der Vijver, 2004). As a result, the advent of new forms of disorder policing can be seen as both a response to factual changes in disorder and to the perceived need for visible reassurance by uniformed officers (Terpstra, 2010b; Terpstra, Van Stokkom & Spreeuwers, 2013; Van Steden, 2017).

A second cause for the rise of new forms of disorder policing is the increased emphasis on anti-social behaviour. Although also caused by higher civic expectations, this emphasis appears to be related more to the changes in the public spaces of large cities. One of these changes is the decline of informal social control and the growth of what is called 'urban anonymity'. Control and guardianship by ordinary citizens and by professionals that fulfilled secondary forms of guardianship next to their primary tasks – such as caretakers or stationmasters – have diminished since the 1970s (Blokland, 2009; Newburn, 2001; Terpstra, 2008b, see further chapters 2, 3 and 5). Other factors contributing to the emphasis on anti-social behaviour are related to changes in urban public space. Security has won great economic significance in many (large) urban areas, for example as a precondition to attract tourists and events. Therefore new forms of policing help convey the message the city is "safe for consumption" (Sleiman & Lippert, 2010). Particularly in city centres, this implies behaviour such as begging, loitering or sleeping in public are more readily considered to be anti-social threats to 'clean, intact and safe' shopping and entertainment areas (Millie 2008, Van Stokkom, 2013a; cf. chapter 3). Van Steden and

---

1.   The overview presented here functions as a preamble to what follows in chapters 2 and 3 of this book.
2.   However, some authors state it is not fear or feelings of insecurity that have increased, but citizens' concerns about the moral condition of society (Spithoven, De Graaf & Boutellier, 2012).

Roelofs (2010) describe the new surveillance officers as "guardians of the hygienic city". The growth of hybrid forms of public and private space in urban areas, such as large office complexes and shopping centres, has further added to the employment of private security officers (Jones & Newburn, 1999; Van Steden, 2007).

A third change that might have caused the rise of disorder policing is formed by the relocating and redefining of police responsibilities. In many Western countries there has been a reconfiguring debate on what comprises police work and what exactly are police responsibilities (Jones & Newburn, 2007; Newburn, 2001; Van Steden, 2007; Terpstra, 2010b; Terpstra et al., 2013). Closely related to this is the establishment of a *security complex* – a situation in which security and policing are no longer provided by the state alone, but by a variety of actors. The result is a network of both public and private suppliers of policing and public and private governing bodies (cf. Terpstra, 2010b). In this new constellation the public police are focusing more and more on so called 'core tasks', like crime fighting and criminal investigation.

In summary, the three developments of a rise in (fear of) crime, the changes in the urban environment and the reconfiguring of police responsibilities have led to more or less comparable developments in disorder policing across Western nations (cf. Terpstra et al., 2013). Adding to these general changes, Dutch security policies have evolved in their own particular ways.

3   Developments in Dutch security policies and disorder policing

Dutch attention to disorder: from Roethof to the present

In the Netherlands issues of disorder in public places have also received more attention in the course of the past thirty years, leading to various new policies.

The need for such new policies was first mentioned around the mid-1970s, but it was not until the 1980s before issues of disorder featured prominently in political debates (Commissie Roethof, 1984: 3). In 1984 the abundance of what were known as 'petty crimes' (*kleine criminaliteit*[3]), such as simple traffic offences, minor damage or vandalism in the streets triggered the establishment of a special governmental committee, the Roethof Committee. This committee was charged with the task of developing a new approach to these petty crimes, not the least because police and judicial authorities did not have enough capacity to deal with these issues (Commissie Roethof, 1984: 4). The ideas of the Roethof Committee and the ensuing gov-

---

3.   It was not only the factual increase of crime that set the stage for the Roethof Committee. Public concerns over crime rates were of equal importance in understanding the increased political attention for 'petty crimes' (Van Houdt & Schinkel, 2014). Moreover, especially in recent years it appears concerns are only loosely connected to these crime rates: although crime rates have dropped and feelings of insecurity have diminished since 2005, the concerns of citizens over public safety have become stronger (cf. Terpstra, 2010b: 20).

ernment policy plan, *Society and Crime*[4], set the focus for the years to follow. The abundance of petty crimes was to be addressed through prevention as well as through the involvement of non-police actors such as youth workers and social workers. In addition, local government authorities were meant to play an important part in the development of these new policies.

In the 1990s the role of municipalities became ever more important, evolving into what became known as local 'Integrated Public Safety Policy' (*integraal veiligheidsbeleid*). This new nomenclature was represented most clearly in the *Integrated Public Safety Report*[5] (Cachet & Ringeling, 2004). The policy aimed for an all-encompassing approach with diverse organisations contributing to the solutions for problems of public safety. Once again, an important reason was that judicial authorities were lacking capacity (Pleysier, 2008; Ministry of Justice, 1990). As a result, public safety increasingly became the concern of local administration. Simultaneously, the discourse changed subtly – 'petty crimes' became 'frequent crimes'.

Towards the end of the nineties and at the start of the 21st century the emphasis in public safety policy shifted, albeit within the framework of integrated public safety policy. In consecutive public safety programmes and reports[6], the tone hardened (Terpstra, 2010b: 39). The most prominent of these is the 2002 policy programme *Towards a Safer Society*.[7] A call for consistent rule enforcement and decisive action became the key feature (Terpstra, 2010c: 29). In addition, the programme indicated that governmental organisations involved in public safety are not visible enough: more surveillance was needed, also by the police (cf. Terpstra, 2010b: 39). In later government policy this tougher stance on public safety and anti-social behaviour was combined with ideas about prevention and the sharing of responsibilities, giving precedence to the regulation of behaviour in public places in society and politics alike (Terpstra, 2010c: 31).[8]

Developments in Dutch policing

These changes in disorder policy and the growing prominence of municipalities in dealing with public safety issues cannot be understood without taking into account the specific changes in Dutch police work.

One of the most important of these is the tendency of the Dutch police to define minor infractions of public order as non-police work. This process, for an impor-

---

4.   *Samenleving en criminaliteit*, 1986.
5.   *Integrale veiligheidsrapportage*, 1993.
6.   *Integraal veiligheidsprogramma* 1999; *Nota criminaliteitsbeheersing*, 2001.
7.   *Naar een veiliger samenleving*, 2002.
8.   See for instance action plan *Disorder and Decline* (*Overlast en verloedering*, 2008). In chapter 2 elements of these changes will be discussed. In chapter 5, these developments will be dealt with chronologically, more extensively and specifically with regard to the changes in municipal disorder policing.

tant part, is the result of what has been named the debate on the core tasks.[9] This debate has resulted in the police increasingly focusing on crime fighting, and partially withdrawing from public spaces, at the cost of visibility, surveillance and general disorder policing (BeBOA, 2010; Crijns, 2010; Haagsma, Smits, Waarsing, & Wiebrens, 2012; Terpstra & Kouwenhoven, 2004; Terpstra, Gunther Moor & Van Stokkom, 2010; Terpstra, 2012).[10]

In addition, new policies and non-police interventions to tackle disorder should equally be understood in the light of a "creeping centralisation" of the Dutch police (Terpstra, 2004). Two vital reorganisations of the police have contributed to this process, starting more or less with the police reorganisation of 1993. Until then, the Dutch police consisted of a central Royal Police force and local, municipal police forces for all municipalities over 25,000 inhabitants. After 1993, the police were organised into 25 districts and one central supplementary force. As a result, the central government gradually became more influential, leading to a growing lack of police involvement in local communities (Terpstra, 2004; Terpstra, 2013; Terpstra et al., 2013).[11] This process seems to be further strengthened by the latest police reorganisation – the re-introduction of a national police force in 2013 (Terpstra, Van Duijneveldt, Eikenaar, Havinga & Van Stokkom, 2016).

The advent of municipal disorder policing

Following these developments, municipalities started looking for ways of replacing the police and dealing with concerns over disorder. The first programmes for municipal disorder policing consisted of surveillance by so-called city wardens. Initially enabled by the subsidies of the Roethof Committee at the end of the 1980s, the work of these wardens, who were drawn from the large numbers of long-term unemployed people at that time, usually amounted to surveillance to prevent petty crimes. Many Dutch cities had their own contingent of these officers (Hauber, 1994; Van Steden, 2012; Van Steden, 2017; cf. chapter 5).

These early forms of municipal disorder policing changed in the first years of the 21st century. Partly as a result of a nation-wide call for strict law enforcement,

---

9. This is known as the *Kerntakendiscussie*. The Netherlands is not unique in this respect. Many Western countries have seen a reconfiguring debate on what comprises police work, and what exactly are police responsibilities (Terpstra et al., 2013).
10. Although this movement can be contrasted with a simultaneous recognition of the need for a police force that is responsive to community needs, this never solidified into a type of officer for general patrol and disorder policing in the Netherlands (cf. Savage, 2007). The function of police surveillance officer (*politiesurveillant*) as an acknowledgement of the growing demand for surveillance in public spaces was abolished fairly quickly after its introduction and for reasons that are not quite clear (cf. Hauber, Hofstra, Toornvliet & Zandbergen, 1996; Terpstra et al., 2013). See further chapter 5.
11. Even though 1993's reorganisation was de-central by objective.

city warden projects were merged with other municipal law enforcement agencies.[12] These new city surveillance agencies were mostly called *Toezicht en Handhaving* or *Stadstoezicht*. In the course of this process, city wardens either resigned, or progressed to become qualified municipal enforcement officers. Thus many of them became *BOAs*, a Dutch abbreviation of *Buitengewoon Opsporingsambtenaar*, freely translated as municipal law enforcement officers (Van Steden, 2017). Nowadays these *BOAs* form by far the largest part of municipal city surveillance agencies (Eikenaar & Van Stokkom, 2014; see further chapter 5) and have the objective of "combating minor annoyances, nuisance and other facts that affect the quality of life" (Ministry of Justice, 2015: 10). As opposed to their predecessors, the city wardens, they have more powers and are expected to impose fines for common forms of disorder and anti-social behaviour, further enabled by the introduction of new administrative penal orders and administrative fines in 2009 (see further chapter 5).[13]

4   MUNICIPAL DISORDER POLICING: SOME RECENT DEVELOPMENTS

By now several studies have shed light on these relatively new municipal officers for disorder policing.[14] These studies address their daily work, education and professionalisation, as well as their relation with the police.

Daily work

On the one hand, municipal officers appear to focus on a limited range of rule infringements (Flight, 2012; Flight, Hartmann, Nauta, Hulshof, & Terpstra, 2012). The fines they impose – mostly administrative penal orders – for instance target non-compliant dog owners who refuse to put their pets on a leash or refrain from cleaning their excrement, or people who pollute the streets, for example by litter or taking out the rubbish too early. In addition, officers often impose fines for parking

---

12. Parking attendance and the policing of environmental offences had been a municipal responsibility since the police reorganisation of 1993 and existed alongside the city wardens. See further chapter 5.

13. Moreover, the role of these officers in criminal law enforcement is getting bigger and "they are increasingly taking over tasks of the police". Letter from Minister Opstelten of Safety & Justice to the House of Representatives: http://www.rijksoverheid.nl/regering/documenten-en-publicaties/kamerstukken/2013/07/01/kamerbrief-samenhang-in-toezicht-en-handhaving-in-de-open-bare-ruimte.html (see also: Ministry of Justice, 2015).

14. There is still a sizable number of municipal disorder policing officers who are not qualified to impose fines. These are mostly called 'surveillance officers' (*toezichthouders*), as opposed to 'enforcement officers' (*handhavers*). To include both officers, the more generic term 'municipal officers' is used here, avoiding the more exclusive terms of 'enforcement officers', '*BOAs*' or 'SIOs' (short for 'Special Investigative Officers') used in other studies (Van Steden, 2017).

violations and check parking permits (Flight et al., 2012; Van Steden, 2012).[15] Hence, if their work must be seen as setting normative standards in public places, this would apply only to a small range of rule infringements and not to anti-social behaviour in general (Van Steden & Bron, 2012).

On the other hand, municipal officers' work comprises of a lot more than fining offenders. Officers have a wide range of strategies and approaches at their disposal to make citizens comply with the rules. Imposing fines is but one of these strategies, and allegedly the least popular (Bervoets & Rovers, 2016; Terpstra, 2012). Other means may be used, ranging from addressing non-compliant citizens without fining them, informing citizens, carrying out general surveillance of public places or signalling and reporting offences that are beyond their authority (Van Steden, 2012). In addition, these officers follow up on citizens' reports, have preventative tasks, provide assistance to the police and cooperate with other professionals (Bervoets, 2013; Bervoets & Rovers, 2016; Eikenaar & Van Stokkom, 2014; Terpstra, 2012). Some state their work is equally imbued with the idea of reassurance, aiming to contribute to citizens' feeling of security by uniformed presence (Terpstra, 2010b).[16] Lastly, their work may be filled with administrative obligations or a rather aimlessly driving around when there is not enough to do (Bervoets, 2013; Terpstra, 2012).

This wide variety in daily activities, for an important part, can be explained by their large discretionary autonomy (Bervoets, 2013). Following the seminal work of Michael Lipsky (2010), several authors state these officers – like other frontline professionals in safety policy (Moors & Bervoets, 2013) – have a considerable amount of room to make autonomous decisions. As a result, some of them might highlight 'service provision', whereas others see themselves more as law enforcement officers (Bervoets & Rovers, 2016; cf. chapter 7).

Education, professionalisation and reputation

In line with the growth of city surveillance agencies, educational facilities and requirements have also developed. Apart from the basic *BOA* certificate that municipal officers are obliged to obtain if they want to become a *BOA*, the most important training is the MTV and HTV courses[17], providing trajectories for respectively officers without and with power to fine. Added to these trajectories, *BOAs* are obliged to complete several courses that differ widely between municipalities, such as violence and de-escalation training programmes or professionali-

---

15. The enforcement of parking permits is done without using administrative penal orders, but as a retrospective collection of taxes.
16. Although other authors highlight that this plays but a minor role in their work (Bervoets, 2013).
17. MTV stands for *medewerker toezicht en veiligheid* (surveillance and security employee), HTV for *handhaver toezicht en veiligheid* (surveillance and security enforcement officer). The prerequisite for the latter is the BOA certificate. As most municipalities only assign BOAs, the MTV education can be expected to lose its relevance (Van Steden, 2012).

sation training for specific juridical knowledge (Van Steden, 2012). As from 2013, the demands for education have increased, leading to a system of permanent schooling and external examination by a national organisation[18] (cf. Mein & Hart-mann, 2013). In addition, occupational organisation *BeBOA* has been initiated as a national consultative body and centre of knowledge.

Nevertheless, various studies point out that municipal officers struggle with their professional level and public reputation as 'good for-nothing city strollers' (Bervoets & Rovers, 2016; Eikenaar & Van Stokkom, 2014; Van Steden, 2012). Some state that the problem of low professional standards is real. In 2012 the Audit Office of Rotterdam indicated its municipal officers generally lacked essential com-municative competencies, mostly with regard to the treatment of non-compliant citizens and de-escalation. Moreover, Mein & Hartmann (2013) state coordinators and police officers often point to the deficient quality of fines and the alleged clumsy interaction with non-compliant citizens (cf. Eikenaar & Van Stokkom, 2014). Apart from these estimations, their reputation seems to be easily influenced by footage on social media that shows rude and tense officers (Bervoets & Rovers, 2016).

Two recent studies found that this reputation is not as bad as many – even some municipal officers themselves – seem to believe (Bervoets & Rovers, 2016; SMV, 2013). A quarter of all citizens appear to be (highly) positive and only ten percent (highly) negative about the presence of *BOAs* in general (including enforcement officers in other domains; SMV, 2013). A study with a more specific focus on municipal enforcement officers found that most citizens do not have pronounced ideas about them. As far as citizens do have an idea, they see municipal officers mostly as 'service providers' (instead of as authoritative officers), particularly valu-ing their helpfulness. In addition, even citizens who did have first-hand experience with municipal officers – for instance, because they were fined or addressed – are mostly positive about that experience (Bervoets & Rovers, 2016).

Relation with the police

Finally, several studies have described the relation between these municipal offi-cers and the police (Eikenaar & Van Stokkom, 2014; Mein & Hartmann, 2013; Van Stokkom & Foekens, 2015). This relation has been enacted formally in the Decree on *BOAs*.[19] Insofar as these municipal officers are *BOAs* – which applies to the vast majority – this Decree designates the Public Prosecutor as general supervisor and the police as direct supervisor (cf. Mein & Hartmann, 2013: 23). Moreover, the police are assigned the operational management of these officers. However, these formal regulations seem to have little meaning in practice (Eikenaar & Van Stok-

---

18. The foundation for Examination Surveillance and Rule Enforcement (Dutch acronym: ExTH).
19. Ministry of Justice (1994) *Besluit Buitengewoon opsporingsambtenaar.*

kom, 2014; Mein & Hartmann, 2013; Van Steden, 2012). The supervision of *BOAs* is mostly regarded as nothing more than a formal obligation, with but few consequences for the interaction between the two organisations. Operational management of these officers by the police proves to be rather complicated, as municipalities are still responsible for 'strategic management', meaning *BOAs* are part of municipalities' local safety policy.[20] This division of responsibilities causes much confusion. Once again, most studies that scrutinise the daily work of these municipal officers find that operational management by the police is poorly developed, not to say absent all together (Bervoets, 2013; Eikenaar & Van Stokkom, 2014; Van Steden, 2012; Van Steden & Bron, 2012).

Daily collaboration between the two organisations seems equally deficient, even though emergency back-up by the police appears rather well-organised in the case of escalating interaction between municipal officers and unruly citizens (Rekenkamer Rotterdam, 2012; Rekenkamercommissie Schiedam-Vlaardingen, 2012; Gemeentelijk ombudsman Amsterdam, 2013; Van Steden & Bron, 2012). Often municipal officers and police officers do not adjust their activities, the police often seems reluctant to share information and quite a few police officers appear to have trouble accepting municipal officers as policing colleagues (Bervoets, 2013; Eikenaar & Van Stokkom, 2014; Gemeentelijke ombudsman Amsterdam, 2013; Mein & Hartmann, 2013; Terpstra, 2012; Van Steden, 2012; Van Steden & Bron, 2012). In addition, collaboration in practice is not stimulated by formal agreements, but largely depends on the willingness of local team coordinators and on local circumstances (Eikenaar & Van Stokkom, 2014; Van Stokkom, 2013b).[21] Hence, both police and municipal officers seem to operate within the confines of their own respective work domain.

5   THIS STUDY

To sum up, recent studies have shown how municipal wardens have developed into policing professionals. These professionals resemble traditional police officers, but they also have their own specific tasks. These tasks fall mainly in the 'quality of life' sphere, a category that is used to indicate the policing of mostly physical disorder issues (cf. chapters 7 and 9). Although professional levels might not always be adequate according to some studies, their reputation as 'city strollers' seems largely unjustified. In contrast, previous studies have provided rich descriptions of

---

20. Letter from minister Opstelten of Safety & Justice to the House of Representatives: http://www.rijksoverheid.nl/regering/documenten-en-publicaties/kamerstukken/2013/07/01/kamer-brief-samenhang-in-toezicht-en-handhaving-in-de-openbare-ruimte.html.
21. Exceptions to these findings can be found in the city of The Hague, where municipal officers are housed at police stations and police constables are assigned as team chiefs (cf. Van Stokkom & Foekens, 2015), or in specific projects where both types of officers collaborate (Eikenaar & Van Stokkom, 2014; Van Stokkom, 2013b).

the multifariousness of their daily work and their professional and deliberate inter-actions with citizens.

However, the wider context in which these officers have to do their work remains under-examined. By focusing on frontline work, previous studies provide insightful descriptions of their work, but leave their historical, societal and organi-sational background aside. They merely give a brief mention of the administrative and political reality in which these officers have to work (Bervoets, 2013). As a result, the image of these municipal officers is largely based on colourful, but somewhat restricted accounts of their daily work and their relation to police offi-cers.

These accounts lack a deeper, more thorough understanding of this relatively new professional group. In addition, few of these studies go into detail on the soci-etal and cultural changes that inform these forms of policing. Generally they merely touch on the observation that the call for social control has become more vociferous, the tolerance of deviant behaviour has declined, or that a hardening of the social climate has occurred. These findings are often not investigated further. The reasons for disorder being seen as a problem and how new forms of disorder policing are assumed to be important remain unclear. Recent studies do not explain how and why municipal forms of surveillance and enforcement have developed. The policy goals and assumptions of municipal disorder policing also remain obscure; neither do these studies show if and how such goals might change in municipal decision making processes or in the everyday practice of these officers themselves. Lastly, current studies do not examine thoroughly which diverging views, expectations and conflicting interests could occur in the field of disorder policing. Possible tensions between different strategies and interests and between policy and frontline work remain under-examined. Municipal management, local politics, citizen groups, municipal professionals and the police are all these parties involved and might have different views on how to shape these new forms of policing.

Based on these points of view, this study aims to contribute to a deeper and richer perspective on the evolution of municipal disorder policing, its changing policies and how these policies relate to the unruliness of a frontline practice.

The main research question is:

Which factors and perspectives are relevant in understanding the policies and practices of municipal disorder policing in the Netherlands?

This question is divided into several sub-questions:
A. Which developments contributed to the establishment and growth of munici-pal disorder policing?
B. What are dominant policy perspectives and how did these change over time?

C. Who decides on disorder policing and how are decisions made?
D. How do municipal officers see their work and strategies and how do they relate to the police?

As a result of this focus, several important aspects of municipal disorder policing are not addressed here. First of all, changes in policy and discourse are given precedence over the juridical background of these officers. Regulations on different penal orders and fines and other developments in administrative law and criminal law are addressed only as far as they are relevant for a better understanding of policy and practice of these municipal officers. Next, several detailed aspects of professionalisation, such as powers, equipment, training and uniforms will not be addressed here. Such questions would need an extensive frontline study of the functioning of municipal officers. Lastly, a detailed examination of their daily work and (daily) collaboration with the police is lacking in this study. Only in a few specific situations (chapter 8) will their daily work be described through close observations, and even there it will be studied mainly in its relation to encompassing policy and its organisational context.

6   OUTLINE

This book is structured as follows.

The first part, which comprises chapters 2 and 3, explores disorder policing theoretically. In **chapter 2** three different strategies of disorder policing are presented, providing insight into underlying views and assumptions. In these strategies, disorder policing is seen as – respectively – a way to reconquer the streets, situational crime prevention and a way to improve informal social control and trust. With every strategy, various police models, as well as the reception in the Dutch context, are discussed. **Chapter 3**, the second theoretical chapter, discusses the wider contexts of disorder policing and presents three sociological interpretations of its advent and growth. As such, it addresses the question which social, political and cultural developments could have contributed to the growth of disorder policing. These interpretations can be seen respectively as benevolent, sceptical and comprehensive readings of disorder policing.

In **chapter 4**, the methodology is introduced. It discusses the research design, the selection of cases and the various methods that are used, as well as several considerations of methodological quality.

The next part is the largest, empirical part and is comprised of five chapters.
    This part starts with the most extensive chapter (**chapter 5**), which answers subquestions A and B above. These questions cannot be answered in isolation: policy

goals and the shifts therein cannot be discussed apart from contextual develop-ments. As a result, this chapter will be structured largely chronologically, alternat-ing between historical developments and changes in the policies of municipal dis-order policing and its underlying assumptions. This chapter will address national developments as far as they are relevant for understanding changes in municipal disorder policing.

The next chapter, **chapter 6**, deals with the organisational context of municipal officers. It takes the analysis from the macro level to a meso level. It describes how decisions on disorder policing are made locally (sub-question C), presenting three different 'logics' – political, managerial, and frontline logic. This leads to highly divergent ideas of how disorder policing is performed and what issues are dealt with.

After this, **chapter 7** addresses on a micro level how municipal officers them-selves think about their responsibilities and the policing strategies they pursue. It serves to scrutinise what municipal officers highlight as the most important aspects of their work. Special attention will be paid to the concepts they use and the extent to which these ideas differ from the earlier described policy goals. As such, this chapter deals with sub-question D.

Whereas chapters 5 – 7 deal with a macro, meso and micro level analysis of municipal disorder policing respectively, **chapter 8** will show that these levels interact in the case of specific hotspots, thereby providing an additional answer to sub-question C. Many of the disorder problems that are subject to the new munici-pal agencies are concentrated on a fairly confined area, with a dynamic that is best studied through the interests of local 'stakeholders' – managers, municipal politi-cians, municipal officers, inhabitants, etcetera. As such, the views of officers can only be understood in the municipal context of political and managerial decision making, a context in which policy and practice interact.

In the last chapter of part II (**chapter 9**) a final aspect of municipal disorder policing is discussed – its relation to police work. However, the approach is not factual, but rather – once again – more fundamental. This chapter deals with the ongoing debate about the proper domain of municipal disorder police in relation to 'traditional' police work. As will become apparent, the determination of tasks and their scope – and thereby the importance that is ascribed to municipal disorder policing – has to this day been the subject of much controversy. By describing four positions on the division of tasks between these two occupational groups, this chapter also provides an answer to sub-question D.

The final chapter, **chapter 10**, sums up the most important findings, presents con-clusions about dominant strategies and goals and reflects on the findings of this study by referring back to the sociological interpretations of chapter 3.

STRATEGIES OF DISORDER POLICING

The previous chapter pointed out that issues of disorder started to feature prominently in political debates in the eighties. In these debates a major role was played
by notions of prevention and social control. Nowadays these notions are still pivotal in municipal disorder policing.

Many of these conceptions have been formulated earlier, especially in the context of American debates on police models. In the seventies and eighties many
police theorists and researchers criticised the standard model of policing (a reactive, incident-driven model, with little attention to citizens' interests) and they
brought about major innovations in policing (Weisburd & Braga, 2006). These
innovations included community policing and broken windows policing, strategies
that attempted to redirect policing efforts to crime and disorder problems about
which residents were worried (Kelling & Coles, 1996).[1] Many of these policing
strategies were introduced and reframed in Dutch policy discourses and policing
practices. As is often the case in 'policy transfer', the original strategies were fil-
tered out to fit them into the new cultural context and implement them in policing
practices (cf. Jones & Newburn, 2007; Savage, 2007; Terpstra et al., 2013).

In this chapter three disorder policing strategies are reviewed, along with the
assumptions that inform these strategies. In the first section broken windows policing is discussed, and in particular its influential zero tolerance interpretation. Section 2 points to situational crime prevention, while section 3 focuses on disorder
policing as a way to improve informal social control and trust. Each of these sections first discusses some relevant assumptions of these policing strategies, and
subsequently the reception of (aspects of) these strategies in the Dutch context.

1   ZERO TOLERANCE AND RECONQUERING THE STREETS

Many accounts of disorder policing start with a short article that appeared in *The
Atlantic Monthly* in 1982. It was written by James Q. Wilson and George Kelling

---

1.   See further Kelling & Coles (1996) for a more extensive discussion of how in the 1960s US police
     had been taken over by a paradigm of "fighting crime", alienating them from mounting issues of
     disorder.

and was called *Broken windows: The police and neighborhood safety*. This article forms the starting point for the influential Broken Windows theory.

The basic assumptions of this theory are as simple as they are appealing: disorder leads to more disorder and even crime, and therefore needs to be addressed. This applies to both physical disorder, such as litter, graffiti, broken windows, and to social disorder, such as rude behaviour, loitering, begging or sleeping in public. The attractiveness of this idea resides in a straightforward causal ratio. If one window is broken in a neighbourhood, more will follow because a broken window that is left unrepaired gives a signal that "no one cares" (Wilson & Kelling, 1982). It will function as an invitation for more people to commit vandalism. In fact, a neighbourhood communicates by way of its tidiness and a general sense of order. Orderly neighbourhoods signal that their inhabitants care, whereas disorderly neighbourhoods, with apparent high levels of vandalism, rubbish and untended behaviour signal that "communal barriers" are absent (*ibid.*).

The key assumption of Wilson & Kelling's basic broken windows theory is that neighbourhoods will decline if seemingly minor issues of disorder are neglected. In fact, disorder has grown *because* the police have neglected this basic feature of policing (Kelling & Coles, 1996: 69). A large part of their short article thus focuses on forms of policing to stop this gradual downward slide, providing a solution that is as simple as its problem definition. Policing should be redirected from reactive crime fighting to paying attention to early neighbourhood decline and maintaining order (Skogan, 1990). Moreover, what applies to unmended broken windows, applies to disorderly behaviour in general. "Street crime flourishes in areas in which disorderly behaviour goes unchecked. The unchecked panhandler is, in effect, the first broken window" (Wilson & Kelling, 1982: 6[2]). An arrest of a single disorderly person may seem unjust, but "a score of drunks or a hundred vagrants may destroy an entire community" (Wilson & Kelling, 1982: 5). Although many forms of disorder strictly speaking are not illegal (sleeping drunks, loitering youths), they have "a considerable impact on the community," and might increase neighbourhood decline (Skogan, 1990a: 3).

Ever since its inception in 1982, the broken windows theory has had an extensive impact on both academic and political discussions, and has been interpreted in many different ways (Harcourt, 2001; Herbert, 2001; Harcourt & Ludwig, 2006). Although the theory can be interpreted in terms of community needs (see the third section below), the 'zero tolerance' interpretation has become the most influential version.[3]

---

2.   For references, the online version has been used: http://www.theatlantic.com/magazine/archive/1982/03/broken-windows/304465/.

3.   The third perspective discussed below shows that the Broken Windows theory is suitable for various interpretations. The zero tolerance model is but one of the more dominant interpretations and some would say undeservedly so (cf. Jones & Newburn, 2007; Van Stokkom, 2008; Terpstra, 2009).

The most famous example of zero tolerance policing was introduced in 1993 by the mayor of New York and the chief of police of the NYPD at that time, Rudolph Giuliani and William Bratton, under the name of the 'quality of life initiative' (Herbert, 2001; Harcourt & Ludwig, 2006).[4] Policing disorder here amounts to tough, hands-on policing of disruptive behaviour and incivilities. Police officers should fine (and arrest) citizens for minor rule-infractions and quality of life offences such as public drinking, vandalism, begging and vagrancy. Thus zero tolerance policing became mainly associated with crackdowns on minor disorder problems (Newburn & Jones, 2007).

Zero tolerance policing starts with defining those neighbourhoods that are at a 'tipping point'. This term was borrowed from Wilson and Kelling (1982) to indicate neighbourhoods "where the public order is deteriorating but not un-reclaimable, where the streets are used frequently but by apprehensive people, where a window is likely to be broken at any time, and must quickly be fixed if all are not to be shattered" (Wilson & Kelling, 1982: 10). In these neighbourhoods public space must be reclaimed.

Within this disorder policing strategy, frontline police officers play a pivotal role, albeit somewhat ambivalently. On the one hand, police officers should be given ample room to make their own decisions when doing their work; they ought to settle problems of disorder by their own estimation of what are appropriate interventions (Newburn, 2007). This would provide plenty of scope for pro-active street-work and a large discretionary authority to police officers. By their presence, they send out messages to disorderly persons and collect information about offenders. On the other hand, through zero tolerance policing police officers have been compelled to adhere to stricter targets and increased performance measures. In New York this happened through the Compstat-system (Newburn & Jones, 2007). This management system was meant to make it easier to review and control officers' activities (Newburn & Jones, 2007).[5]

Reception

Zero tolerance has become immensely popular in policing policies and practices, and is "probably the largest 'policy transfer' in criminological history," according to some (Van Swaaningen, 2005: 292, cf. Beckett & Herbert, 2009; Harcourt, 2001; Herbert and Brown, 2006; Van de Bunt & van Swaaningen, 2012). Other cities copied and adapted this initiative of the city of New York. This happened first in the

---

4.   As a result of the use of the term 'quality of life' in this context, the restrictive forms of policing described here might come to mind. However, the chapters that follow will show that the term 'quality of life' and the related Dutch term *leefbaarheid* has another relevance in the context of Dutch municipal disorder policing: it is used to designate certain tasks are the responsibility of municipal officers rather than police officers (cf. chapters 5 and 9).

5.   See also Eterno and Silverman (2012) for distortions and negative consequences of this system.

United States and eventually also in other cities in the Western, and even non-Western world, albeit rarely in a strict zero tolerance variant (Harcourt, 2001: 57; Harcourt & Ludwig, 2006; cf. Newburn & Jones, 2007). As several scholars claim, this popularity is not due to the alleged effectiveness of zero tolerance policing, but to certain cultural and political circumstances that influenced the adoption of this theory (Herbert, 2001; Mooney & Young, 2006).[6]

Likewise, representatives of the Dutch police travelled to New York to learn from this 'miracle', leading to an adaptation of several zero tolerance elements in the Netherlands (Punch, Hoogenboom & Williamson, 2005; Schuilenburg, 2013).[7] Thus the Dutch police embraced elements of zero tolerance policing, albeit mostly in specific neighbourhoods of Rotterdam, Amsterdam and Utrecht (Punch, 2006). These policing practices differ from the strict New York prototype discussed above because, for instance, the approach to drug addicts who cause disorder problems, often also involves healthcare. Zero tolerance policing is restricted to measures taken in deprived neighbourhoods with severe issues of disorder. Nevertheless, Dutch examples of 'Very Irritating Policing' or the Amsterdam Streetwise programme are unmistakably influenced by overseas "vigorous law-enforcement" strategies to combat disorder and decline (Newburn & Jones, 2007: 226; Punch, 2006; Terpstra, 2009; Van Stokkom, 2005).

These tendencies should equally be understood in the light of the changing security policies at the beginning of the 21st century in the Netherlands. After 2002, the general political stance in the Netherlands tended toward a tougher approach of issues of security and public safety. In its 2002 policy programme *Toward a safer society* the Ministers of Justice and of the Interior at the time stated issues of security and disorder had been 'festering too long' (Ministry of the Interior and Ministry of Justice, 2002). The programme further claimed that citizens' feelings of insecurity had been neglected for too long and called for a turn away from the leniency and the policy of too much tolerance of the past, for offensive plans and action programmes (cf. Martineau, 2006). In doing so, this new policy programme seemed to make a clear distinction between those that cause incivilities and crime

---

6. Although zero tolerance policing was received differently in the UK, the US and the Netherlands (Mooney & Young, 2006; Newburn & Jones, 2007; Terpstra, 2009) several factors can explain the overall popularity of this approach. Hence, the popularity of zero tolerance policing might not only be explained by its basic, appealing idea of a causal relation between disorder, fear and crime, but also by a simultaneous drop in crime rates in New York at the time of the introduction of broken windows policing (Herbert, 2001; Herbert and Brown, 2006). In addition, several cultural and political circumstances contributed to its acceptance. These encompass inherent traits of police culture, such as an affinity with the use of force, and the "moral purpose with which police officers imbue their work" (Herbert, 2001: 453; Taylor, 2006), and zero tolerance's accordance with a wider societal understanding of crime as something that is inflicted upon the community from outside (Herbert, 2001). Lastly, similar changes in the political climate might have contributed to its acceptance, as various countries have embraced a tougher approach on crime (Herbert, 2001).

7. Some state that the term 'zero tolerance' is rarely used or even rejected by the Dutch police and as such mostly limited to political slogans (Martineau, 2006; Punch 2006; Van Dijk, 2012).

(the disorderly) and those who go about their daily lives peacefully (the orderly). By removing these 'notorious sources' from the streets or by excluding 'bothersome individuals' from public transport insecurity and incivilities were thought to diminish and the decline of public space to be halted (Ministry of the Interior and Ministry of Justice, 2002: 35). The renewed stress on visibility and visible enforcement also provided a new perspective (*ibid.*: 34 ff.), for instance to enhance rule enforcement and surveillance in public places such as "railway stations, nightlife districts, shopping centres, the areas surrounding coffee shops, areas where youth assemble" (*ibid.*: 34). Moreover, this recalibration of public safety policy would have to be done mostly at a "local level" by local governments and their way of enforcing laws. Thus, employment of enforcement officers other than traditional police for disorder policing is mentioned for the first time in a government plan (*ibid.*: 37).

The city of Rotterdam is often mentioned in this respect. Rotterdam apparently underwent a sea change from previous lenient ideas about public safety issues to a tough approach. Tops (2007) speaks of a regime change, backed by an electoral landslide from the long reigning social democratic party (PvdA), to the right-wing populist party LPF, and with more attention being paid to the insecurities, fears and annoyances of its inhabitants. In Rotterdam this led to a new municipal policy in which "public safety becomes the primary lens" (Tops, 2007: 68; see also Schuilenburg, 2013; Van Swaaningen, 2005). What is more, then mayor Opstelten – dubbed Rotterdam's Giuliani, and well known for his clear break with previous policy – played a crucial role. The Rotterdam approach includes a fixation on targets (the 'Safety Index'), "action logics", an "almost fanatic longing for concrete and visible results" (Tops, 2007: 212), intrusive house calls (Dutch: *huisbezoeken*), 'firmness' and a priority of the frontline over policy.

The national policy programme *Towards a Safer Society* claims the Rotterdam approach provides a guide. This municipality has been investing in what is termed the 'social reconquering' of public space in its 'deprived neighbourhoods'[8], specifically defining those neighbourhoods that have passed a 'critical limit', reminiscent of Wilson & Kelling's tipping point (Engbersen, Snel & Weltevreden, 2005). This decisive strategy appears to leave little room for the classical social worker, as security and justice personnel are expected to cover all the bases, together with municipal neighbourhood professionals, intervention-teams, housing associations and the private sector (*ibid.*: 19). Moreover, frontline professionals were meant to become 'streetwise', to be 'de-bureaucratised', and they were given the room to rediscover what is happening on the streets. Their intrusive approach also aimed at setting moral standards, leading some to see this as a 'civilisation-offensive' (cf. Van den Brink, 2004). Although this policy of "social reconquering" involves concerns about social disadvantages and encompasses social support, the emphasis on

---

8.   A loose description of what in Dutch are termed *achterstandswijken*.

strict enforcement and repression of disorder is undeniable (cf. Schuilenburg, 2013).

2   SITUATIONAL CRIME PREVENTION

Summing up the first section, zero tolerance strategies aim to nip the process of neighbourhood decline in the bud by addressing the hitherto neglected issues of disorder and incivilities and by making a clear distinction between orderly and disorderly persons.

In many ways the second strategy of disorder policing suggests the opposite. The strategy of situational crime prevention sees disorder as a problem that could be caused by anyone. Whereas the zero tolerance model draws a clear line between insiders as honest citizens and outsiders as loitering youths, tramps or drunks, this theory assumes that *everyone* might be inclined to commit crime and that all citizens tend to make the same choices under similar situational circumstances – "all people have some probability of committing crime", and "situational prevention does not draw hard distinctions between criminals and others" (Clarke, 1997: 4, see also Felson, 1998; Newman, 1972).[9] Theories of situational crime prevention assume that crime can be reduced effectively by altering situations rather than the personal dispositions of the offender.

Rooted in socio-ecological theories and theories on opportunity reduction, this approach to disorder is mainly concerned with the question how local situations could influence the rational choices individuals make (Clarke, 1997; Felson, 1998; Newman, 1972). High rise buildings for example, with a lot of anonymous space and little opportunity for surveillance by residents will have more risk of becoming locations with a high incidence of crime and disorder (Newman, 1972). Felson (1998) elaborates these basic premises in his theory of the chemistry of crime: the incidence of crime is dependent on three variables, all contributing to define the probability of someone actually committing an offence. A likely *offender* and a suitable *target* must be present, whereas a "capable *guardian*" must be absent (Felson, 1998: 53). Taking these three basic conditions into consideration, the probability of a crime can easily be determined, according to Felson. As such, guardianship is only one of several elements that might predict crime.[10]

---

9.   However, some authors state that theories of situational crime prevention do make a clear distinction between insiders and outsiders, the normal and the pathological (Herbert & Brown, 2006: 758). Newman for instance, seems to suggest that residents should be given more opportunity to guard their neighbourhood from "intruders" (Newman, 1972: 72). This evidently influences Newman's commitment to rational choice theory, in which good and bad moral options do not play a role, but simply the individual considerations on whether or not to commit a crime or (here) act in a disorderly manner (Herbert & Brown, 2006: 763).

10.   Albeit an element that does not get as much attention as victim/target suitability and the motivation of the offender (Hollis-Peel, Reynald, Bavel, Elffers & Welsh, 2011).

Theories of situational crime prevention propose solutions that revolve around changing the rational choices of possible offenders. This applies equally to forms of guardianship: guardians are important as they change the opportunities for criminal or disorderly behaviour.[11] In the initial writings on situational crime prevention this is mostly understood as *informal* guardianship. Public spaces should be designed in such a fashion that there are more possibilities for inhabitants *themselves* to control their own environment so they will be less reluctant to deal with "the problem of security" (Newman, 1972: 49). This in fact is "the traditional responsibility of the citizenry" (*ibid.*: 14). The 'defensible space' approach to crime and disorder is even aimed at previous models of urban design and the allegedly ineffective forms of policing that came along with it: "[t]he high-rise prototype, with its myriad of resident janitorial and security staff" (*ibid.*: 7).

Nevertheless, several forms of disorder policing are in line with the situational approach. Formally guarding against the opportunities for offences might well be a reply to weakened informal guardianship by citizens themselves. Thus policing disorder is meant to reduce the probability individuals will behave in a disorderly fashion at given times and given places. Examples of such formal guards are security guards, urban citizen patrols, place managers (e.g. bus drivers or car park attendants), actively monitored CCTV and neighbourhood watch groups (Hollis-Peel, Reynald, Bavel, Elffers, & Welsh, 2011: 61 ff.). All have a (situational) role to diminish the risk of crime and disorder.

The theory of situational crime prevention has also influenced several policing strategies. One example of this is *problem oriented policing*. In the explanation of Goldstein (1979), problem oriented policing is based on a "detailed analysis of the everyday problems [the police] handle and the devising of tailor-made solutions" (*ibid.*: 9).[12] The police are there to deal with a series of problems, not just to enforce the law in the coded, bureaucratic way they tend to do (Goldstein, 1979: 246). Thus, Goldstein makes explicit reference to situational crime prevention and the theory of Newman (*ibid.*: 251), as 'smart forms of guardianship' might be good alternatives to prevent issues of crimes and disorder. A second example of policing influenced by situational crime prevention is *hotspot policing*. Opportunities for crime and disorder are reduced if certain places are 'painted blue' at certain times and possible offenders are deterred by the presence of uniformed personnel. This approach focuses equally on both inquiring extensively into local problems and on the most effective forms of uniformed interventions in the places with the most problems – the hotspots. Thus, hotspot policing and problem oriented policing

---

11. Here guardianship by and large is understood as a notion that is in accordance with situational crime prevention thinking, but guardianship may be equally associated with strategies that highlight trust and informal social control (see further below).
12. According to Goldstein (1979), problem oriented policing first and foremost should be seen as an answer to previous, allegedly ineffective ways of policing and provided an opportunity to reorient policing on "the primary purposes for which they were created" (*Ibid.*: 237).

might have a lot in common in their (empirical) assessment of what works best at certain times and in certain places and their embrace of situational crime prevention (Weisburd & Braga, 2008).[13]

Reception

In the Dutch case, theories of situational crime prevention influenced local safety policies mostly in the form of administrative prevention. This is most clearly represented in the solutions proposed by the Roethof Committee and the ensuing 1986 national policy programme *Society and crime* that have already briefly been mentioned in chapter 1.

Both this Committee and the *Society and Crime* policy programme noted the need for a combination of preventative and repressive measures.[14] To address the abundance of petty crimes the committee proposed solutions that were strongly influenced by situational crime prevention theories, highlighting a reduction of opportunities by redeveloping the built environment and by fortifying functional surveillance for instance, by conductors, caretakers or shop attendants (Ministry of Justice, 1985: 9; cf. Van Dijk, 2012).[15] Likewise, these ideas of opportunity reduction found their way to Dutch policy makers (De Haan, 2001). The popularity of these theories was further strengthened by the widely shared idea that opportunities for crime and disorder abounded due to a loss of informal guardianship by citizens themselves (Hauber et al., 1996; Ministry of Justice, 1985). As a result, the first municipal city wardens, police patrol officers and surveillance officers in public transport seemed to find an important legitimation in the compensation for this loss (Hauber et al., 1996; Van Andel, 1989).

By contrast, the Dutch police seemed to have a minor role in these administrative ideas of situational crime prevention (Straver, 2006: 202). Only with the later government paper *Towards a Safer Society* (2002) was the police's role in order maintenance reintroduced, albeit more in terms of (reactive) law enforcement (see above). That does not mean however, that situational crime prevention wholly disappeared from Dutch police policy. Through the innovations of problem oriented policing and hotspot policing a situational approach did find acclaim within the Dutch police. The vision elaborated in police policy document *Police in Development* (*Politie in Ontwikkeling*; Projectgroep visie op de politiefunctie, 2005) for instance,

---

13. These approaches allegedly 'work' better than "misdemeanour arrests and social service strategies" (Braga & Bond 2008; see also Harcourt & Ludwig, 2006; Weisburd & Braga, 2008).
14. As the Roethof Committee did not provide a clear theoretical or juridical definition of these 'petty crimes', their abundance seemed more important than their exact definition, which was proved by the later shift in focus from 'petty' to 'frequent' (in Dutch: *veelvoorkomend*, cf. Boutellier, 2008).
15. The third prominent solution proposed by the Roethof committee deviates from these situational interventions. Inspired by Travis Hirschi's theory of social bonds, it highlights that petty crimes can also be prevented by improving the integration of (mainly) youth in society (Commissie Roethof 1984, see also Hirschi, 1969).

highlights the breach with traditional concepts that was already evident in the earlier report *Police in Transition* (*Politie in Verandering*; Projectgroep Organisatie Structuren, 1978; see also below). The former document highlighted – among other things – "situationally determined action" (Projectgroep visie op de politiefunctie, 2005: 73), provided room for problem oriented variants of policing and greater visible presence of police on the streets (Straver, 2008).[16] In addition, other recent police concepts also lean on some of the basic premises of situational crime prevention, such as the notion of *tegenhouden* (obstructing) as a preventative crime fighting strategy (Hoogewoning, 2004).[17]

3   IMPROVING INFORMAL SOCIAL CONTROL AND BUILDING TRUST

A last strategy that is discussed here focuses on the disruptive effects of disorder on neighbourhood residents' feelings of security. Disorder leads citizens to avoid public places, or even move away from their neighbourhood. As such, it induces fear and aloofness. If police addressed the basic signs of disorder that matter to neighbourhood residents, *and* if they invested in relations with residents, citizens might regain trust in them and might eventually be willing to address seemingly minor disorder issues themselves. Thus, disorder policing can help to restore informal social control.

This interpretation can be seen as an alternative reading of the broken windows thesis and as such can be contrasted to the abovementioned zero tolerance approach. Instead of seeing disorder as a precursor to crime and repressively focusing on "the subset of incivilities" (Taylor, 2006: 107), this strategy targets underlying causes of neighbourhood decline that lead to *both* disorder and crime: "Lack of social control might cause *both* graffiti and robbery" (Sampson & Raudenbusch, 1999: 608, emphasis added, see also Bottoms, 2006). Even if disorder has a cascading effect, "encouraging people to move [...] or discouraging efforts at building collective responses," merely fighting disorder is a "simplistic and largely misplaced" way of fighting crime (Sampson & Raudenbusch, 1999: 637).

However, that does not mean that issues of disorder are irrelevant (Bottoms, 2006: 268; Sampson, Raudenbusch, & Earls, 1997; Sampson & Raudenbusch, 1999; Taylor, 2001; Taylor, 2006). On the contrary, when residents see that the police are fighting disorder, they might feel less insecure and helpless, gain trust and eventually even the willingness to address disorder themselves. The work of Sampson & Raudenbusch (1999) proves especially insightful here. They define the preparedness to intervene in public space and to settle issues by informal social control as 'collective efficacy'. Or, to put it somewhat more elaborately: "the ability of [a]

---

16. Although some of these interpretations seem closer to zero tolerance policing than to problem oriented or hot spot variants, see also below.
17. See also Versteegh, Van der Plas & Nieuwstraten (2010) for an elaboration of problem oriented policing as a solution to crime in the wider region of The Hague.

community to regulate its members and to realize collective goals such as control-ling group processes" (Atkinson & Flint, 2004: 335). As disorder leads to aloofness and fear in public space, directing policing attention to disorder will assumedly strengthen a community's collective efficacy.[18]

This emphasis on collective efficacy echoes with some conceptions of *community policing*. Although the first ideas of community policing predate the broken win-dows theory, and its ideas vary greatly between countries, all conceptions of com-munity policing point at the disrupting effect of disorder. In effect, disorder polic-ing understood from this perspective mainly aims at restoring trust of citizens, but also at (re)building police legitimacy.

First and foremost, community policing focuses on priorities of neighbourhood residents and what bothers them most (Punch, Van der Vijver, & Zoomer, 2002; Skogan, 2006a). In general, this means the police are prepared to be involved with more (disorder) issues and to widen their scope (Skogan, 2006a: 8). The main rea-son for this approach is that addressing disorder has an important psychological relevance: "visual cues matter" (Sampson & Raudenbusch, 1999: 605; Innes, 2004). The restoring of visible order involves visible surveillance, foot patrols, neighbour-hood storefront offices and physical presence – a "maximalistic" strategy of polic-ing (Van Stokkom, 2008; see also Kelling and Coles, 1996; Skogan, 1990; Wilson and Kelling, 1982). In this respect, community policing is closely related to the notion of *reassurance policing*, as this is also a strategy that aims at taking into account the problems that matter the most to feelings of insecurity of citizens (Terpstra, 2010b). Giving prominence to these feelings and how they are related to visible signs of disorder implies that policing aims to reassure residents. Policing might even regain public trust by engineering 'control signals'. These are acts of social control that communicate to citizens that disorderly behaviour is regulated (Innes, 2004; Van Stokkom, 2007). It is claimed that investing in these signals would eventually bolster informal social control (cf. Bottoms, 2006). In other words, identifying those problems that matter most in the eyes of neighbourhood residents and showing that something is done about these issues, not only reassures residents, it might also invite them to address these problems *themselves*.[19]

Secondly, this perspective on disorder policing aims at restoring police legiti-macy, involving a strengthening of bonds between citizens and police in general (Taylor 2006: 105, Punch et al., 2002: 69). Past policing strategies such as incident-driven crime fighting and rapid response have generally failed because they

---

18. Some authors warn against seeing disorder and fear as necessarily causally related, as disorder is perceived differently at different times and in different places (Matthews, 1992; Hancock, 2001 in: Van Stokkom, 2008: 56).

19. Especially in American interpretations of community policing the emphasis is on the strengthening of informal social control, and even re-invigorating lost ideals of community and social cohesion. In this respect, disorder policing would be an opportunity to strengthen or remobilise 'the com-munity' in general (Skogan, 1990).

neglected both the importance of interaction with citizens, and their concerns, and because they estranged the police from "the communities they serve" (Skogan, 1990: 89, see also Kelling & Coles, 1996). In some cases, it is also assumed that police auxiliaries – such as the Police Community Support Officers in England and Wales – can play an important role in this respect. These officers might provide an opportunity to "instigate informal, and even innovative, means of engagement to improve dialogue with diverse populations within local communities through their enhanced visibility, familiarity and accessibility" (Cosgrove & Ramshaw, 2013: 82, cf. Crawford & Lister, 2004). These auxiliaries function as intermediaries between the police and the public, reconnecting the two in times of mounting distance and distrust (Cosgrove & Ramshaw, 2013; Crawford, 2006; Paskell, 2007).

Reception

In the Netherlands the perspective that highlights reassurance and trust can be found in various forms of community policing. Although it differs notably from its American counterparts, Dutch community policing can also be seen as a response to the standard, incident-driven policing model. At the start of the 1970s the Dutch police were seen as drifting too far from the Dutch populace. In addition, they were considered ineffective, too reactive and overtly bureaucratic. Through several developmental phases (cf. Terpstra, 2008b) – and with an important role for the abovementioned report *Police in Transition* – this change involved several ambitions that distinguish it from previous policing models. Terpstra (2010a) mentions five – enhancing citizens' trust in the police, broadening the scope of the problems with which the police is involved, using preventative and proactive strategies, cooperating with other agencies and cooperating with citizens. With these changes in policing strategies the Dutch police have taken the concerns and feelings of insecurity of neighbourhood residents more seriously.

What sets Dutch community policing apart from American ideas of community policing is its geographical orientation. Whereas the American variants of community policing (among other things) highlight notions of community building and social cohesion (Herbert, 2006), Dutch community policing prioritises the embedding of officers in geographical areas. It is mainly for these reasons that Dutch community policing is known by the name of 'area specific operating' (*gebiedsgebonden werken*; Terpstra, 2008b). This has little to do with the reinvigoration of romantic or classic ideals of community. Dutch ambitions seem more pragmatic and centred around notions of being a familiar presence in the neighbourhood ('to know and to be known'), and what might "work" (Van der Bunt & Van Swaaningen, 2012: 501). In addition, informal social control is emphasised less than proximity and the idea that citizens could *join* the police in preventing and fighting minor infractions of public order.[20] Dutch community policing seems related more to reassurance policing than to American variants that stress social cohesion and informal social control. This is all the more relevant for an interpretation of munici- pal disorder policing in the Netherlands, as municipal officers appear to be influ- enced by the idea of reassurance (Terpstra, 2008a, 2010b; see further chapter 5).

Nevertheless, notions of community and cohesion *do* play a role in Dutch public safety policy. Van Houdt & Schinkel (2014) for example, note that national Dutch safety policy incorporated concerns about "the morality of citizens and their nor- mative attachment to society" (2014: 6). In this case, the policy paper *Law in Motion*[21] leads these authors to conclude that the "Dutch government of crime has been influenced by the rationality of communitarianism" (2014: 54, see also Van Stokkom & Toenders, 2010). On a local level too, Van Houdt & Schinkel (2014) pro- vide the example of safety policy in Rotterdam where the wish for citizens to become more active was connected with the concern over "responsible communi- ties" and "vital coalitions" (*ibid.*: 11). Furthermore, prominent examples of local policy that is aimed at bolstering informal social control can be found in citizen participation projects in public safety. In these projects, residents are for instance stimulated to patrol their own neighbourhoods or set up their own network for reporting issues to police or municipality (cf. Van der Land, Van Stokkom & Bou- tellier, 2014).[22]

4   CONCLUSION

This chapter has presented a theoretical exploration of three strategies of disorder policing. For each of the strategies, the main assumptions were discussed, as well as the reception of (parts of) these strategies in the Dutch context.

The first strategy is based on a specific interpretation of the broken windows theory. The basic premises of the theory, as well as the way its most famous exam- ple – 'the New York miracle' – was advertised, makes this one of the most popular and most discussed theories in the field. This zero tolerance strategy centres on the police being supposed to crackdown on minor forms of disorder, because this would prevent these minor infringements from leading to worse forms of disorder and crime. This amounts to a repressive way of policing, in which a distinction is

---

20. The thesis that policing disorder could enhance informal social control is not supported by the daily practice of community policing in the Netherlands. Moreover, citizens are only summarily involved in everyday police work in the Netherlands. Whereas ideals might highlight the involve- ment of citizens through citizen panels or beat meetings, or else involve an elicitation to 'decent citizenship' (Nap & Van Os, 2006), in their daily work, community police officers are involved with contacting citizens only to a very limited extent. In fact, "there is only one form of citizen participa- tion which community officers are generally prepared to support: citizens as a source of informa- tion for the police" (Terpstra, 20010a: 69).
21. *Recht in Beweging* (Ministry of Justice, 1990).
22. Although such projects mostly concern a rather pragmatic activation of informal networks for the problems defined by the police or the local government.

made between orderly insiders (neighbourhood residents) and disorderly outsiders.

The second prominent strategy of disorder policing is the situational crime prevention approach. This theory is the most pragmatic of the three. Assuming any act of disorder is preceded by rational considerations, such acts can be prevented by reducing the opportunities for crime and disorder. In the case of disorder policing, this amounts to an investment in guardianship. The policing practices that bring these assumptions to mind are forms of problem oriented policing and (some) forms of hotspot policing.

The third strategy of disorder policing aims at improving informal social control and trust. By inviting residents to indicate the most pressing disorder problems and showing that these problems are tackled, residents might feel reassured. By accentuating visible cues of order, residents might even be persuaded to address these problems themselves, thus restoring informal social control. This interpretation is most evident in different variants of community policing. Although the expectation that informal social control can be restored is not prominent in every variant, these variants share a concern about reassurance.

Finally, it should be noted that this exploration of different strategies contains abstractions and simplifications. Although these strategies and their assumptions in theory can be distinguished, in practice many conceptions cross-sect and overlap (see also Onrust & Voorham, 2013; Terpstra, 2008b).[23] Hotspot policing for instance, is often a preventative practice, but it may also adopt the contours of a repressive and zero tolerance intervention, especially where it concerns the temporary increase in the number of police officers to suppress and deter disorderly behaviour (Rosenbaum, 2008). Likewise, in community policing different policy perspectives might intertwine. Here it has been explained mainly as valuing citizens' concerns and priorities, but a problem-oriented intervention may equally be dubbed community policing (Braga & Bond, 2008; Skogan, 2006a).[24] Moreover, some variants of community policing might even border on zero tolerance approaches (Punch et al., 2002: 71). In practice various policing strategies intermingle. As will be elaborated in the second part of this study, Dutch municipal disorder policing is characterised by a sometimes confusing mix of approaches to disorder, showing the influence of diverging policing strategies.

---

23. Even in theory there is a large overlap and similarity between these perspectives. Newman for instance, has been presented here as a founding father of theories of situational crime prevention, but his work also emphasises informal social control and the importance of paying attention to early disorder and decay (Newman, 1972).
24. Some even state that community policing derived its basic methodology from problem oriented policing (Punch et al., 2002).

Sociological interpretations of disorder policing

As stated in the first chapter, this study aims to develop a better understanding of Dutch municipal disorder policing by addressing *both* its dominant perspectives *and* the social and cultural context that contributed to its growth. Having explored three strategies of disorder policing in the previous chapter, this second theoretical chapter deals with the broader societal developments that might have contributed to its emergence. It does so by discussing various sociological interpretations of urban disorder and disorder policing. Nevertheless, some of these readings are closely related to what has previously been discussed, as some strategies of disorder policing appear to relate to specific societal developments, such as the weakening of informal social control.

In the first section disorder policing is interpreted as a response to changes in the urban social fabric. Largely based on the writings of Jane Jacobs, this section discusses readings that take up disorder policing as a benevolent response to a changed informal social order and to other aspects of what is called an 'urban crisis'. The second section discusses sceptical interpretations. Instead of interpreting disorder policing as an intervention to invigorate the quality of life, it is seen as a part of revanchist and exclusionary policies. In the third section, disorder policing is understood as part of what David Garland calls the 'culture of control'. Garland provides a comprehensive theory of changes in crime and disorder and governmental responses, ranging from risk management to rhetorical and emotionalised political reactions. The fourth section provides an overview by summing up the most important characteristics of these three interpretations.

1   Benevolent interpretations: disorder policing as a response to changes in the urban social fabric

The first interpretation presented here regards disorder policing as a well-meaning response to various urban changes – the decline in informal social order and the lack of trust between citizens and police forces. Part of these transitions in the social fabric of large cities in the last seventy years or so are famously captured by Jane Jacobs in her seminal work *The Death and Life of Great American Cities* (1962). In this book Jacobs provides insight into how concerns over rising segregation, the loss of informal social control and animosity in large, anonymous cities might be at the base of urban disorder.[1]

Her concerns are rooted in a somewhat nostalgic remembrance of city life as it used to be, noting how cities increasingly become segregated, uninviting places, where different people have stopped meeting or interacting in public (cf. Zukin, 2010). Jacobs mainly blames urban planners for this as they intend to reshape cities, creating a division between different functions and different types of residents, leading to a demise of vital and diverse cities into homogenous, characterless and open cityscapes, a "monotonous, unnourishing gruel" (Jacobs, 1962: 7). Moreover, these cities become increasingly segregated, with affluent citizens living in secluded suburbs and deprived citizens residing in ghettos. Through the demise of diversity, and through segregation of different functions and different groups of people, street life is lost. Jacobs laments in particular that pavements are less and less used, citizens withdraw from public space and cities are increasingly homogenised and compartmentalised into areas in which different lifestyles are isolated from each other (cf. Sennett, 1971). Jacobs essentially seems to grieve over the loss of a truly public space, in that it is less and less a meeting place for strangers or what she calls a 'sidewalk ballet'.

Most important for the point made here, *The Death and Life of Great American Cities* also discusses the preconditions for a more vibrant public space. According to Jacobs, a livelier and inviting street-life can only be attained by re-centring citizens' own interests and ways of maintaining order. Thus, an important part of her ideas about city life concerns the social order that accompanies these city scenes as "theatres of differences". Cities can only be vital if there is a healthy degree of informal social control among different users of public space: "there must be eyes on the street, eyes belonging to those we might call the natural proprietors of the street" (Jacobs, 1962: 35). Particularly this latter perspective became increasingly popular in later thinking about disorder and how to police it.

Although there is an evident rift between Jacobs' longing for informal social control and formal disorder policing, the establishment of disorder policing can equally be seen as an answer to a lack of trust among city residents and to their fear to enter public space. Thus disorder policing might be a way of controlling the 'publicness' of public places. Focusing on predictability, reliability and maintaining a level of 'normality', disorder policing enables people to trust others in their environment and to interact freely in public (cf. Misztal, 2001). Understood in these terms, the later advent of disorder policing is a contribution to basic ordering that

---

1. Although Jacobs herself does not mention *formal* social control, her thinking seems to have notable influence on later theories of disorder policing, especially the broken windows theory (Ranasinghe, 2012).

"makes possible a basis for action" (Lofland, 1973: 95, see also Bottoms, 2006).[2] Other authors relate this to what they call the "domestication" of public spaces, helping people "to be at home in cities" (Koch & Latham, 2012: 19). City land-scapes that have changed into uninviting spaces can be revitalised. Often this is done by physical design-led interventions, such as putting up benches, opening up dark and secluded parks or creating other interventions to enhance "pleasurable encounters" and stimulate "convivial forms of sociality" (Koch & Latham, 2012: 7, Van Stokkom, 2008). The term domestication here in a sense refers to what Lofland would call "creating home territories" (1973: 119). Surveillance and control by uni-formed wardens might be seen as part of this domestication.[3]

Jacobs' thinking does not stand alone. In fact, it seems indicative of a wider aware-ness of the urban issues in the 1960s and 1970s, albeit this awareness was expressed in various terms. Other writers refer to, for instance, "the urban problem" (Wilson, 1969) or "the urban crisis" (Banfield, 1970, in: Ranasinghe 2012) and see the omni-presence of "improper behaviour" as a result of "the failure of community" (Wil-son, 1969). Yet other studies and reports address racial segregation, the frequent occurrence of riots and widespread distrust between citizens of lower-income neighbourhoods and the police in the 1960s (Taylor, 2006).

These observations, diverse as they might be, also form the intellectual founda-tions of later, more elaborate concerns about community policing and the first for-mulations of disorder policing in the broken windows theory (Ranasinghe, 2012; Skogan, 2006b; Taylor, 2006). New forms of (disorder) policing would provide an opportunity to involve communities in crime fighting and to enhance trust between police officers and neighbourhood residents. Thus, already these early conceptions of disorder policing are characterised by a wish to provide a solution to different problems – distrust between police and (deprived) citizens on the one hand, and changes in the urban environment and informal social control on the other hand (Taylor, 2006; see also Rosenbaum, 1988).

Although the Dutch situation is not comparable to the widespread antagonism in some large American cities in the 1960s, early Dutch forms of community polic-ing in fact were also a response to changed urban conditions and a wish to restore the relation with the "societal environment" (Terpstra, 2008b). Police forces were seen as bureaucratically isolated, as focused too much on (reactive) law enforce-ment, and therefore needed to be brought closer to the communities they were supposed to serve (even though these ambitions were generally not related to

---

2.   Some actually assume an important role for 'intermediary' plural policing functions in this respect. Neighbourhood wardens for instance, can create the conditions for 'vibrant communities', quite contrary to "a narrow state police-centred focus on law enforcement in the promotion of civility" (Crawford, 2006: 974).

3.   Although domestication also has a pejorative ring to it, privatising or 'colonising' interventions seclude unwanted people, enhance exclusion and limit the use of public spaces by multiple and diverse cultures (Atkinson, 2003; Lofland, 1973). See further below.

notions of a growing underclass). In this respect, especially the 1977 police policy document *Police in Transition* (*Politie in Verandering*) led the way for a more decentralised police organisation that was better integrated in society and could regain the police's legitimacy (Terpstra, 2008b: 16).

2   SCEPTICAL INTERPRETATIONS: DISORDER POLICING AS AN EXCLUSIONARY
           RESPONSE

Although rooted in diverse observations, disorder policing may predominantly be interpreted as springing from citizens' concerns or worries over urban communities. In this respect, disorder policing is seen as an inclusive intervention, aimed at involving different residents, defending 'the publicness of public space', and at its core concerned with diversity.

    By contrast, a more sceptical interpretation points out that the rhetoric of citizen oriented policing merely shrouds the exclusionary practice of disorder policing. Hence, disorder policing may be seen as defending narrowly defined interests. It sees disorder policing as part of 'urban revanchism', as the extension of the interests of middle-class citizens at worst, or as a mistaken response to problems of marginality at best. Other sceptical readings highlight its exclusionary character, especially where it concerns the policing of incivilities or anti-social behaviour.

One such sceptical reading pointing to disorder policing as an exclusionary practice can be found in the work of Neil Smith (1996, 2002). Smith describes initiatives that are meant to improve the quality of life of neighbourhoods, but his analyses and conclusions are at odds with the abovementioned benevolent readings. In fact, quality of life initiatives are part of what Smith calls 'urban revanchism'.

    Smith specifically targets urban policies that are advertised as 'gentrification'. By these policies, governments stimulate well-to-do people to move into streets and neighbourhoods on the verge of 'tipping', of sliding into further decline (Smith, 1996). The influx of these residents is thought to help improve neighbourhoods and create an upward spiral of amelioration (Smith, 1996: 15). The effect however, is that the less well-to-do allegedly lose their "right to the city" (Mitchell, 2003). Thus the quality of life this policy aims at is not meant to benefit all populations in the city, but has an exclusionary character. Here, 'quality of life' becomes an instrument to condemn other, marginal life styles. Urban upgrading, regeneration and gentrification thus benefit only middle class citizens (Smith, 1996: 89). Crucial to understanding this revanchism according to Smith, is the loss of middle class optimism in times of economic setback (Smith, 1996: 47). Revanchism "represents a reaction against the supposed "theft" of the city, a desperate defence of a challenged phalanx of privileges, cloaked in the populist language of civic morality, family values and neighbourhood security" (*ibid*.: 211). Moreover, processes of gentrification and revanchism are closely intertwined with neo-liberal tendencies, as consumerist values prevail. Thus, influenced by the predominance of global capital and neo-liberalist values, various cities across the globe are now characterised by an exclusionary regulation of public space, changing large areas into what might be termed 'pseudo-private spaces' (Mitchell & Staeheli, 2006; Smith, 2002).

In this respect, disorder policing can also be seen as a mistaken response to issues of marginality (Wacquant, 2008).[4] French sociologist Loïc Wacquant for instance, opposes the view that urban disorder is the result of a moral crisis of the working class (*ibid*.: 24), or – in Jacobsian terms – of a loss of eyes on the streets. Instead, Wacquant sees the "public disorders caused by dispossessed youth"[5] as a result of "massive structural violence unleashed upon them by a set of mutually reinforcing economic and socio-political changes" (*ibid*.: 24), resulting in "mass unemployment", "relegation to decaying neighbourhoods" and "heightened stig-matisation" (*ibid*.: 25). Even though American 'hyper-ghetto's' and French *banlieues* are not comparable to Dutch deprived neighbourhoods, the gist of Wacquant's interpretation might equally apply to forms of disorder policing found here. Entrusting the police with providing the solution to complex problems of margin-ality transforms feelings of *social* insecurity to problems of *criminal* insecurity (*ibid*.: 12). Hence, disorder policing might exacerbate social tensions, urban unrest and marginality, especially where the police are prone to violence and intimidation themselves. One could even go so far as to say that sending in police as a response to marginality might be no more than a way to give state authorities the "comfort-ing feeling that it is responding to the demands of the 'people' while at the same time exculpating its own historic responsibility in the making of the urban outcasts of the new century" (*ibid*.: 12).

Closely related to Smith's ideas of urban revanchism, various studies are equally sceptical of disorder policing. However, these studies limit themselves to specific contexts and mostly refrain from the revanchist terminology altogether, instead focusing on the process of exclusion as such.

Some authors point to the increase in social control and the criminalisation of minor forms of disorder (Crawford, 2006; Hughes, 2007, in: Devroe, 2012), a proc-ess that is also referred to as 'net widening'. This term, first coined by Stanley Cohen (1979), implies that an increasing array of incivilities or disruptive behav-iour is criminalised. Others see this as proof of the criminalisation of everyday

---

4.   Some oppose the terminology of classes altogether, as this merely obscures a more profound and nuanced analysis of "struggles over the city," where notions of inclusion, identity and the 'civilis-ing' of the urban poor are of more importance (Van Eijk, 2010; Uitermark & Duyvendak, 2008). In fact, the labelling of different 'classes' itself springs from a state-led "moulding" of marginality (Wacquant, 2008: 8) in which 'the underclass' is a category imposed from outside and used to define "groups who are socially and morally disconnected from the rest of society with different values; the 'depraved rather than the deprived'" (Crawford, 2006: 959).

5.   In Wacquant's case, large scale disorders such as mass rioting, or looting.

behaviour (Bannister, Fyfe & Kearns, 2006), or of a process of 'defining deviancy up' (Devroe, 2012; Krauthamer, 1993). Yet other authors point out that the quest for a new urban aesthetics, and the ensuing focus on anti-social behaviour use questionable definitions of what exactly is anti-social (Cook & Whowell, 2011; Millie, 2008; cf. Mitchell, 2003). In some studies new forms of disorder policing are discussed as part of such dubious exclusionary practices. Often these forms of disorder policing target homeless people, such as in Beckett & Herbert's (2010) account of banishment by the use of off-limit orders in the city of Montreal. Van de Bunt & Van Swaaningen (2012) point out that such exclusionary tendencies can also be found in the Dutch context.

This interpretation provides a contrasting perspective on what was earlier called the domestication of public space. Instead of opting for diversity, state actors privatise public places and choreograph urban landscapes in a fashion that sends a clear signal that certain people and lifestyles are not welcome (Allen & Crookes, 2009; Macleod & Johnstone, 2012). In doing so, they create new "dwelling scapes" meant for consumerist middle class households, thereby both sanitising these backward areas and instilling civility and control (Allen & Crookes, 2009). In addition, other authors see exclusionary disorder policing as limited to specific urban areas, or see negative consequences as concomitant with specific localities and times, such as the night-time economy – a reading that is of equal relevance for developments in the Dutch context (Van Aalst & Van Liempt, 2012; see also Hae, 2011, Hobbs, Lister, Hadfield, Winlow & Hall, 2000). Hence, the outcomes of state-led strategies to enhance the quality of life of poorer neighbourhoods might in fact include "deepened social cleavages and growing indifference" instead of creating a public space that is accessible to anyone (Uitermark, Duyvendak & Kleinhans, 2007: 137).

3   COMPREHENSIVE INTERPRETATIONS: DISORDER POLICING AS RISK
         MANAGEMENT AND 'ACTING OUT'

The two interpretations of disorder policing discussed hitherto leave us with two sharply opposing views. Whereas the first interpretation sees disorder policing as a benevolent reaction to urban problems, the second set of interpretations assumes that the structural causes for disorder do not tally with the exclusionary reasons why state actors would invest in disorder policing in the first place.

A third and final interpretation of disorder policing presented here unites these two contrasting visions into one comprehensive theory. David Garland's *The culture of control* (2001) provides an opportunity to see both developments in crime and disorder *and* the diverse responses to those as part of a larger cultural framework (Young, 2003). Vital in understanding this framework is Garland's notion of a 'criminological predicament'. Put simply, crime has been rising over the years, whereas the capacity of the criminal justice system to deal with it is limited (Garland, 2001: 106). Garland states that any crime policy (and rhetoric) basically can be seen as a response to the governmental "loss of sovereignty" over issues of disorder and crime. Thus this predicament of high crime and limited state capacity functions as the organising principle of his theory and encompasses contradictory state responses, a schizoid form of policy and a portrayal of man torn between different ideologies.[6]

Garland accounts for these contradictions by stating that in this newly emerged culture of control, several opposing 'criminologies' inform policy simultaneously; multiple ideologies conflict over crime and punishment. In this way the culture of control is characterised by both a primacy of rational choice on the one hand, and strong and punitive interventions for moral wrongs on the other hand. Garland frames these distinct state responses to the abovementioned criminological predicament by calling them 'adaptive' or 'non-adaptive' (Garland, 2001: 106 ff.).

Disorder policing as risk management: a criminology of the self

Adaptive state responses to the abovementioned predicament can be characterised by their move away from previous rehabilitative penology. Instead of a welfarist belief in the malleability of man, adaptive responses to the loss of state sovereignty over disorder are led mostly by administrative actors, trying to *control* instead of structurally *change* disorder. Hence managing the risks of crime and disorder is seen as a viable alternative to alleged unrealistic reformation and rehabilitation of offenders. Since offenders are seen as "rational actors who are responsive to disincentives and fully responsible for their criminal acts," crime or deviancy regarded as the result of individual pathology or abnormality with a role for "faulty socialisation or social dysfunction" have no more validity (*ibid.*: 16).[7]

An important result of this focus on control is the administrative 'defining down' of deviance. By reducing the number of acts that are penalised, limited state capacity is dealt with in an adaptive way. As a result, governments try to minimise the harm caused by offenders, without a true interest in rehabilitation or correction (O'Malley, 2010). This adaptive strategy can explain the strong influence of a paradigm of rational choice and the popularity of situational crime prevention strategies (Garland, 1999). As everybody is thought to act in the same way under the same circumstances, disorder and crime are controlled by anticipating how possible offenders might make their choices in specific situations. For this reason, this adaptive response may equally be called a 'criminology of the self'.

---

6.   Garland presents a highly ambitious and all-encompassing theory. Here I do not have the room to explore this theory in all its refinedness. For a more extensive discussion of his theory and how it applies to new legislation on incivilities in Belgium, see Devroe, 2012.

7.   Just as poverty or social exclusion is the result of "poor choices made by uninformed, unmotivated, incompetent or irresponsible individuals" (Crawford, 2009: 814).

Two other characteristics of this strategy are of interest here. The first is the relocating and redefining of responsibilities for dealing with crime and disorder in "an enhanced network of more or less directed, more or less informal crime control, complementing and extending the formal controls of the criminal justice state" (Garland, 2001: 124). The formation of a "strategic relation to other forces of social control" is crucial (Garland, 2001: 124). A second characteristic concerns the aim of preventing crime, as an alternative to reactive strategies. In Garland's view, these preventative goals and the tendency to relocate responsibilities for crime and disorder control are closely connected. Non state-actors, such as the private sector or communities themselves, share in the management of crime and thereby make it easier to manage security (Ashworth & Zedner, 2014: 10). Thus one can see an expanding infrastructure of crime prevention and community safety in the form of "preventative partnerships" (Garland, 2001: 17; cf. Newburn, 2001). In Dutch public safety policy these developments can also be noted, especially in the aforementioned *'Integrated Public Safety Policy'* (cf. chapter 1; Van Houdt & Schinkel, 2014).

These tendencies to control can also be linked to an expanding system of legal and administrative regulatory innovations. In recent years the criminal justice system of several countries (most research focuses on US and UK examples) has seen the ascendance of preventive orders (Ashworth & Zedner, 2014; Beckett & Herbert, 2008; Crawford, 2009; Koemans, 2011; Simester & Von Hirsch, 2006). These relatively new orders are used as partly rhetorical alternatives to dysfunctional reactive punishment, moving the focus from punishment to regulation (Ashworth & Zedner, 2014; Crawford, 2009). Here the drive to control deviancy and the tendency described above to banish unwanted people are interconnected, as these orders provide an opportunity to deal with disorderly conduct that escapes criminal law (Crawford, 2009). Possibly deviant persons are confronted with an contract-like agreement that restricts their behaviour in public places. Some of these preventive orders specifically target 'disorderly behaviour', the most well-known being the 'Anti Social Behaviour Order' (ASBO; Ashworth & Zedner, 2014; Koemans, 2011; Macdonald, 2006). In the Dutch context, restraining orders used by Dutch local governments to deal with anti-social behaviour of unruly juveniles are reminiscent of these British preventive orders. The most notable example is the Dutch soccer law (Dutch: *Voetbalwet*[8]), meant to impose restrictive preventive orders on football hooligans and other deviant persons, but in reality used mostly for preventing disorder in residential areas by banishing troublesome persons (Van de Bunt & Van Swaaningen, 2012; see also Becket & Herbert, 2008).

---

8.   In Dutch known as *Wet maatregelen bestrijding voetbalvandalisme en ernstige overlast.*

Disorder policing as 'acting out': a criminology of the other

Contradicting these adaptive responses, state actors respond equally in a 'non adaptive' way to the loss of state sovereignty over crime and disorder. In this respect, and as opposed to the primacy of rational choice and the management of disorderly behaviour, the 'culture of control' also encompasses absolute ideas about moral good and bad. State actors – in this case politicians rather than administrative actors – vocally respond to high crime and disorder by 'acting out': they vent emotionalised and rhetorical reactions that suggest decisiveness. Thus disorder policing can also be seen as part of an emotional reaction to threats by outsiders, a 'criminology of the other', with a clear depiction of the "fearsome stranger" (2001: 137):

> As crime and punishment came to be highly charged election issues, government and opposition parties competed to establish their credentials as being tough on crime, concerned for public safety, and capable of restoring morality, order and discipline in the face of the corrosive social changes of late modernity (Garland, 2001: 131).

Many of these reactions have a highly symbolic significance, especially those that involve political attention to 'the public'. On the outset of *The Culture of Control*, Garland mentions several changes that show the emotional tone of crime policy. Thus not only crime in itself is targeted, but also and chiefly, its effects in terms of fear and the emotional reactions of the public. In other words, "[c]rime has been re-dramatized" (*ibid.*: 10), conjuring up "stereotypical depictions of unruly youth, dangerous predators, and incorrigible career criminals" (*ibid.*). This leads to stronger reactions from an emotional public, a "righteous demand for retribution" (*ibid.*). Closely related is "the return of the victim" (*ibid.*: 11), a discursive emphasis on the victim's experience as representative for the whole population and the notion that "the public must be protected" (*ibid.*: 12). Lastly, and likewise closely related, there is a tendency to distrust expert knowledge on crime fighting, instead emphasising 'common sense' and the "authority of the people" (*ibid.*: 13) as reflected in a "politicisation of crime policy and a 'new populism'" (*ibid.*).

As such, this interpretation has some similarity to the urban revanchist and exclusionary interpretation mentioned above as it puts an equal emphasis on clear boundaries between insiders and outsiders, between order and disorder. However, it is informed by different reasoning. Whereas the urban revanchist interpretation highlights disorder policing as the result of a neo-liberal and rights based middle class pressure on local government, Garland's idea of this non-adaptive strategy has an emotional, neo-conservative tone and should be understood more as an act to reinvest in the impression that the state is in control of crime and disorder. These responses therefore should be seen as informed by symbolical interests of state actors themselves. What has been described in chapter 2 about the influence of zero tolerance thinking in Dutch security policies could be seen as concurring with this non-adaptive reading. Especially the rhetorics of decisiveness and of a 'turn to the people' that are inherent in the policy plan *Towards a Safer Society* appear to be in line with what Garland calls a "criminology of the other". Moreover, several authors have shown such a non-adaptive reading might be of relevance in understanding the establishment of new legislation for controlling disorder (cf. Devroe, 2012).

4   OVERVIEW

In this chapter several sociological interpretations have been discussed to provide support for a better understanding of the growth of disorder policing. Expanding on the exploration of various strategies of disorder policing in the previous chapter, it has provided a more thorough understanding of various cultural and social factors that may have led to these strategies.

The first set of interpretations of the establishment and advent of disorder policing might be termed benevolent responses to changes in the social order of large cities. Firstly, by addressing Jane Jacobs' seminal writings on the disappearance of 'eyes on the streets' that once made a vibrant urban life possible, disorder policing may be understood as a governmental response to a decline of informal social control. This interpretation emphasises that public spaces will lose their 'publicness' when they lack such basic ordering, as they will devolve into uninviting and unpredictable spaces, avoided by most citizens. Viewed from this perspective, disorder policing might be a form of domesticating public space, keeping it open for a diverse public with diverse interests. Secondly, the initial forms of disorder policing were informed by concerns about the alienation of police officers from urban communities. Thus disorder policing can be seen as attempts at police reform and at improving the relation between police and society.

The second set of interpretations, in many respects, opposes these readings. Instead of the benevolent view of disorder policing as a sincere and inclusive response to a changing urban environment, it sceptically regards disorder policing as the defence of more narrowly defined interests. In the most radical of these interpretations, the urban revanchist view of Neil Smith and the like, disorder policing is the result of the strong influence of the middle class on the local agenda. Moreover, disorder policing seems a mistaken solution to problems of marginality that beg for other approaches. Addressing marginality through such solutions might only heighten social tensions, increase urban unrest and encourage segregation. Other authors assert that 'quality of life' initiatives or 'anti-social behaviour' agendas are cloaked attempts at excluding or banishing marginal groups of citizens. This might be of equal relevance to the Dutch context, especially with regard to shopping districts and the night-time economy.

The last sociological interpretation of disorder policing combines the preceding theories by acknowledging both the commonality of crime and disorder issues *and* state responses. David Garland's *Culture of Control* proved to be of help here. By encompassing both adaptive and non-adaptive responses to the predicament of high crime and limited state capacity, his theory provides an opportunity to understand contradictory tendencies in disorder policing. Thus where disorder policing on the one hand might be an example of risk management in which the abundance of crime and disorder are merely controlled through a variety of preventative measures and interventions, on the other hand it might be characterised by an emotional, politically incited acting out against threats from the outside. Both these reactions are part of the same inherently contradictory 'culture of control' and thus could provide ample support for interpreting various forms of Dutch municipal disorder policing yet to be unearthed in this study.

4 | METHODOLOGY

After the theoretical exploration of disorder policing, this chapter deals with the methodological design and approach of this study.

In section 1 the general research strategies and process are described. Next, section 2 deals with the research design and the selection of respondents and cases. This is done by describing the two different phases of research and the various elements that constitute these phases. Section 3 focuses on the specific methods. Finally, section 4 reflects on the methodological quality of the study in terms of validity and reliability.

1   APPROACH

Research strategies: case studies and ethnographic research

The main questions of this study as described in chapter 1 demand a research design that allows for an open approach of the phenomenon of municipal disorder policing. This approach helps to find out how this subject is "locally constituted," how those involved define it and give meaning to its practice (Silverman, 2011: 17). Only a qualitative research design provides this opportunity. Within that design I chose two research strategies: case studies and ethnographic research.

A case study design allows studying a phenomenon in a specific locality and as part of a network of relations, perceptions, attitudes and behaviour (Swanborn, 2010). As the research interest concerned the context of municipal disorder policing and the divergent perspectives that might inform it, case studies seemed appropriate for studying relatively confined cases of municipal disorder policing (cf. Leys, Zaitch, & Decorte, 2010). In addition, this strategy provided the best opportunity for studying the changes *within* certain cases, as well as for a cross-comparison between different localities (Swanborn, 2010). Finally, as a case study is best suited for *how* and *why* questions, this matched the abovementioned division in two consecutive phases (Leys et al., 2010; Yin, 1984). The first phase contained six case studies of municipal disorder policing in six different cities (see below) and was aimed at developing a better understanding of *how* municipal disorder policing is done in the Netherlands. The second phase involved two case studies, focused on

local policy, and dealt with *why*-questions and the in-depth description of local circumstances, interests and views that determine municipal disorder policing. Thus,
what exactly constituted a single case differed between the first and the second
phase of research.

The second research strategy is that of the ethnographic study.[1] This strategy
partly overlaps with case study design, but deserves to be mentioned separately
here.[2] On various occasions in this study, municipal officers or municipal disorder
policing was approached as a "cultural or social group or system" (Creswell, 1998).
As such, the enquiry was not always led by the cases of local policy, but also by an
interest in what municipal officers as members of an occupational group think, say
and do (Creswell, 1998). As will become more evident below, this is of specific
importance for chapters 7, 8 and 9.

A cyclical research process

As a result of the exploratory approach, this research had a notably cyclical character (Spradley, 1980). Whereas linear research designs have a clearly defined and
chronologically ordered research pattern of hypotheses, operationalisation, data
collection, analysis and reporting, a cyclical approach is characterised by the possibility to frame new questions or fine-tune existing questions after data has been
collected (*ibid.*). Hence questions were (re)focused at several key moments during
this research. At the outset of the first phase for instance, questions were formed to
provide direction and scope for the case studies (Simons, 2009: 31). These initial
questions allowed room to develop into more focussed questions, depending on
the first findings. Consequently, they were adapted as a result of new insights.
Thus, refocused research questions helped to define interesting cases and spot
those situations that urged a more thorough description and explanation.

This cyclical process impacted equally on the use of literature. On the one hand,
studying literature helped to focus the research questions. On the other hand,
exploratory intentions demanded an open approach, implying the research was
not purely theory-led. Thus, this study contained phases of a more theory-generat-
ing character (Glaser & Strauss, 2012). This implied that theoretical reflections were
often involved only *after* the patterns of the empirical findings had been assessed,
analysed and coded. This approach – loosely inspired by the notion of *grounded
theory* (*ibid.*) – will prove to be of importance for several aspects of the methodology described below. Moreover, it implies that the theories that were discussed in
chapters 2 and 3 served mainly to provide a framework for orientation and retrospective interpretation.

---

1.   Although not all text books define it as a separate strategy (cf. Marshall & Rossman, 2006).
2.   Some define ethnographic case studies as a particular subtype of case studies (Simons, 2009).

2   RESEARCH DESIGN AND CASE SELECTION

As the organisational and political context of municipal disorder policing has received only scant academic attention, I only gradually developed an idea which respondents could provide most insights. This implied that the research evolved gradually, relying on initial insights to develop a better understanding of the most important stakeholders. In the first phase of research, this happened through relying on 'gatekeepers'. These are initial, well-versed contacts who are part of the municipal city surveillance agency or the encompassing organisations. These persons were of great help in extending contacts within their organisation. This way of designing fieldwork resembles what is known as 'snowball sampling', implying the use of first respondents' accounts to find other important and influential respondents (Bernard, 2006).

Phase 1: Study of municipal disorder policing in six cities

The first, most extensive phase concerned the study of municipal disorder policing in six major Dutch cities. As mentioned above, this initial phase was motivated by a special interest in local policy and collaboration with the police.

For this initial study I used purposive sampling to select city surveillance agencies in the largest Dutch municipalities (Leys et al., 2010; Silverman, 2011). Large cities were selected as they involve their own, specific type of public safety problems. These are mostly concentrated in central areas, surrounding central stations, in night-life areas and close to tourist attractions. In contrast, residential areas have their own particular problems of public safety. This variety makes large municipalities interesting locations for in-depth studies of municipal disorder policing.[3]

Focusing on city surveillance agencies as an initial unit for case selection implies that the emphasis is on a meso level, in between macro and micro developments (Leys et al., 2010: 186). These agencies have to deal with national and municipal (macro) developments in policy and legislation. At the same time, studying these agencies as cases gives many opportunities to study views and developments on a micro-level, such as ideas of local (neighbourhood) stakeholders, the views and expectations of municipal officers or specific (nested) cases of local policy.

The most important criteria for selecting the six agencies mentioned below concerned the characteristics of the cities and of the agencies themselves. Hence, the size of the city, its geographical location and the presence of a variety of notable public safety and quality-of-life issues were considered. I selected six cities with

---

3.   As such, the findings in this study apply exclusively to the development of municipal disorder policing in these larger municipalities. Municipal disorder policing in middle-sized and small Dutch municipalities might not be comparable to its counterpart in larger cities, not in the least because police reorganisations of late may have had more of an impact in these municipalities (see also: Bervoets, 2013; Terpstra et al., 2016).

relatively similar public safety issues. In addition, the city surveillance agencies themselves were relatively well developed and professionalised. In contrast, the selection was varied in terms of the geographical location of the cities, and the policy and approach of the different agencies (insofar this could be ascertained based on initial orientations). This combination of a number of equal characteristics, with variety in other aspects, allowed comparison between different cases of municipal disorder policing (Simons, 2009: 30).

The following six cities and their city surveillance agencies were selected as cases, in order of size and their place on the list of largest municipalities in the Netherlands:[4]

–   Rotterdam (2nd),
–   Den Haag/The Hague (3rd),
–   Utrecht (4th),
–   Eindhoven (5th),
–   Tilburg (6th), and
–   Nijmegen (10th).

The most remarkable absentee in this list is the city of Amsterdam. As one of the few cities in the Netherlands, Amsterdam has been the subject of a relatively large number of studies in recent years (cf. Van Steden & De Groot, 2011; Van Steden & Bron, 2012; Van Stokkom, 2013b, Van Stokkom & Foekens, 2015). Both to avoid a possible burden of too much research and overvaluing insights from this city, this selection starts with the 2nd largest city, Rotterdam. Furthermore, the largest Dutch cities can be found in the urban conglomeration in the central West area, indicated as *Randstad*. I included three cities in this area – Rotterdam, The Hague and Utrecht. The three other cities in this study are outside this administrative and political region – Tilburg, Eindhoven and Nijmegen. Tilburg and Eindhoven were chosen as large, provincial cities and because of the prominence of public safety issues in these cities (Fijnaut et al., 2008). Furthermore, as these cities are both located in the province of Noord-Brabant, the sixth city was selected outside this province – Nijmegen, 10th on the list of largest municipalities in the Netherlands.[5]

In each city, approximately 16 persons were interviewed, totalling 98 individuals. These respondents were spread over four different types of organisations. First, and obviously, interviews were held with representatives of the city surveillance agencies – municipal officers, coordinators and managers. Second, to get a proper view of the organisational and historical context, interviews were conducted with

4.   https://nl.wikipedia.org/wiki/Lijst_van_grootste_gemeenten_in_Nederland; indicating the largest municipalities as per 1-4-2016.
5.   Almere, the 7th city on the list, was not involved due to its proximity to the Randstad area. Breda, the 8th city on the list, was not selected as it would have been another city from the province of Brabant. Groningen, number 9, was not involved due to practical circumstances (mainly: its relative remoteness – an example of "convenience sampling"; Leys et al., 2010: 187).

respondents from the wider municipal organisation, such as senior managers from policy departments of public safety, neighbourhood managers and employees from other municipal units (e.g. public maintenance). Third, police representatives of various ranks were interviewed.[6] Lastly, several political respondents and representatives of the local offices of the public prosecutor were interviewed. In addition, policy documents were scrutinised in each city, especially those that provided insight in policy and organisational structure. In section 3, I will explain more about the study of available policy documents, the nature and type of the interviews and their analysis.

Phase 2: In-depth study – renewed analysis, historical development, and two in-depth case studies

The next phase of this study comprised additional in-depth research and was divided into three different elements.

First of all, part of the material collected during the first research phase was re-analysed. Due to the use of an exploratory approach and semi-structured interviews in this first phase (see below), many respondents reflected freely on a variety of themes during interviews. Thus, these initial interviews proved to be rich in insights that had remained unearthed. Through a renewed analysis of existing material, these elements were given more attention in the second phase, resulting in a new set of findings. For this renewed analysis, I selected those interviews that were particularly rich in views about the importance of disorder policing and that provided the most information on how decisions about disorder policing are made locally.

The second element of the new research phase consisted of extra research to find out more about the historical developments of municipal disorder policing in the Netherlands. Earlier interviews and previous studies supported some general notions of these developments, but these remained of a somewhat unspecific nature and demanded extra study. As this extra study concerned the history and development of municipal disorder policing, it involved both the study of documents (see below for a further explanation), and interviews with some managers and researchers who were involved with early forms of Dutch municipal disorder policing.

The third element of the new research phase consists of two case studies on municipal disorder policing in situations of urgent disorder. The main reason to involve case studies is again informed by the wish to deepen earlier analyses of municipal disorder policing. After having developed a better understanding of dif-

---

6.   The initial research design preserved more space for studying the relations and collaboration between municipal and police officers. Although the views of police representatives were of vital importance for chapter 9, insights from these interviews are discussed more thoroughly elsewhere (Eikenaar & Van Stokkom, 2014).

ferent stakeholders and their respective views, case studies provided the best opportunity to obtain insight into how these stakeholders might actually influence each other and the practice of municipal disorder policing. In addition, the first phase of the research showed that many of the disorder problems are concentrated in fairly confined areas. As such, the agendas for disorder policing differ to a great extent and are constantly (re)defined on local levels, especially if disorder is seen as an urgent issue.

For this part of phase 2 in the study I returned to two previous cases of 'target group policing' in which the activities of municipal officers are directed at specific groups. One case concerned street youth, the other concerned drug dealers, drug users and homeless people. In these cases a total of 12 extra respondents were interviewed. In addition, I joined municipal officers on their daily (or nightly) work. During these shifts I was able to observe the way these officers fulfil their tasks, and had the opportunity to conduct what are called walking (or informal – Bernard, 2006: 204) interviews and have conversations with approximately 15 different officers.

3   RESEARCH METHODS

Interviews

To answer the research questions, my most frequently used method was the semi-structured interview. This form of interviewing allowed me to conduct the interview with a topic list, but provided sufficient space for following new leads and incentives, and prevented the impression of "excessive control" (Bernard, 2006: 205).

Due to the variety in the design of the enquiry, respondents from various backgrounds and affiliations were questioned, both about facts and their views on relevant matters. This was often because of their specific expertise, but in several cases also to collect a wide variety of opinions. As noted, I specifically aimed at involving respondents from various organisational affiliations to develop an all-encompassing view of the policy and practice of municipal disorder policing. This applies to both the first and the second phase of the research.

Interviews were generally conducted at the work place of the respondents and in an unconstrained atmosphere. This was created using relatively little interference with the respondents' accounts by "get[ting] people on a topic of interest and get[ting] out of the way" (Bernard 2006: 209) and by assuring the respondent of anonymity. On average, the interviews lasted one hour. They were generally recorded, with one or two exceptions, depending on respondents' requests. In a few cases, respondents were interviewed in pairs, sometimes because work schedules did not allow two interviews, and sometimes because interviewees could complement each other's answers. In general, respondents showed willingness and openness to talk about their experiences and ideas.

In order to structure the interviews (Bernard, 2006), topic lists – based on relevant topics and questions – were prepared in advance. These topic lists were adapted to suit the variety of respondents. As a result, topic lists for the initial research phase were grouped in four categories, depending on the respondent's organisational affiliation (see above). Then I developed topic lists for each function in the respective organisation, for instance frontline worker, coordinator or (senior) manager. In the second phase, obviously other topic lists were needed.

Document study

A second research method was the study of documents. Policy documents were collected to get a better understanding of policy goals, organisational structure and the municipal organisation of disorder policing.

Several types of documents were used. First of all, policies on a national level were studied by involving a range of policy plans and policy statements. Among them were the policy plans that announced nation-wide changes in public safety policy, written to the Lower House and also the letters that the Minister for Safety and Justice wrote to inform the Lower House were used on several occasions. Other policy documents that transcend local policy are the BOA note (*BOA circulaire*) and its successors, its juridical backing (the Decree on BOAs and the Police Act of 1993, article 142), as well as statements, for instance by the Dutch association of municipalities (VNG) or vision documents from occupational organisation *BeBOA*. Second, local policy was scrutinised by studying 'enforcement plans' and documents that targeted the (re)development of municipal surveillance and enforcement. In addition, several documents with a more political stance were analysed – coalition agreements and policy programmes insofar they concerned the development of local safety policy and the role of municipal officers. Next, documents were studied that provided more insight into the approach of the city surveillance agencies themselves. These included what the Dutch mostly refer to as *plan van aanpak* (action plan) and the evaluations of defined projects. Organisation matrices and departmental schemes provided further grip on the organisational structure of the city surveillance agencies. Lastly, on several occasions – especially in chapter 5 – literature study and empirical study were combined. Thereby the results of previous studies, for instance on early administrative prevention were merged with new insights from policy documents and the accounts of respondents.

It proved hard to obtain certain documents: in none of the cases was an easily accessible or coherent collection of policy documents available. Not least, so it seems, because explicit policy theory is poorly reflected in municipal disorder policing.[7] For this reason, I had to rely on a variety of resources to develop a better understanding of policy and how it developed. It implied that (early) thoughts on municipal policy in some cases were best acquired through interviews. In some cases, I was able to access municipal archives, obtaining documents on the development of municipal disorder policing itself or on the political debates that are relevant to understanding its background. In other cases, municipal archives were not accessible until a relatively recent date or did not yield any relevant results on the subject of municipal disorder policing. My account of the history of municipal disorder policing therefore is based on a somewhat varied and disparate assembly of resources and earlier insights recorded by previous researchers.

Observation

Observation was the final method used in this study; and it was used only in the two in-depth case studies of the additional research phase. The reason for the modest amount of time dedicated to this approach is that observation was mainly meant to deepen prior insights. Joining the shifts of municipal officers was of vital importance to develop a better understanding of how the daily work of frontline professionals is influenced by different stakeholders. During the shifts on which I joined municipal officers I was able to observe what they do and how they spend their time during their shifts. This enabled me to put these officers' views in the context of their daily work. Moreover, their acts provided the occasion to ask more in-depth questions (cf. Agar, 2008). As such, observation in these two cases did not only provide the chance to get a better understanding of the daily work of a specific group of municipal officers, but also allowed a large number of walking, improvised and informal interviews and conversations (Bernard, 2006). Talking to municipal officers on a number of informal occasions – be it on the street, at the coffee machine or during breaks – offered an opportunity to question them in a completely unconstrained atmosphere. During all of these observations and conversations – or shortly thereafter – I meticulously took notes of details and ideas (Agar, 2008).

Analysis

Due to the mixed methodological strategies and goals mentioned above, the material was analysed by using both inductive and deductive coding (Decorte, 2010). Although part of the codes followed directly from pre-given theoretical notions, most of these codes were the result of inductive analysis – generating codes from within the text (Glaser & Strauss, 2012). At times, this implied I was walking a tightrope during the analytical process, as sticking too much to respondents'

---

7.   Something also observed by Mein & Hartman (2013).

accounts would not yield a great amount of analytical insights, whereas too much labelling in terms of theoretical insights would mean a loss of detail (Silverman, 2011). I dealt with this issue by doing the initial coding – or open coding (Boeije, 2010) – partly by using a group of codes that was based on theoretical insights, but expanding it constantly with codes that were generated from interview material. In addition, writing memos during the coding process proved helpful to develop the first contours of later, more or less theoretical or conceptual notions (Silverman, 2011). Thus, the analysis of material – both interviews and documents – was done in several steps.

The first step was already taken during the periods of fieldwork. After each interview, the recording of it was transcribed immediately, and analysed and coded quickly thereafter by using the qualitative analytical *Atlas* programme (Boeije, 2010). Thus interview material was divided in different sections, for instance in parts about tasks, opinions, organisational embedding or collaboration with the police. In addition, an important part of the coding was done inductively, by using grounded theory (Glaser & Strauss, 2012). This analytical method was of particular relevance since the overarching approach was mainly exploratory. Documents were analysed in a similar vein, although the results of this document analysis – obviously – concerned only formal policy.

The next steps in the analytical process followed quickly after each other. After the initial (open) coding phase, material was further analysed through a process called axial coding (Boeije, 2010). Axial coding refers to a more abstract analysis of the different categories and (potential) subcategories (*ibid.*). Therefore, I considered whether the initial codes covered the empirical data. Subsequently, I moved to a phase of selective coding, in which the relations between different categories were scrutinised (*ibid.*). This step was taken after most interviews were conducted. Next, these categories formed the basis of extensive case reports that described the situation in each of the six cities, the historical development of municipal disorder policing, or the situation in the two case studies. By collecting themes in case reports that took cities as a unit, I was equally able to compare cities and cases for similarities and differences. The last analytical step consisted of rereading these case reports and collecting insights 'horizontally' to develop a "cross-case report" (Yin, 1984: 51). Thus, I was able to develop an overview of different patterns, occurring in several cities. Lastly, by reassembling the material and involving the memos I had written during the analytical process, I was able to lay the groundwork for later chapters.

For the additional research in the second phase, I took a few steps back in the analytical process by re-examining initial codes and underlying text fragments. Some interviews were wholly re-analysed for this phase: these included all the interviews with municipal officers and many of the interviews with coordinators and municipal managers. New interviews that were conducted to obtain more information about the history and development of municipal disorder policing were analysed as in step two and three. Finally, the interviews and participatory observations for the two in-depth case studies were also analysed as described above, leading to two extensive reports for the respective cases that were eventually reread and combined to form chapter 8.

4   RELIABILITY AND VALIDITY

In comparison with *quantitative* approaches, doing *qualitative* research implies other challenges have to be met to assure methodological quality. Whereas the former relies on standardised procedures for the reliability and the validity of results, these are lacking in qualitative research (LeCompte & Goetz, 1982).[8] In this study, several steps were taken to safeguard methodological quality, both in terms of validity (internal and external) and reliability (internal and external).[9]

Internal validity – in qualitative research the issue 'whether I observe what I think I am observing' (cf. LeCompte & Goetz, 1982) – was firstly enhanced in this research design by using multiple data sources to answer the research questions. Hence, by using policy documents, interviews, and previous research insights, data triangulation was pursued (Denzin, 1970, in: Maesschalck, 2010: 134). This was further enhanced by the involvement of respondents with various organisational affiliations and positions. Interviewing managers, coordinators, policy makers or frontline professionals, and – in general – respondents from various organisations provides multiple perspectives on the same issues. For the document study, I also involved various resources – policy plans, statements, organisational schemes and evaluative reports. This array of written resources enriched insights on formal policy and how it might evolve throughout time. Moreover, so-called 'member checks' formed a vital element during various moments of the study; both during the first phase and the second phase, case reports or conclusions were discussed with representatives of the city surveillance agencies (Seale, 1999). Secondly, theoretical triangulation was attained by studying a number of possible interpretative frames for disorder policing (Maesschalk, 2010: 135). This provided various theoretical angles to interpret views and statements and prevented any premature interpretation of interview material.

The chosen research format has important consequences for external validity. External validity concerns the question whether insights can be generalised to other cases and circumstances. Although the number of interviewees was too limi-

---

8.   In fact, as the notions of reliability and validity are derived from quantitative research, several
     authors have suggested alternative indicators for methodological quality in qualitative research
     (see also: Maesschalck 2010: 122).
9.   It should be noted that this line of work in general, and the city surveillance agencies in particular,
     is constantly changing. This means that some of the insights might have changed as soon as a case
     study was closed. These changes concern mostly the organisational embedding, but also the
     employment of officers for special projects or occasions. Therefore, many of the observations are
     limited to the specific time span during which fieldwork was conducted.

ted for statistically valid statements, the variety of views and perspectives did provide an opportunity for theoretical generalisation (Maesschalk, 2010: 130). Through
a 'thick description' of cases (Geertz, 1973), these could be compared and categories and patterns that were discovered in one case could be transferred to the next
(Simons, 2009; Yin, 1984). Hence, the variety of perspectives, views and developments allowed for theoretical statements about the growth and development of
municipal disorder policing as such.

Striving for reliability provided an additional set of challenges, as is common
for all qualitative research (Seale, 1999). Claims about internal reliability – the issue
whether other researchers would arrive at the same conclusions based on the same
data (LeCompte & Goetz, 1982) – cannot be substantiated unequivocally, as this
research was done for a large part by me. However, the first part of the research
was done in consultation with a fellow researcher, and initial case reports and
interviews were also read by him (resembling 'peer examination', *ibid.*: 42). In some
cases, this researcher joined the interviews I conducted. Furthermore, intermediate
conclusions were discussed thoroughly and at several stages of both the first and
the second phase with other researchers as well.

External reliability concerns the question whether "independent researchers
would discover the same phenomena or generate the same constructs in the same
or similar settings" (LeCompte & Goetz, 1982: 32). This claim is harder to support.
Especially since this is the first time municipal disorder policing has been
approached from the perspective chosen here. Nevertheless, external reliability has
been approached (*ibid.*: 37), by being as reflexive as possible (Seale, 1999), by opening up on the choices I made concerning my informants, by explaining the social
context of data collection (see above) and by identifying the assumptions and theories through which I approached this subject matter (LeCompte & Goetz, 1982: 37
ff.).

5 | Policy goals of municipal disorder policing: past and present

1   Introduction

As the first of five empirical chapters, this chapter begins by exploring the development of municipal disorder policing, its policy goals and their backgrounds. The main point here is that changes in policies are due only in part to changes in the manner of thinking about actual disorder. Such changes are determined also by managerial ambitions, police collaboration and the dynamics of an evolving occupational group.

This chapter primarily addresses local developments, although a complete understanding of changes in public safety policy necessitates discussion of national changes. In order to characterise initial developments, therefore, Section 2 starts with a discussion of early concerns about disorder, the build-up to the Roethof Committee and its thoughts on functional surveillance. Section 3 continues with the first city warden projects, as well as their goals and how they gradually changed throughout the 1990s. These first two sections are based largely on interviews with early managers and researchers, as well as on policy documents and literature. Section 4 serves as an interlude, addressing national developments in public safety policy. Section 5 addresses the first major change in municipal disorder policing – the end of the city warden phase, a local 'call for surveillance' and the growing pains of the newly established municipal departments for city surveillance. Section 6 describes the most recent phase by highlighting policy perspectives, as well as how and why they differ from previous phases, and by describing the most prominent tasks of recent municipal officers. These two sections are based on material from policy documents and interviews in the six cities that were introduced in chapter 4. Section 7 offers a conclusion.

2   EARLY DUTCH CONCERNS ABOUT DISORDER: THE 1980S

The perception of a changed scene: norm erosion in the 1980s

The 1980s represent a watershed in Dutch thinking about disorder with the Roet-hof Committee appearing as a concrete manifestation of this change (see also chapter 1).

The establishment of this committee was preceded by the awareness of a changed urban scene and the strong growth of what was referred to as 'petty crime'. This "acceleration of crime" – as one respondent describes it – concerned relatively low-level offences (e.g. petty theft, shoplifting, bicycle theft), as well as general forms of rule infringements (e.g. fare dodging on public transport, littering or other 'disorderly behaviour'). In retrospect, some respondents associate these types of crime in part to the growth in drug-related crimes. Although such crimes were limited to specific areas in the central districts of large cities, some respondents emphasise the notable impact of these changes on the collective perception of disorder:

> People really started to be bothered by bicycle theft, car burglaries, you name it. Basically, a lot was being nicked. At that time, the use of heroin was increasing greatly. […] I remember Amsterdam in the eighties, walking on the *pillenbrug* [the bridge of pills] or the Zeedijk. Every-where people were hustling, dealing drugs. And people considered it a normal situation. Kruis-kade, Rotterdam, the same, loads of drug trafficking.

In many accounts, the growing awareness of petty crimes and disorderly behaviour are mentioned in one breath with generic changes in social cohesion and social control. The decline of informal social control is thus mentioned as one of the most important explanations for the rise in petty crimes: 'Back in the day, people used to correct each other'. As recounted by a manager who had been involved with early surveillance by municipal wardens:

> I used to get a slap on the wrist now and then by someone who knew me. That just happened. But these forms of correction became a lot less common in the course of the seventies. People retreated behind their front doors, and the streets became empty. That gap was filled by all kinds of groups, like drug users. And eventually no one dared to intervene when someone broke a car window or something.

Emancipation had gone too far, he adds, and the liberation from restrictive norms and overt social control had led to an abundance of disorderly behaviour.

According to these accounts, Dutch society seemed to be in something of a transition in the 1980s, both in terms of the factual growth of disorder and in the perception of that disorder.[1] A general consensus emerged that compliance to rules in public space was eroding, petty crime was becoming widespread, and the informal ways of correcting deviant behaviour had largely vanished. The perception of disorder also changed through enhanced police registration and subsequently new victim surveys that were created to measure crime, especially in terms of victimisation (cf. Roethof, 1984; Boutellier, 2008: 122 ff).

These developments in awareness provided the backdrop for the Roethof committee and the 1986 national policy plan entitled *Society and Crime* (in Dutch, *Samenleving en criminaliteit*), as described in chapter 2.

As noted previously, this committee suggested that parties other than the police and the public prosecution agency should be made responsible. Such thinking is rooted in the acknowledgement that the police and the public prosecution agency did not actually know how to address the plethora of these issues (Commissie Roethof, 1984; Van Houdt & Schinkel, 2014).[2] To stimulate the involvement of non-police actors, the Dutch national government decided to provide local governments with funding for new projects. It led to an unprecedented number of projects, "a period of let a thousand flowers bloom", an early researcher remembers – the Roethof projects (cf. Polder & Van Vlaardingen, 1992; Terpstra, 2010b). Most importantly, these projects approached issues of petty crime as *societal* problems, and not exclusively as *criminal* problems. Consequently they addressed petty crimes primarily by changing the behaviour of perpetrators and less so by punishing them, as an early researcher recalls. In addition, new solutions were to be defined according to prevention instead of repression. Early researchers highlight the undeniable influence of several well-known Dutch criminologists in this respect, most notably Jan van Dijk and Josine Junger-Tas.

The projects supported by the Roethof subsidies included new forms of functional surveillance (Polder & van Vlaardingen, 1992). These projects were designed primarily according to the philosophy of situational crime prevention, as discussed in chapter 2. One of the projects for new functional surveillance included the first forms of Dutch municipal disorder policing (*ibid.*; cf. Van Dijk & De Waard, 1991).

---

1.   Vuysje captures this change in *Lof der dwang* (In praise of coercion, 1989), linking it to the advent of the 'calculating citizen', the non-compliant citizen who took advantage of the lack of social control to engage in fare dodging, shoplifting or other activities that Vuysje understatedly refers to as 'proletarian shopping'.
2.   This brings to mind the words of Garland (2001) with regard to the predicament of the judicial apparatus (cf. Van Houdt & Schinkel, 2014).

3   EARLY MUNICIPAL DISORDER POLICING BY CITY WARDENS: THE 1990S

City wardens: a solution to two problems

Most of the Roethof undertakings ended as the result of a predefined project length. Likewise, most projects for functional surveillance were temporary. For example, there was the case of a project for surveillance officers in a shopping district in Utrecht (Colder & Nuijten-Edelbroek, 1987) and one involving surveillance in several neighbourhoods in Amsterdam (Polder & Van Vlaardingen, 1992). Schemes involving city wardens were granted a longer lifespan however, and they continued long after the Roethof subsidies ended.

Reasons for the relative success of city warden projects are varied. Although many of them were evaluated as effective in reducing the number of petty crimes or as having a positive effect on decreasing feelings of insecurity (Hauber, 1994),[3] their relative success was only partly related to these results. Another aspect that appeared to be of at least equal importance was that these officers provided a solution to the major problem of unemployment existing in the Netherlands at that time. Without exception, city wardens were long-term unemployed individuals who had been assigned surveillance tasks as part of a work reintegration trajectory. As recounted by one researcher:

> They made a plan for two problems, one a problem of criminal justice, the other one of employment. We can give those unemployed people control tasks in the cities. Give them a suit so people can recognise them [...] Then they were trained for a bit, so they knew what they were allowed to do – no more than ordinary citizens. We can all stop someone and hand him over to the police. Only their means to get in touch with the police were improved a bit.

After the first Roethof projects for functional surveillance, various unemployment arrangements thus enabled municipalities to establish foundations for city wardens (Hauber, 1994, Ministry of the Interior, 1996: 12). Initially, employment usually took place through the Job Pool (in Dutch, *Banenpool*) arrangement (*ibid.*). From 1995 onwards, city warden projects received additional funding through the 'Melkert arrangement' (named after the initiator, Ad Melkert, the Minister of Social Affairs and Employment at that time), which was another subsidy programme for

---

3.   In the course of the 1990s feelings of insecurity came to play a greater role in public safety policy (see below).

long-term unemployed people.[4] Therefore, from then on city wardens were also called *Melketiers*.

The city of Dordrecht was the first to experiment with using long term-unemployed people for general surveillance tasks in 1989. Many more cities quickly followed this example. In addition, a national foundation was initiated in 1992 and continued in 1993, with financial backing from the Ministry of Justice – the Dutch City Warden Organisation (*Stichting Stadswacht Nederland*).[5] After 1995 the Melkert arrangements allowed ever more cities in the Netherlands to employ city wardens, even those that had initially opposed 'half-baked police officers'.[6] In 1996 115 municipalities were involved with city warden projects, employing at least 2,000 officers in total, all with a background of long-term unemployment.[7]

City wardens: situational crime prevention or more?

The city warden foundations established in the 1990s show a lot of similarity in policy and approach, irrespective of differences in organisation (Hauber, 1994).[8] Nevertheless, these goals are rather multi-faceted.

Firstly, city wardens were meant to prevent crime by their sheer physical presence. In Rotterdam for instance, this idea was first implemented in the Maas-tunnel. This corridor was seen as a particular unsafe spot due to loitering drug dealers and users. Rotterdam's early city wardens, called 'public safety assistants' (*Veiligheidsassistenten*), were supposed to help address this problem through a simple solution, as an early manager explains:

---

4.   This arrangement was formally known as the Arrangement for extra employment of long-term unemployed people (In Dutch, *Regeling extra werkgelegenheid voor langdurig werklozen*; Ministry of Social Affairs and Employment, 1995). The actual scope of these Melkert jobs was even broader. The jobs were intended to provide long-term unemployed people with additional work experience in a relatively low-pressure environment, ranging from public garden maintenance and street sweeping to positions as shop assistants and factory employees. The goals of the early city warden projects were well-suited to these Melkert jobs, and the national subsidy for this new regulation provided many municipalities with a good opportunity to continue their city warden projects. In 1999, these jobs were changed to 'ID jobs' (Dutch: *Instroom/Doorstroom banen*), referring to the wish to have more output towards the job market. The latter variant of subsidised employment was discontinued in 2004.

5.   This organisation later changed its name to the Netherlands Interest Group for City Surveillance (In Dutch, *Belangengroep Stadstoezicht Nederland*), and later to the Public Safety Sector Organisation (In Dutch, *Brancheorganisatie Publieke Veiligheid*; Ministry of the Interior, 1996; Van Steden, 2011).

6.   Pels, J. (2010) Stadstoezicht in de lift. *Masterthesis*. Retrieved from http://www.hetccv.nl/binaries/content/assets/ccv/dossiers/boa/stadstoezicht_in_de_lift.pdf.

7.   Not all of these officers were known as city wardens (in Dutch, *stadswacht*): a sizeable proportion was known as surveillance officers (in Dutch, *toezichthouder*). Moreover, the total number of 2,000 city wardens/surveillance officers might be a low estimation, as this overview of the Ministry of the Interior includes only those city warden foundations that were associated with the national Dutch City Warden Organisation (Ministry of the Interior, 1996: 16).

8.   Due to a lack of available policy documents on city warden foundations, this overview is largely based on the spoken accounts of early managers and researchers.

> Those city wardens couldn't do a thing, they didn't do a thing. They didn't *want* to do a thing.
> They were just standing there like living dolls. But it certainly stopped the trouble. Things were
> clean, intact, nothing happened.

These forms of functional surveillance were also developed in other cities. In relatively small areas, groups of surveillance officers walked around as guardians to diminish the number of petty crimes (Hauber, 1994). 'Being there' and deterring perpetrators of petty crimes was the main goal of these first wardens, a manager of the early period states.

Secondly, some city wardens were expected to interfere in cases of misbehaviour. "They could address people who were misbehaving, were messing around with cars. People who threw garbage on the street were addressed," a manager explains. As such, city wardens had the task to reproach people who committed offences, or more generally, disregarded the rules. Their powers however, were limited to those of any citizen. In addition, it was believed that correcting unacceptable behaviour would be easier if it was done by officials who were known by inhabitants. "They knew their area, and the area knew them," said an early manager. However, the suggestion many city wardens were eventually supposed to be led back to regular (other) work seems at odds with the expectation they would familiarise themselves with particular neighbourhoods and its inhabitants.

Thirdly, city wardens were seen as the 'eyes and ears' of the police. The police would be informed when situations were considered too dangerous for wardens (cf. Hauber, 1994; Ministry of the Interior, 1996). Sometimes the police had a more prominent role and city wardens were even employed as police support officers. In Utrecht for instance, the city wardens of *Stichting Stadstoezicht* were managed by police constables, had a more thorough police training than their colleagues in other cities and wore police uniforms. Hence, they were a "police extension", the "first point of reference on the streets", and "eyes and ears" for noting offences, informing the police, but also to make citizen arrests when individuals committed offences, a manager in Utrecht recounts.

Lastly, surveillance by city wardens was expected to diminish feelings of insecurity. In some accounts of city wardens, this idea of reassurance even seemed to have been more important than the actual fighting of petty crimes or anti-social behaviour. An early manager points out:

> Certainly, in some neighbourhoods there was quite a bit of trouble. But a large part of that
> image [of insecurity – TE] was equally caused by old ladies that were peeking from behind their
> [curtains] and only saw [black people] leaning against lamp posts. So, the experience of safety
> was something new.

In this respect, some municipalities highlighted the notion of 'hosting'. These wardens had a task to make visitors and residents feel at home in their city. A police officer in Eindhoven remembers how this worked:

> We used to say jokingly they were there to point the way to the local department store. [...] But for a citizen it's clear, he sees a uniform and appreciates that. [...] They didn't have too much know-how. They couldn't do a lot more than have a chat, talk to some people. But for a citizen that mattered. At least it gave a feeling of security.

In summary, city wardens were employed for divergent goals. These ranged from rather passive goals, such as merely being present to deter possible perpetrators or to diminish citizens' feelings of insecurity, to more active interference with 'disorderly persons' or reporting on issues.

Moreover, the general impression of their work is that their occupational goals were but little elaborated. Not only are there but few policy documents or statements providing clarification, also many respondents brush aside the impact of city wardens in terms of public safety. Thus, it remains unclear what behaviour exactly might have to be dealt with, how this relates to goals of crime prevention, in what cases the police should be informed, or if, and when reassurance is more important than actual crime reduction. As such, goals concerning public safety appear undefined and subordinate to other considerations.

Undefined goals

This lack of clear goals seems partly attributable to the primacy of other ideas. As most respondents claim, ideas about situational crime prevention or correcting behaviour were subordinate to the goal of gaining work experience for long term unemployed people – the more important the social reintegration goals, the less important policy goals in terms of surveillance or public safety, a manager states. He explains:

> Employment came first; it didn't matter if it did any good for public safety. We gave those people a suit, and they were walking around in flocks of eight, with their hands behind their backs, looking downward, continually smoking filter cigarettes, hundreds of them. Didn't matter at all.

In addition, there was widespread uncertainty about the competence of these surveillance officers being seriously occupied with public safety issues. "It was the bottom end of the catalogue, psychiatric patients, criminals," as a manager explains. "We called those guys penny-seekers," he adds, referring to city wardens' alleged tendency to constantly look down.

Yet, it was not only the primacy of social reintegration goals that caused vagueness in their occupational goals. It was also the result of the reluctance of police chiefs to manage them. In most cities these chiefs were provided with city wardens and sometimes they were even housed in their station, as they were seen as a police replacement for lower level surveillance. However, police chiefs were often reluctant to adopt these new officers, as they were quite simply placed under their command without their consent. As a result, many chiefs used wardens for the chores that police officers were reluctant to do. "Why don't you go walk around for a bit, or do something," a respondent from Eindhoven recalls the police's general attitude towards these wardens. A respondent in Utrecht points out that city wardens were often called "the police's postmen". This also impacted on tasks and occupational goals of early municipal officers, leading to differences between cities, depending on the willingness of local police constables to invest in these 'new colleagues'. Moreover, it led to difficulties in the relations between these new surveillance officers and the established police forces. Most police officers did not see long term unemployed people as fit for any sort of surveillance task. Sometimes police officers downright rejected their new colleagues. An early researcher recounts the situation in Amsterdam: "The police vehemently opposed them. Even in the local press, articles appeared [in which police representatives addressed citizens in terms of], 'you don't have to bother about those city wardens'."[9]

To sum up, the basic ideas that accounted for city wardens – inspired by notions of functional surveillance and a growing attention to feelings of insecurity – can but partly explain how these officers worked. A certain indefiniteness in their work, or even ineffectiveness as many maintain, cannot be understood without taking into account the primacy of work reintegration goals for unemployed people, their subordination to local police forces, the widespread cynicism among police officers to these new surveillance personnel and the image of an otiose group of 'caretakers'.

Shifting public safety policies

Apart from these internal factors, the work of city wardens was also determined by several shifts in the encompassing public safety policy in the 1990s. These changes were already addressed briefly in previous chapters. Here they are discussed in their relevance for municipal disorder policing.

First of all, municipal public safety policy, now called '*integrated public safety management*', grew in importance and changed considerably in the years after the foundations for city wardens were established. During the 1990s, the perspective on petty crime became broader, both semantically and practically (Cachet & Ringe-

---

9.   As such, the animosity of police towards municipal officers noted by Van Steden (2011) and Eikenaar & van Stokkom (2014) could be observed even in the 1990s; possibly it might even originate in the police's rejection of early city wardens.

ling, 2004; Van de Bunt & Van Swaaningen, 2004). 'Crime policy' became 'public safety policy' or 'security policy' and local governments broadened their scope from prevention to pro-action (Ministry of the Interior, 1993). Van Steden (2011) states safety became the "centrifugal force of our society", a concept around which different policy fields became organised: anti-social behaviour, neighbourhood decline and crime all had to be fought with combined forces (2011: 45).

New concepts were also introduced in municipal safety policy. *Petty* crimes became *frequent* crimes and eventually the notion of 'minor annoyances' (*kleine ergernissen*) was staged, reflecting local governments' care for the alleged minor, but yet most vexatious issues. Another term reflecting this renewed orientation was the stronger prominence of the heading *overlast*,[10] a Dutch word referring to various forms of incivilities and especially the annoyance and hindrance these cause (Ministry of the Interior, 1993).[11] Moreover, these terms were part of a more moralising discourse, especially in government policy programme *Law in Motion* (*Recht in Beweging*; Ministry of Justice, 1990) and the ensuing *Integrated Public Safety Report* (*Integrale Veiligheidsrapportage*; Ministry of the Interior, 1993). The 'moral tissue' of society was for the first time explicitly diagnosed as being in decline, bringing about various incivilities. Instead of suffering from insufficient ties between youngsters and society or a lack of functional surveillance, society was diagnosed as struggling with a 'blurring sense of values' (*vervagend normbesef*, cf. Van Houdt & Schinkel, 2014).

Other concepts reflect how certain fashions in criminology were 'dutchified' (cf. Newburn & Jones, 2007). The broken windows theory for instance, is present in the Dutch idea of *schoon, heel en veilig* (clean, intact and safe), as an early manager states. The basic psychological assumption that one broken window that is left unrepaired will lead to more serious crime informs these accounts. This manager states,

> Clean, intact and safe then became popular. The police too, said: make sure things are intact. If one thing breaks down, more will follow.

In addition, citizens' feelings of security gained prominence on local municipal agendas. The popularity of this notion seemed to partly overlap with the broken windows assumption that physical decline does have negative impacts on such

---

10. Although Hauber (1994) observes the term *overlast* also informed the first city wardens.
11. *Overlast* is a Dutch term that is usually translated as 'a nuisance'. However, this English term has a more limited meaning (mostly in singular form and referring to a temporary situation). In contrast, *overlast* refers to a broader experience and is mostly related to various incivilities. It may be associated with all kinds of annoyances, both caused by physical circumstances, such as poor maintenance of public roads, and social circumstances or anti-social behaviour. Municipal officers almost exclusively concern themselves with the latter variant – the general discomfort caused by anti-social behaviour. See further Devroe (2012) for a more extensive discussion of *overlast* and its various interpretations.

feelings.[12] This idea was further enhanced by new ways of measuring. A manager recounts how the idea gained ground that in general people felt more insecure in neighbourhoods with a low level of maintenance and a lot of rubbish (cf. Bruinsma, Bernasco & Elffers, 2004; Maas-de Waal & Wittebrood, 2002; RMO 2004; Van Stokkom, 2008; see further chapter 6). Feelings of insecurity grew in importance as a policy issue through the introduction of the Police Monitor in 1993, accentuating victim risks (Bruinsma, Bernasco & Elffers, 2004; RMO, 2004).

Lastly, the 1990s saw an increase in popularity of the comprehensive term *leefbaarheid*, mostly translated in English as 'quality of life' or 'liveability'.[13] Mostly associated with what has been called the 'neighbourhood approach' (WRR, 2005; Reijndorp, 2004), this term became popular during the 1970s, when urban welfare policies were increasingly decentralised, with a greater focus on neighbourhoods, urban renewal, opposition to anonymous 'bricklaying' and paying closer attention to the correspondence between the experience of social quality and physical characteristics of a neighbourhood. *Leefbaarheid* became a term to capture this new awareness (among many other things – De Hart, 2002) and grew in popularity under the new large city policy of the 1990s (VROM, 2004: *Grote Steden Beleid*).[14]

On the one hand, these shifts and new terms seemed to change city wardens' work in the course of the 1990s. The goal of preventing petty crimes was gradually replaced by more generally correcting behaviour that had gone astray. This is represented by a change from targeting illegal acts to intolerable or in-civil acts (WRR, 2003, in: Van Stokkom, 2008), and by a transition from initial concerns about bicycle theft, purse snatching or shoplifters, to worries over a 'clean and intact' public space that is liveable and free from incivilities (*overlast*). City wardens were meant to play an important role in correcting people who breached these norms.[15] Moreover, several respondents state city wardens were assigned to a large number of

12. Although this was no new thought either, cf. Commissie Roethof, 1984: 20.
13. The most usual translation of *leefbaarheid* is 'quality of life', although this term seems to entail more and other notions than its Dutch counterpart (cf. De Hart, 2002; Leidelmeijer & Van Kamp, 2003). Chapter 9 will discuss the semantic indefiniteness of the notion of *leefbaarheid* that often enables stakeholders to define and redefine the work of municipal officers, especially where it concerns the distinction with police work. Leidelmeijer & Van Kamp (2003) provide a thorough overview of the conceptual similarities and differences between *leefbaarheid*, liveability and quality of life.
14. Although terms in neighbourhood policy changed every few years, *leefbaarheid* would be persistent and even develop into an important and measurable indicator in so called 'quality of life' monitoring (leefbaarheidsmonitoren, WRR, 2005). Increasingly it became defined in relation to the day to day problems citizens experienced (WRR, 2005: 37). Bruinsma, Bernasco and Elffers (2004) state that Dutch municipalities started measuring residents' experience of public safety and quality of life from 1996 onwards. According to a Dutch ministerial report *leefbaarheid* refers to at least three different themes – the physical living environment, the social environment (interaction with other residents) and last but not least, the impact of crime, incivilities and issues of public safety (VROM 2004: 15).
15. Although not the main focus here, the decrease in crime and disorder in itself obviously has a large impact on these new officers (cf. Wittebrood & Nieuwbeerta, 2006).

areas, thus diluting the effect of 'familiar faces' patrolling confined areas. They were a victim of their own success, as an early researcher states. Because they were successful in preventing petty crimes in relatively small areas, other area managers started demanding city wardens for their own neighbourhood, but spreading a limited amount of officers over more neighbourhoods had a negative impact on this effect.

On the other hand, this change in discourse and encompassing public safety policy had but little effect on what city wardens were actually doing in practice. A researcher recounts how new terms became fashionable. They were invented or copied from other movements in a somewhat casual way, but had a relatively small impact on practice. He recalls the term 'social safety', which was yet another term to highlight citizens' feelings of insecurity:

> Social safety was more general. It had to do with the built environment, the relation between environment and crime, urban planning, parks, tunnels. Social safety, it was also a term from the feminist movement. It sounded good, you have to feel safe, yeah, why not? It used to be called fear of crime. These things are conceptually mingled […] in our reports we added those terms. Well alright, we thought, as long as something happens.[16]

As such, he states, it was mostly the discourse that changed. Others underscore that the practice of city wardens remained the same in terms of their limited powers, the prominence of social reintegration goals for unemployed people, subordination to the police and alleged ineffectiveness. A larger change was yet to come.

4   INTERMEZZO: NEW LEGISLATION AND CHANGES IN SECURITY POLICIES

Summing up the previous sections, the first period in municipal disorder policing was dominated by theories of situational crime prevention and social control, growing concerns about feelings of insecurity, and a gradual shift to other terms and concerns, at least in discourse. Likewise, the decision to appoint long-term unemployed people as city wardens, the somewhat indefinite surveillance goals and subordination to the police had great influence on the work of early city wardens.

This first phase came to an end at the beginning of the 21st century. Since the early 2000s municipalities started to develop professional municipal policing services and to transform city wardens into professional officers who were expected eventually to actually fine for rule infringements. This process took several years, but to understand this shift some important changes in Dutch legislation and security policies in the 1990s and the 2000s need to be discussed. First, a national 'call for strict law enforcement' is addressed, together with the enlarged role for the

---

16. For a more extensive discussion of the roots of the Dutch focus on victims, see Boutellier, 2008.

mayor in local safety policies and the introduction of new administrative fines and penal orders. Next, the larger role of *BOAs* or enforcement officers (see also chapter 1) is discussed. Lastly, the trend of the police withdrawing from public spaces is considered.

A call for strict law enforcement

As mentioned in chapters 1 and 2, the start of the 21st century was marked by a nation-wide change in tone and approach concerning public safety issues, most clearly visible in the 2002 national policy programme *Towards a Safer Society* (*Naar een veiliger samenleving*).

In chapter 2 this programme was discussed as the most evident Dutch example of zero tolerance thinking in policy. Apart from being a 'deviation from the trend' in terms of more and stricter law enforcement and the targeting of 'notorious sources' of disorder and crime, it can also be seen as the result of the growing focus on citizens' feelings of insecurity.[17] Hence the programme states "society will become safer, at the latest in 2006, not only objectively as will be evident from statistics, but mainly subjectively, where it concerns the feelings of citizens [*de gevoelstemperatuur voor de burgers*]" (Ministry of the Interior and Ministry of Justice, 2002: 11). As such, this policy plan mainly nurtured ambitions to address those offences and incivilities that directly impact upon citizens.

This relatively harsh stance on incivilities and issues of public safety was later continued in the 2008 action plan *Disorder and Decline* (*actieplan Overlast en Verloedering*), albeit with a more communitarian twist to it (Terpstra, 2010b; Van Houdt & Schinkel, 2014). This plan is an elaboration of one of the main themes of the policy programme of 2007s new government (Terpstra, 2010b), and part of the project 'Public safety starts with prevention' (*Veiligheid begint bij voorkomen*). This plan and its predecessors resulted in a wide range of measures to further "regulate behaviour in public space" (Terpstra, 2010b: 123), particularly granting police and local government more powers.

These national changes had a large impact on local governments. Municipalities, and particularly mayors, were granted more powers to fight various kinds of disorder and incivilities (Sackers, 2010). Mayors were granted the power, for instance to introduce camera surveillance, to assign areas for preventative stop and search actions by the police or to administer area restraining orders in case of drug abuse (see also chapter 8; cf. Sackers, 2010). In addition, changes in administrative law enabled governments to administer fines or penal orders for recurring incivilities. These are the administrative penal order (*bestuurlijke strafbeschikking*) and the administrative fine (*bestuurlijke boete*; Terpstra & Havinga, 2005; Terpstra et al.,

---

17. It should be noted that this 'breach' seems partly rhetorical, as tendencies to strict enforcement could already be observed in some of the policy plans of the preceding coalition (cf Terpstra, 2010b).

2013). These legal inventions provided municipalities with means to fine people for rule infringements that caused annoyance, such as dog excrement, anti-social behaviour of street youth or household waste (cf. Flight et al., 2012).[18]

BOAs: Special Investigative Officers

A second development that is important in this respect is the increased use of *BOAs* as municipal law enforcement officers (*Buitengewoon opsporingsambtenaren*: Special Investigative Officers). Officers with more powers than city wardens were needed to administer fines or penal orders.

Local governments have been able to appoint these *BOAs* since 1994.[19] In close relation to the major police reorganisation in 1993 involving the abolition of municipal police forces, several police tasks such as controlling parking offences and the policing of environmental offences were transferred to municipalities. This led to the introduction of a new type of non-police enforcement officers. In Rotterdam for instance, environmental control was planned as part of a municipal organisation called Roteb, in addition to the parking wardens with their own agency. Likewise, in most cities that were selected for this study, the municipality had its own independent agency for parking surveillance. The municipality of Utrecht for instance, established an agency with environmental police (called 'cleaning police' – *reinigingspolitie*) and a team of officers that addressed rule infringements associated with dog owners, such as dog excrement or dogs that are left unleashed (called 'dog wardens' – *hondenwachters*).

The Decree on Special Investigative Officers was issued in 1994 to enable these new municipal officers to issue fines for offences, something city wardens were unable to do. This Decree followed an adaptation of article 142 of the new Police-law of 1993 (cf. Brouwer & Van Rest, 1996). The new *BOAs* replaced two types of investigative officers that were part of the municipal police forces (Roodzant, Van Oosterhout & Bouwmeister, 1994). The 1994 decree determined their functions and tasks, for instance in terms of the legal grounds of their special investigative pow-

---

18. Dutch municipalities have been introducing administrative fines for a variety of offences since halfway through the nineties. After 2009 specific administrative fines and administrative penal orders for 'incivilities in public spaces' were introduced. Until recently two third of all Dutch municipalities had chosen to introduce the administrative penal order. This seemed due to the fact administrative penal orders involved a relatively low administrative burden, to the fixed amount of money municipalities receive for every penal order they write (from the 'Central Collecting Agency of the Ministry of Security and Justice' CJIB), and to the relative transparency of this system (Flight et al., 2012, Terpstra et al., 2013). This system however, has changed from January 2015: the compensation for administrative penal orders was abolished. As a result, the municipalities of The Hague and Amsterdam have decided to reintroduce the administrative fine from 1-1-2017 after all.

19. The introduction of these officers was based on the ministerial decree on Special Investigative Officers of 1994: *Besluit buitengewoon opsporingsambtenaren* (http://wetten.overheid.nl/BWBR0007013/geldigheidsdatum_19-02-2013).

ers, as well as the requirements regarding capacity and reliability (Mein & Hartman, 2013). Later the *BOA*-note (*BOA circulaire*) organised this system of non-
police enforcement officers further.[20] Only after the turn of the millennium did
municipalities start to replace city wardens by *BOAs*.

Developments within the public police

A third national development that added to a more prominent role of municipalities in local enforcement is the redirection of the police to so-called 'core tasks',
resulting in less police attention to minor offences and disorder policing (see also
chapter 1).

After the police reorganisation in 1993, it still had ambitions to monopolise
enforcement in public spaces. This is reflected in the introduction of new police
surveillance officers for law enforcement in public spaces in 1993. In fact, this function of *politiesurveillant* – a function that is similar to the English 'Police Community Support Officers' (PCSO's, Terpstra et al., 2013) – can be seen partly as the
result of the police's rejection of surveillance by city wardens and what they called
the fragmentation of policing. This may be seen as "a strategy for the police forces
to recover lost ground" (Terpstra et al., 2013: 27). The Amsterdam *Streetwise* programme, running from 1998 until 2005, provides a good example of the employment of these officers, when large numbers of police officers were deployed to
address minor offences and rule infringements (Van Stokkom, 2005). In addition,
growing pressure on the police organisation for better results during the 1990s led
to the introduction of performance management. First raised in the 1999s *Policy
Plan Police* (*Beleidsplan Politie*), concrete indicators for performance were introduced
in 2003, as a result of the national policy programme *Towards a Safer Society* (Terpstra & Trommel, 2006). Although these were received differently across police districts, this led to more enforcement efforts and a growth in fines for minor offences
– mostly traffic violations – in many districts (Sluis, Cachet, De Jong, Nieuwenhuyzen & Ringeling, 2006: 70 ff.).

Although the police continued using the performance management indicators,
the fine quota were side-lined in 2006 by Minister Remkes (Van Stokkom, 2016). In
2010 these indicators were abolished altogether. The police role in the enforcement
of municipal bye-laws and traffic rules dropped dramatically in the 2010s (Van
Stokkom, 2016). Another indication for the police reorientation on core tasks is the
disappearance of the function of *politiesurveillant*. In the last decade these patrol
officers received more and more back-office tasks and there was no provision for
this function in the last police reorganisation in 2013.

---

20. By now *BOAs* can be found in various other sectors. There are six different legal spheres for *BOAs*.
     This categorisation was developed in response to the fragmentation of surveillance and law
     enforcement by non-police actors (Mein & Hartman, 2013). The number of *BOAs* in the public
     domain (domain 1) – relevant for this study – is about 3,600 municipal officers.

5   THE ADVENT OF NEW MUNICIPAL DISORDER POLICING: 2002 – 2007

These three national developments proved to be relevant for changes in municipal disorder policing. They provided the conditions for the establishment of new city surveillance agencies with new officers that were able to "make a difference".

Local developments: A call for surveillance

On a local level, the start of the 21st century is characterised by a notable demand for 'more blue on the streets', for more police or police-like officers. This is commonly referred to as a 'call for surveillance'. Although several respondents claim this call was incited by the alleged retreat of the police, these demands reach beyond changes in the police apparatus.[21] Especially since, as described in the last section, police developments have been somewhat ambiguous. As such, it is mainly the clearer political urge of local city councils for 'more blue' that sets this period apart from earlier phases.

In this section, first local developments are scrutinised, based on findings derived from the six cities introduced in chapter 4. Next, the introduction and initial growth of the new municipal city surveillance agencies (*Toezicht en Handhaving*) is discussed.

The tougher national stance on disorder had a clear local echo. Mostly, this call for more surveillance was voiced by political representatives in terms of the annoyances and feelings of insecurity of neighbourhood residents, expressing a heightened awareness of citizens' concerns.

In Eindhoven for instance, the urge for more surveillance solidified in the coalition agreement following the 2006 municipal elections. In this agreement the political parties that would form the new coalition underscored they wanted more control over local public safety issues. In the coalition agreement for 2006-2010 this is connected with changing police priorities as follows:

> Our city is in increasing need of general surveillance in neighbourhoods and at hotspots, not least because the police are partly retreating from surveillance tasks as a result of the national debate on their core tasks. We want a unit City Surveillance, under [our own] direction and organisational management that will comprise seventy to eighty city wardens, from 2010, and employed by the municipality.[22]

---

21. Some state this 'call' could already be noted during the early 1990s and especially in the countryside (Terpstra et al., 2013).
22. Eindhoven (2006), *Coalitieakkoord 2006-2010: Eindhoven Eén. Slagvaardig op weg naar een sociaal, sterk en betrokken Eindhoven.*

Likewise, the Tilburg city council increasingly started to take note of 'minor annoy-ances'. Political debates on what bothered citizens the most, centred on alleged minor issues of physical disorder.[23] A manager in Tilburg said

> There is a debate in the council on these minor annoyances. By their very nature, these are
> minor environmental rule infringements, for instance dog litter, or incivilities that haven't been
> a police priority in recent years.

In some cases, this attention can be ascribed to the efforts of individual decision makers. In Nijmegen for instance, one of the aldermen made a case for neighbour-hood residents and the feelings of abandonment they purportedly experienced. According to a respondent who was a manager at the time, this alderman was "a highly inspiring man, saying, 'go into those neighbourhoods, have a look at what is going on', and [scolding] the police, 'you don't show up enough'. As local gov-ernment we are responsible for these neighbourhoods, and that includes public safety'."

Although the call for surveillance coincided with the withdrawal of the police, according to these accounts, this urge for more blue on the streets is also related to other developments; the extra police investment in the first years of the 21st century contradict a simple explanation of municipal officers replacing police officers.

An additional explanation might be found in the fact that the concerns of citi-zens became more visible. In these years the means to measure citizens' concerns and feelings of insecurity improved greatly. Rotterdam for instance, started using the safety index from 2002 onwards (cf. De Leeuw & Van Swaaningen, 2011). As one manager states

> Those safety indexes, they really were an issue back then. It was the only thing that transcended
> the gut feeling […] What's happening in those neighbourhoods. […] They really played a role at
> that time as a point of reference.

Other cities were either inspired by Rotterdam's example of measuring public safety through such indexes (such as Tilburg), or came into focus as scoring partic-ularly badly on other indicators. The crime monitor of the national newspaper *Algemeen Dagblad* (AD) for instance, indicated the cities of Tilburg and Eindhoven were among the Dutch cities with the largest public safety issues (cf. Fijnaut et al., 2008). Equally, quality of life monitors were growing in importance in these years (cf. Van Dijk, Flight & Oppenhuis, 2000; Bruinsma, Bernasco & Elffers, 2004). As a result, residents' valuation of their living environment became more visible, as

---

23.   Council debate Tilburg, 26th April, 2006; Tilburg (2006) *Algemeen Beleidsplan College.*

well as their chief annoyances. Thus, for quite a few local political decision makers "a call for surveillance" was supported by these indicators.

In The Hague for instance, this led to more attention for notable hotspots, which were determined by analysing complaints about decline and public safety from 2003 onwards.[24] In Rotterdam the physical deterioration and gradual downward slide of neighbourhoods became a political item somewhat earlier. Due to Rotterdam's electoral landslide in 2001 and the ensuing period with Opstelten as the mayor (see also chapter 2), a lot of political attention was paid to the quality of the urban living environment. A manager points out

> [New policies] concerned the decline of this city. Keeping it clean and intact. Then you're talking about household waste. Opstelten also made a stand against people throwing their chewing gum on the pavement. These things were really characteristic for that time, because it needed more surveillance, while the police were gradually moving to tougher crime fighting. So a gap arose between those minor offences in the neighbourhood, leading to decline, frustration, annoyance, that didn't quite promote social cohesion. That's what we were used for.

In summary, public safety policy developed in a similar fashion in large Dutch cities in the first years of the 21st century. Influenced by a turn in the national debate on incivilities and disorder and aided by a clearer image of what bothers citizens the most, local political debates revolved around the ideas that more surveillance would be needed and that the police were not willing to take this responsibility.

City wardens: unfit?

Simultaneously a broad consensus ensued that city wardens would be unable to meet these demands. These officers were seen as incapable of "making a difference", as was commonly noted. Some say, not only because the lowest level of long term unemployed people populated the ranks as the basis for city wardens, but also because the foundations for city wardens had trouble to retain faithful employees. As one researcher explains, the private security sector was emerging at that time and also started offering surveillance services, luring away the better part of the personnel.

Added to this combination of more demands and lack of trust in city warden's abilities, was the phased abolition of subsidies for unemployment arrangements from 2004 onwards.[25] This new situation forced municipalities to discuss whether

---

24. The Hague (2003) *Veiligheidsplan*.
25. From January 1, 2004, the national government decreed the ID jobs, the follow up to the previous Melkert arrangements, were to be abolished.

municipal disorder policing had a *raison d'être*.[26] Most councils decided that they wanted to continue a form of surveillance by municipal personnel: although providing old city wardens with a new option for employment did play a role in this decision, city councils noted that surveillance in itself also had to change for the better.

New city surveillance agencies

Between roughly 2001 and 2007 new municipal city surveillance agencies were established. In Dutch these new agencies had different names, mostly *Stadstoezicht* ('City Surveillance'; Rotterdam, Eindhoven, Tilburg), or related, such as *Bureau Toezicht* ('Bureau for Surveillance'; Nijmegen), *Toezicht en Handhaving Openbare Ruimte* ('Surveillance and Law Enforcement Public Spaces'; Utrecht), or *Leefbaarheid en Toezicht* ('Quality of life and Surveillance'; The Hague).

With these new agencies, municipalities generally put different officers into one organisation, thus including both city wardens and other municipal enforcement officers, such as parking wardens and environmental rule enforcement officers, into one organisation. Moreover, they generally implemented a more robust policy to tackle issues of disorder and annoyances. New municipal officers were expected to act more resolutely and firmly to be able to "make a difference", as opposed to the allegedly ineffective, unprofessional and 'soft' city wardens. To this end, new officers were expected to issue fines. As stated above, these powers were enabled by further adapting the possibilities of the Dutch *BOA*-system that was introduced with the police reforms of 1993, and later by new administrative penal orders and fines.

Rotterdam provides the clearest example of such firmness, resulting in municipal officers with more powers (in the peculiar Rotterdam patois called *doorzettingsmacht*), officers that would be able to interfere actively and fine people, equally referred to in the hardly translatable term of *doorpakken*: "acting tenaciously". Thus, Rotterdam's early *Stadstoezicht* was clearly informed by the new coalition's programme *Towards a New Engagement* (Dutch: *Naar een nieuw elan*), as a manager explains,

> One of the things in that programme was we are going to enlarge the power (*doorzettingsmacht*)
> of the city surveillance agency. We are going to hire 250 general law enforcement officers [*brede*

---

26. Some municipalities noted that the cut-backs on these unemployment arrangements were at odds with the "proposed policy to improve safety in cities" (Policy plan *Naar een veiliger Den Haag*, 2003: 4).

handhavers]. Basically that means, we have 550 [city wardens], but they're worthless. We need much tougher guys.[27]

Although Rotterdam seems to be the forerunner, the same ambition to achieve a firmer approach to disorder can be found in other cities. In Utrecht for instance, the coordinator who headed the newly established city surveillance agency in 2007, "cleaned up the whole thing," a municipal manager remembers. Moreover, under municipal responsibility, they were assigned more public safety tasks. Approximately 75% of their work would involve for instance addressing street youth, visiting victims of burglaries or fining cyclists in pedestrian zones. This also meant that municipal officers would be held more accountable for how they contributed to the goals of the municipal safety programme through what was then the new 'enforcement plan' (see further chapter 6).

In Nijmegen, a new prospect for new municipal officers was especially due to the efforts of the aforementioned alderman in close cooperation with the coordinator of the city surveillance agency at the time. This coordinator recounts that in 2002 he was asked by the alderman for more investment in officers with public safety tasks and authority to impose fines.

I asked this alderman back then 'what is it you want?' 'Well, more blue on the streets'. He said, 'more parking attendance, more environmental police. And more public safety tasks'.

Again, city wardens without powers were not seen as being capable of "making a difference", or "having a lot of meaning in public spaces," as another senior manager recounts. Their replacements would be called surveillance officers. The same manager states, "With sixty surveillance officers a lot more is possible than with sixty city wardens [...] they have more powers, another education, another level". Hence, most municipalities expressed the ambition for a new organisation with "profound competences".[28]

Nevertheless, not all municipalities saw their city wardens as instantly capable of law enforcement, and some municipalities took several years to change their wardens into enforcement officers. As a result, the first years of developing a new form of municipal surveillance were characterised by profound growing pains. At the very least, new municipal officers would have to be managed in a more task specific way through clear assignments. "General tasks, such as general preventive

---

27. Rotterdam's old municipal officers were called 'surveillance officers' and the *new* municipal officers who do have powers for fining are called 'city wardens'. These terms are used in reverse in other cities, using the term city wardens to indicate previous, and alleged ineffective workers. To prevent confusion, Rotterdam's pre-2001 municipal officers are here also called 'city wardens'.
28. Tilburg (2006) *Professionalisering toezicht in het openbaar gebied*, Tilburg (2006) *Actief, buurtgericht en creatief*. The Hague (2003) *Veiligheidsplan*.

surveillance, are no part of that," as a policy document on professionalisation of Tilburg's city surveillance agency remarks, implying that only clearly circum-scribed tasks with a measurable output or outcome would count (see further chapter 6).[29]

Thus coordinators and managers gradually started to emphasise that their human resources and organisation needed substantial re-working. Therefore, the political call for more blue on the streets was countered by civil servants trying to convince political decision makers of investing more in these agencies. A Rotterdam manager recalls this moment.

> At a certain point we had a meeting with the mayor and the alderman. […] We took them with us [and showed them] not only the people, but also the equipment. It was terrible, the housing too. We showed them how bad the organisation was […] Because we were dealing with an employment project, but the city council was demanding things from us as if we were the Navy Seals. And that really bothered us.

These deficits in professional standards in many cases were deepened by a lack of occupational pride, according to some respondents. City wardens did not seem to bother about their work.

Moreover, early managers had to create a new organisation out of a rather diverse workforce. Different officers, all with their own visions and task descriptions, "different blood types," as a manager in Eindhoven calls it, had to be merged into one agency. Parking wardens or environmental rule enforcement officers were accustomed to clearly defined tasks and to more powers, sometimes resulting in an eagerness to highlight the difference with their new colleagues. As a manager points out, this might be related to the fact that these officers were part of the municipal police forces until the 1993 re-organisation (see chapter 1): "these men saw their status as ex-police officers as highly important". Therefore many of them did not want to be merged into one agency with city wardens who allegedly had no authority, no powers, and a bad image. "It caused problems, because, well, 'we are police officers'," as an early manager replicates the ideas of these officers. It was urgent to create one's own municipal disorder policing identity, as one of the first managers relates.

> Both city wardens and parking attendants were talking about the municipality this and the municipality that, as if they were no part of it. In their perception they were still part of the police. And the municipality was something distant from them.[30]

---

29. Tilburg (2006) Professionalisering toezicht in het openbaar gebied.
30. This seems a somewhat peculiar vision, as the municipal police forces were equally part of the municipalities until 1993. Apparently their status as 'ex-municipal *police* officers' nevertheless set them apart emotionally from the encompassing municipal organisation.

According to most respondents it took a lot of energy and frustration to develop these officers into fully professional municipal officers who could meet political demands. To this end, these managers generally took a clear stand on the previous city warden phase and looked for a new and own 'municipal identity'. Thus, work reintegration as a goal was opposed and municipal officers were supposed to become independent from the local police forces: "Not as much *away* from the police, but *towards* a new identity," a manager in Eindhoven explains. In some cities, a lot depended on individual managers, who were ambitious and keen to develop their agency to a top-of-the-bill municipal disorder policing apparatus.

In several cities new self-assertion for the city surveillance agencies and its officers seemed to be an important part of these first years. Occupational pride for instance, developed in a remarkably short period of time in some cities. This applies especially to Rotterdam, as a senior manager explains,

> They fixed it up really nicely, so they could be proud of it, something that was lacking with a lot of these people. They were neither proud of themselves, nor of what they were doing. City wardens were just softies. But that totally reversed.

Part of the effort to highlight the break with previous phases was the development of a new vocabulary and name for the newly established agencies. The new municipal city surveillance agency in Utrecht for example, chose to abolish the name *stadswacht* (city warden), as that was seen as tainted by the association with arrangements for long-term unemployed people. For similar reasons, several municipalities chose to abolish the name *Stadstoezicht* (City Surveillance).

In the years following their initiation, the new agencies strove for a more professional image and more professional forms of disorder policing. In Utrecht new officers and coordinators were employed after 2007; workers who were seen as dysfunctional were encouraged to leave the organisation and all new officers were supposed to have the *BOA* qualification. Also in Rotterdam a thorough reshuffling of human resources occurred. Particularly in this city early managers took the stage to establish their new organisation as a new unit that needed to be taken seriously. Although it took several years after the initiation of Rotterdam's city surveillance agency in 2002, it became known as one of the best equipped and largest of the Netherlands. A Rotterdam police officer states that the officers of the new agency were even better equipped than the police: "Anything was possible. They'd be walking around with I-pads, making us really jealous. In our eyes they were the lesser ones, but they had material that was a whole lot better". Equally typical for that phase, according to another respondent, is that this new municipal agency tended to take on more and heavier tasks, bordering on police work. As a consequence the Public Prosecution office and the Police (as official Supervising authorities) told them "to step on the brakes all of the time" (see also chapter 1). Hence,

these ambitious developments also implied some city surveillance agencies ran up
against their limits.

6   RECENT POLICY GOALS AND TASKS: 2007 – 2014

The previous section again showed that political ambitions to enhance public
safety might explain the outlook of municipal disorder policing, but only in part.
Ambitions that are related to the forging of new agencies and an orientation on
occupational pride equally define these new municipal agencies.

   After this initial phase the city surveillance agencies further developed their
ideas of disorder policing. This most recent phase appears as one of professional
maturation – a more conscious application of newly attained law enforcement
powers and reflection on what means could serve the end of compliance with the
rules. As such, city surveillance agencies developed more pragmatic goals, as
opposed to (overt) ambitions to highlight the differences with city wardens. It
seems city surveillance agencies and their officers became more aware of what they
had to offer and how this would match the demands they met.

   In Rotterdam for instance, this was informed by a critical report of the local
Audit office, which concluded that the enforcement activities of municipal officers
were not matched by sufficient professional standards.[31] In The Hague and Tilburg, although their city surveillance agencies seemed less keen on new and ambitious tasks, (internal) reports and audits also targeted the professional level of local
municipal officers. In fact, many respondents state that these officers were unable
to use their discretionary autonomy in a satisfactory way. Hence, quite ironically,
new municipal officers that seem – at least partly – occupied with proving their
status as a viable municipal alternative to a withdrawing police force, were reprimanded for lacking in these vital professional competences. A Rotterdam coordinator recalls the complaints that abounded about this strict rule enforcement.

> We were supposed to enforce the rules, so we did. But the thing is, our officers know how to be
> nuanced only to a certain extent. You can tell them, 'If you see someone in the park drinking
> alcohol, he is done for'. You can't say, 'You can leave alone harmless, left wing, intellectual
> types with a glass of rosé'. Things would get really complicated. Apparently, there was a prob-
> lem with drinking in that park; apparently there were bacchanalian orgies going on there, creat-
> ing a terrible nuisance. So the rules were enforced. But it didn't last for another eighteen months
> for the first debates in the city council: 'You can't even drink a glass of rosé in that park for
> those stupid officers to fine you'.

Such criticism led to a 'recalibration' (Rotterdam: *herijking*), a 'City surveillance
agency 3.0' (Tilburg: *Stadstoezicht 3.0*) or a new plan for 'Rule enforcement on a The

---

31. Rekenkamer Rotterdam, 2012.

Hague level' (The Hague: *Handhaven op Haagse hoogte*). Without exception, these revisions highlighted a renewed orientation in terms of both tasks and approaches, in general – a move away from unquestioningly adopting police-like work and imprudent rule enforcement, and an emphasis on more conscious and professional forms of policing.

Again, there are great similarities between the city surveillance agencies in these most recent developments. In this last section before the conclusion, these similarities in recent policy and tasks of municipal disorder policing are analysed.[32]

Neighbourhood decline and physical disorder

Firstly, the recent policies of various city surveillance agencies are similar in their emphasis on physical disorder, mostly referred to as 'quality of life tasks'. The Hague's new plan provides a clear example of a stricter determination of tasks. More than any other of the municipal agencies in this study The Hague's *Leefbaarheid en Toezicht* has been troubled by issues concerning organisation, vision, professionalisation and the relation with the police. In 2011 this led to the policy plan *Handhaven op Haagse hoogte*, written under direction of the alderman for City maintenance (*stadsbeheer*) of the time. This document proves to be a clear example of a focus on physical disorder and presents one of the most vivid examples of the halting of neighbourhood decline through policing of physical disorder. The Hague opts for a city "where inhabitants feel at home and comfortable," and "where the quality of life attracts new inhabitants, companies and visitors".[33] The introduction provides some lively images of why disorder policing is relevant.

> Unfortunately the people of The Hague do not feel safe all the time and everywhere, they are terribly annoyed by discomforts such as dog litter and garbage bags that are torn apart and they do not have a blind faith in local government in its battle against misbehaviour in public places.[34]

Whereas it is these public places, so it is stated, that are vital for a city where people can feel at home.

---

32. In the appendix a short overview of the differences between the six city surveillance agencies in this study are presented.
33. Gemeente Den Haag (2011). *Handhaven op Haagse hoogte. Beleidsplan voor de handhaving van de leefbaarheid van de openbare ruimte.*
34. *Ibid.*

> The Hague strives for public places that are inviting to dwell in. Next to a high quality of the
> design [*inrichting*] and good maintenance, this demands behavioural rules for the use of public
> places.[35]

'Minor annoyances' [*kleine ergernissen*] have a disrupting effect, the plan maintains, especially since signs of physical decline [*verloedering*] are an early warning of further deterioration of neighbourhoods. In fact it is stressed that addressing misbehaviour by regulation should be combined with cleaning or repairing to show "discomfort and annoyances are taken seriously". As such, this plan represents one of the clearest examples of the influence of broken windows thinking (see also chapter 2).

This vision fully defined the priorities at the time of research. *Handhaven op Haagse hoogte* culminated in a strict determination of the three aspects The Hague's municipal officers should focus on – litter, dog litter and parking issues. These subjects lie at the heart of what bothers The Hague's residents most, and thus what allegedly hinders an inviting public space.

A strict allegiance to a well-defined set of physical disorder issues can be noted in other cities as well. However, this does not always mean officers were told to refrain from fining. Enforcement of rules is still expected – something that seems at odds with the next characteristic of recent policy.[36]

Behavioural compliance

The second corresponding characteristic of recent policy also seems to be influenced by the turn away from intensive enforcement. A term that came to define this is 'behavioural compliance'. This notion seems to imply that municipalities try to be more aware of what can be done to let people obey the rules in public places.

Coordinators and municipal managers stress that the number of fines should be less important than the idea of behavioural compliance and these should no longer be a goal in itself. A municipal manager from the city of Tilburg, states they "really shifted emphasis to the setting of normative standards and […] behavioural compliance". In other municipalities too, behavioural compliance is deemed highly relevant. In Utrecht for example, municipal officers are meant to "stimulate and monitor desired conduct in public places" and "legislation in public places should be complied with as much as possible".[37] Ideally municipal officers would issue a fine only after other means have been tried, as can be read in a policy plan of the city of Nijmegen.[38] Equally, the city of The Hague highlights this basic principle in its

---

35. *Ibid.*
36. Moreover, not all cities were as devoted to these tasks related to physical disorder (see also the appendix).
37. Gemeente Utrecht (2012). *Afdelingsplan THOR.*
38. Gemeente Nijmegen (2012). *Handhaving fysieke leefomgeving. Beleidskader 2012-2016.*

year plan for the municipal officers. "Enforcing the law in public places by coercion is the final resort in a list of efforts to keep the city clean, intact and safe".[39]

As not all city surveillance agencies were under scrutiny of audits or politically initiated 'recalibrations', other reasons might equally well explain why intensive and strict rule enforcement is opposed, at least in policy rhetoric.[40] Tough rule enforcement is not always seen as effective, for instance. The psychological rationale that people have a tendency to behave better under social control is still a key idea for the later approaches of these agencies. The ideal municipal officer is a 'behavioural influencer' [*gedragsbeïnvloeder*], as depicted in a vision document of the city of Rotterdam.[41] In some cases managers have found inspiration in psychological and criminological theories for guidance in this influencing of behaviour, for example an enforcement cycle called 'the big 8', the *tafel van elf* (the table of eleven) or the pyramid of Braithwaite, all meant to gain insight into why specific types of citizens do not comply with the rules and what could ideally be the most effective means to realise behavioural compliance.

Citizen oriented policing

A last recurring policy goal in recent municipal disorder policing concerns the relation with citizens. Again, this goal seems to be a result of criticism of previous approaches. Allegedly, the initial bureaucratic specialisation of city surveillance agencies has led to the alienation of municipal officers from citizens. If some officers deal only with parking offences, others only with stray litter and yet others only with street youth, this does not contribute to 'what the citizen is expecting', many respondents point out. A manager explains:

> I'm only for this, I'm only for that. It's inefficient as hell and it doesn't match what the citizen is expecting […] is there an overview of the neighbourhood? Do you know what that neighbourhood needs?

In contrast, several agencies have started to develop their own ideas of what they call "holistic municipal officers".[42] These are officers that are meant to address any

---

39. Gemeente Den Haag (2012). *Jaarwerkplan 2013. Bedrijfsonderdeel: Leefbaarheid en Toezicht. Gemeente Den Haag – Dienst Stadsbeheer*.
40. Chapter 8 in particular discusses the policy emphasis on behavioural compliance and "enforcement as a last resort" forms a sharp contrast with the strict politics and practices of some municipal officers.
41. Gemeente Rotterdam (2012). *Visie stadswachten: Vertrouwd op straat. Positionering, aansturing en inrichting van de Rotterdamse stadswachten van (voormalig) Stadstoezicht*: p. 5.
42. In Dutch this is referred to with *integrale handhaving* ('integrated law enforcement'). The word 'integrated' [*integraal*] is used interchangeably (and quite confusingly) for at least two different matters. On the one hand to indicate the collaboration of different partners in public safety policy under the nomenclature of 'integrated public safety management', on the other hand as it is used here for officers with an all-encompassing task description.

rule infringement they come across, and operate as neighbourhood wardens. The city of Nijmegen for instance, has instituted such officers. Moreover, municipal officers who are assigned to their own neighbourhood should generally know its residents and should be known by most residents. Equally, Tilburg's revision of the city surveillance agency emphasises that employees should be visible, recognisable and approachable. In the latter case, this is also seen as a way for residents to feel more secure.[43]

More specifically, several city surveillance agencies purposefully aim at familiarity in the neighbourhoods in which they are operating. A clear example of this can be found again in Rotterdam. In its new vision document the agency not only made the case for a renewed focus on behavioural compliance, but municipal officers were also meant to become "well-known faces", neighbourhood wardens, enhancing both compliance with the rules and 'trust in the neighbourhood':

> Citizens are constantly informed about the developments in their neighbourhood. Conversely, municipal officers are easily contacted by citizens. Familiar officials add to the trust in the neighbourhood. Likewise, their closeness stimulates people to address one another on the streets in the case of undesirable behaviour. This is stimulated by indicating which behaviour is the norm, by being alert for signs of anti-social behaviour and to have citizens take their responsibility.[44]

In other cities, policy dictates that citizens should be allowed to set the agenda in a more direct way. This implies not only the predetermined lists of most common annoyances are in use, but more directly, the issues on which citizens report. In Tilburg, it is worded as such:

> To make sure the city is clean, intact and safe, citizens will take part in agenda setting more and more. Their contribution to surveillance and enforcement will become more important and complaints will weigh more heavily in determining the annual priorities.[45]

In Eindhoven this is even taken further. In a special project, citizens are invited to determine directly what should be the tasks of Eindhoven's municipal officers (see also the next chapter).

The emphasis on residents' concerns occasionally leads city surveillance agencies – literally – to define citizens as customers. In Eindhoven for instance, a policy document states "customer friendliness" should be firmly upheld.[46] Likewise in

---

43. Hence, reassurance still appears as a policy goal, albeit it seldom.
44. Gemeente Rotterdam (2012). *Visie stadswachten: Vertrouwd op straat. Positionering, aansturing en inrichting van de Rotterdamse stadswachten van (voormalig) Stadstoezicht*. In fact this vision is loosely inspired by certain criminological insights and reports that thematise the involvement of citizens in policy making, such as the WRR report *Vertrouwen in burgers* ('trust in citizens'; WRR, 2012).
45. Gemeente Tilburg (2013). *Collegeadvies doorontwikkeling stadstoezicht*.
46. Gemeente Eindhoven (2006). *Uitwerking collegeakkoord*.

The Hague, the city surveillance agency aims at a better and more intensive relation with neighbourhood residents, to be capable of addressing "the annoyances
and discomfort of The Hague's inhabitants",[47] and ideally the city surveillance
agency is "serviceable to residents".[48] As such, something of a 'customer orientation' can be noted – addressing the most important annoyances and trying to give
residents a feeling of more security.[49]

Prominent tasks

For a part these policy goals are commonly translated into a set of formal tasks.
Thus, upon asking municipal officers and their coordinators about formal requirements, a specific list of tasks is often mentioned.

Most of these tasks can be regarded as addressing incivilities that are related to
'physical disorder'. A category that might be best summarised as comprising all
(physical) objects that are left soiled, broken, obstructing or hindering, and in particular involving disorder that is high on the municipal list of annoyances: 'dogs
and household waste', and a specific list of traffic offences (mainly parking).[50] This
physical disorder should be man-made in order to attract their attention; officers
deal with the things that are intentionally *left* 'disorderly' by citizens. Thus, discomfort with physical causes, such as street lightning that has broken down due to
a short circuit, potholes or badly maintained public parks, are not considered to be
their tasks.

However this is not a strict category. It comprises forms of incivilities as diverse
as bad parking habits (double-parking, parking on the pavement, etc.), negligence
of car, caravan and bicycle wrecks, illegal dumping of household waste, littering in
general, reluctance to leash dogs or clean their excrement, cycling on the pavement
or in pedestrian zones. In some cities the enforcement of paid parking regulations
is added. In Nijmegen for example, this is the most important task. Also in Rotterdam, patrolling paid parking zones is an important part of their tasks.[51] In addi-

---

47. Gemeente Den Haag (2011). *Handhaven op Haagse hoogte, Beleidsplan voor de handhaving van de leefbaarheid van de openbare ruimte.*
48. Gemeente Den Haag (2012). *Jaarwerkplan 2013. Bedrijfsonderdeel: Leefbaarheid en Toezicht.* Gemeente
Den Haag – Dienst Stadsbeheer.
49. These three characteristics might be presented here as separate entities, but in many explanations
they appear closely intertwined. It is thought for example, that in an ideal situation interaction
with neighbourhood residents and being well known in the neighbourhood increases behavioural
compliance.
50. Flight (2012) and Flight et al. (2012) use the comprehensive terms of 'dogs' and 'waste' to refer to
infringements for which most administrative orders for incivilities were issued (*bestuurlijke strafbeschikking overlast*). As their study concerned only such administrative penal orders and administrative fines for incivilities (*overlast*), it did not encompass the administrative fines and penal orders
for traffic violations (see also chapter 1).
51. At the time of research several cities – such as Rotterdam and Utrecht – decided to have parking
attendance automated, making the use of municipal officers for this task largely redundant.

tion, municipal officers have several extra administrative legal tasks and responsibilities. In some cities they have coercive means to have bicycle and car wrecks
removed. Often they also supervise shop displays and the pavement terrace size of
cafés and restaurants.[52]

For another part, these municipal core tasks in many cities are supplemented by
other tasks (see also chapter 9). A prominent example of this is the policing of 'disorderly persons'. Instead of focusing primarily on disorderly physical circumstances and subsequently addressing whoever might have caused them, the focus here
is on certain groups that are seen as most prone to causing (physical) disorder or
feelings of insecurity. Thus municipal officers are deemed to specifically police certain categories of persons and sometimes have extra powers to address the incivilities caused by, for example homeless people, street youth or nightlife public, such
as alcohol consumption in public places, loitering in doorways and sleeping on the
streets.

In addition, some city surveillance agencies are prepared to fulfil tasks that
stretch the concept of disorder or disorder policing itself, sometimes even leaving
the initial focus on disorder policing aside altogether. In several cities municipal
officers are used for the prevention of criminal offences, such as burglaries or carjacking. Sometimes this happens by situational prevention through walking beats
in neighbourhoods with high levels of such offences. In other cases, employees
visit the victims of carjacking and burglary to provide information on prevention,
assist the police with the preventive control of motorists for burglary tools or with
their 'dark days offensive' (during the days in autumn and winter when most burglaries are reported), running additional surveillance shifts.

Finally, there is quite a large category of other tasks and chores that are handed
to municipal officers, such as the managing of the bicycle depot in Eindhoven, the
removal of bicycle wrecks in Tilburg, noise measurement at events in Nijmegen or
market supervision in Rotterdam. In addition, in some cities municipal officers
have a role in CCTV rooms. For example, in Tilburg and Rotterdam specially
trained employees are responsible for camera surveillance. Lastly, municipal officers are involved in community participation projects in a number of cities.
Although this remaining category depends on local preferences and agreements
between municipal management, police and mayor, it appears to be expanding.
From January 1st, 2013 for instance, municipalities also need to assign municipal

---

52. In this list are rule infringements that need some creativity to be called 'physical disorder', but nev-
     ertheless occupy municipal officers in many cities, such as dogs that are unleashed outside desig-
     nated areas or cycling on the pavement. With regard to the enforcement of traffic offences, munici-
     pal officers are qualified to enforce only a limited set of traffic laws, and in general these do not
     involve moving traffic, such as speeding, ignoring one way traffic signs, or ignoring red lights by
     pedestrians and cyclists. However, the fact that these lower level traffic violations are seen as caus-
     ing a lot of annoyance among citizens leads to debate in several cities. Sometimes law enforcement
     in these cases is made a 'passive power', meaning offenders may be fined if they are 'caught in the
     act', but not as part of a focused action.

officers to enforce the laws on age restrictions in pubs and bars or permits of bar owners.

7   Conclusions

This chapter dealt with the policies of Dutch municipal disorder policing and how it developed throughout the years.

First of all, it described how thinking about crime and disorder changed in the 1980s. This shift can be associated both with a noted rise in petty crime and with risks of victimisation. This renewed focus eventually led to the Roethof Committee and its funding of preventative projects. Among these projects were the first forms of municipal functional surveillance. Putting theoretical notions of prevention into concrete forms of disorder policing, these projects mostly emphasised opportunity reduction through uniformed surveillance.

The most popular of these projects were the first city warden projects. Many cities established a city warden foundation in the first half of the 1990s. The city warden projects for an important part should be placed against the background of the widespread unemployment problem. City wardens were long term unemployed people, and thus were paid through various unemployment benefit schemes. Their work consisted of rather basic forms of situational crime prevention, in some cases correcting behaviour, in any case serving as "eyes and ears" of the police and reassuring citizens. However, the development of a professional habitus was hindered by the prominence of social reintegration goals and wardens' subordinate position to (reluctant) police officers. In addition, the 1990s witnessed a gradual shift towards a different terminology, with a more prominent role for municipal public safety policy, an emphasis on minor annoyances, incivilities (*overlast*) and ideas inspired by broken windows thinking, such as 'clean, intact and safe' or the notion of *leefbaarheid* (quality of life). These terms also impacted on early city wardens.

The first big change in municipal disorder policing took place at the start of the 21st century. Both nationally and locally, a general tendency towards more toughness and stricter interventions to correct deviant behaviour can be noted – a call for more surveillance and rule enforcement. Aided by emerging safety indexes and quality of life monitors, this often translated into the urge to address citizens' concerns more thoroughly. City wardens however, were not seen as adequate for this. As ineffective 'city strollers' they would be unable to "make a difference". Thus, the idea that something had to change spread quickly, helped by the nation-wide abolishment of subsidies for unemployment benefit schemes and increased pressure on municipalities to realise rule enforcement policies. It led to the establishment of city surveillance agencies and enforcement, gradually filled with new municipal officers (known as *BOAs*), who have the power to fine. In addition, in many municipalities they were given more public safety tasks. An important part of this emphasis on firmness was also related to concerns about the development of new occupational pride and the building of an occupational identity from divergent types of municipal officers and city wardens.

In the last phase, the city surveillance agencies further professionalised and seemed to reflect more consciously on tasks and approaches. In quite a few cities the city surveillance agencies were either reprimanded by critical audits or managers realised that professional disorder policing needed more than officers who were capable of fining. As a result, several city surveillance agencies distanced themselves – at least rhetorically – from imprudent rule enforcement so characteristic of the previous phase. It resulted in a renewed focus on tasks of physical disorder, behavioural compliance and more attention for citizen oriented policing, sometimes with consumerist tendencies.

Reflecting on this chapter, it seems that the working goals of municipal officers have changed considerably and rather tortuously. Much of it was caused by factors that are unrelated to disorder in itself. Most importantly, the initial decision to appoint long-term unemployed people as city wardens has proven to be highly influential, both in terms of the alleged lack of effect of these wardens in the 1990s, and in terms of a reputation of unprofessional employees that continues to haunt them to this day. Consequently, overt ambitions and the pursuance of tough enforcement by the first managers of the city surveillance agencies have contributed to the aim of 'making a difference'.

As a result of different policy goals and starting points, municipal officers often appear to have multiple roles at the same time. As such, they sometimes appear as a vehicle for various ideas, expectations and ambitions, both related to public safety policy and to wholly other motives. They are supposed to be officers that address minor annoyances, they are meant to be 'smart' and efficient and know how to induce citizens to behave in the proper way and they are supposed to be 'familiar and trustworthy faces'. Simultaneously they should know how to enforce the rules, in contrast to their allegedly ineffective predecessors.

In the following chapters I will address the question of what happens with such multifarious goals in local decision making processes and the everyday practice of municipal officers. In the next chapter it will become clear that the focus on effectiveness and measurement, and the proximity of municipal politicians are highly influential, implying that some of the aforementioned policy goals will prove to be more rhetorical than realistic.

DECIDING ON DISORDER POLICING ON A LOCAL LEVEL

Chapter 5 dealt with the origins and development of municipal disorder policing in the Netherlands. By discussing nation-wide changes in disorder policies – such as the Roethof subsidies – and the similarities in municipal public safety policies, that chapter addressed the subject of municipal disorder policing on a macro level.

Discussing such macro developments, however, does not reveal a great deal about how policy is made *within* municipalities. Local policy does not depend only on executive decisions made on a national or central level, but is the result of various players who try to influence decisions and put forward different claims. This chapter discusses this 'meso level' of *local* stakeholders and addresses the questions how and by whom disorder policing is decided upon (sub question C). It does so in four sections. Section 1 introduces several concepts that will guide the enquiry into local decision making on disorder policing. Section 2, the main part of this chapter, deals with three different 'logics' through which local decisions on disorder policing are made – political logic, managerial logic and frontline logic. In the third section, two examples of conflicts in deciding on disorder policing are highlighted. Section 4 presents conclusions.

1   STUDYING LOCAL DECISION MAKING

In a classic model well-known in the field of public administration the creation of policy is seen as the result of a rational, central and top-down decision making process (Kickert, Klijn & Koppenjan, 1997; Kingdon, 2014; Rhodes, 1997). In this model, public policy making and implementation are divided into two distinct realms: a strong central actor (the 'agent') makes substantial choices on policy and efficiently steers the objects for the implementation of that policy, "a non-political, technical and potentially programmable activity" (Kickert, Klijn & Koppenjan, 1997: 7).

This linear model of decision making has been widely criticised and researchers of public policy generally agree it is not suited for the study of public policy in practice (Kickert, Klijn & Koppenjan, 1997; Laws & Hajer, 2006; Rhodes, 2006). Rather than being a hierarchical top-down process of decision making and docile implementation, policy is the result of various actors engaging in the implicit or explicit exchanges of resources, interests, problems and solutions (Compston, 2009; Rosenthal et al., 1996). Without wanting to claim the centre is fully hollowed out (Rhodes, 2006), this chapter is largely based on these ideas of policy creation.

Three different theoretical notions guide the enquiry here – network theory, the influence of street level bureaucracy, and the notion of decision making as organised anarchy. These different theories are first briefly introduced before moving to the empirical part of this chapter.

First, local decisions can be seen as the result of various policy networks. This theory points out that public policy is the result of several organisational actors, often depending on other actors in inter-organisational networks (Compston, 2009; Kickert, Klijn & Koppenjan, 1997). In this approach to decision making, the capacity of central actors to steer policy processes is challenged, thereby seeing government as one of multiple actors in policy creation and suggesting the replacement of *government* by *governance* (Kickert, Klijn & Koppenjan, 1997; Rhodes, 2000; Rhodes, 2006). Among other things, this implies that the strife over goals, interests and resources continues in the implementation of policy (Compston, 2009; Rosenthal, 1996; Rhodes, 1997; Rhodes, 2006). Likewise, this approach enables attention to be given to the internal divisions of organisations. Instead of seeing organisations as monoliths with uniform interests and an unambiguous relation with their environment, they can be divided in numerous sub-groups with their respective interests and diverging relations with actors outside the organisation (Rosenthal, 1996: 214). This idea of various networks with their own interests and resources will inform all three 'logics' discussed below.

This network approach is supplemented with the notion that frontline professionals have a particular influence on public policy. Loosely based on Michael Lipsky's seminal work on street-level bureaucracy (2010, [1980]), this second approach takes the beliefs and routines of frontline professionals as a base for understanding local decision making (Laws & Hajer, 2006). Here Lipsky's basic observation that professionals have a relatively large amount of "discretion and relative autonomy from organizational authority" is a guide-line (Lipsky, 2010: 13). Hence, decisions on disorder policing can only be understood if the way frontline professionals adapt, implement and even make policy is taken into account (*ibid.*) and practice must be seen as a "site of joint action and learning constituted around shared problems" (Laws & Hajer, 2006: 412). Many studies have shown this applies equally to policy implementation in public safety (see for instance: Moors & Bervoets, 2013). This chapter will show that professionals form their own networks with associated meaning making and policy creation.

A last theoretical notion refers to local decision-making as the result of a relatively chaotic and unstructured process, a result of 'organised anarchy'. Most insightfully worded by Kingdon (2014), decisions on local policy are the result of the interaction of various problem definitions, solutions and political processes

(Kingdon, 2014).[1] Instead of seeing policy as the alleged best solution available *after* a problem is identified, solutions (potential policy) could exist even before problems are formulated. Various solutions lie in wait and problems could be formulated in different ways. Only when the 'streams' of solutions and problems meet and interact with independent political processes, aided by policy entrepreneurs who highlight certain problems or solutions over others, a window of opportunity for specific policy opens, actual choices are made and policy changes (Kingdon, 2014). Conceived as such, specific policies of municipal disorder policing may be seen as a solution that had been waiting for an appropriate problem. This model will be of use, both in describing part of political logic below, and in two case studies discussed in chapter 8.[2]

2   THREE 'LOGICS' IN DECIDING ON MUNICIPAL DISORDER POLICING

Before turning to a description of the 'logics' that influence decisions in municipal disorder policing, a description of the formal bureaucratic organisation and the different players is needed.

First of all, and as stated above, political decision making and implementation may be seen formally as two separate realms, with municipal management subservient to the decisions of politicians. Hence first in line of the formal hierarchy are political decision makers. Executive decisions on municipal disorder policing are the responsibility of the mayor and aldermen and are subject to political (council) debates.

Second in this formal, hierarchical line are senior municipal managers, mostly from a Public Safety policy department. These senior officials draw up annual plans and reports, thereby developing concrete policies for the decisions made by the municipalities' administrations. In addition, other policy departments such as Public space or Mobility also develop a (mostly minor) part of the plans for municipal officers.

Third in line are the city surveillance agencies themselves. These agencies do not develop their own policy, but implement annual plans made by the aforementioned policy departments. The city surveillance agencies are mostly clustered in a

---

1.   Kingdon partly uses a theory first developed by Cohen, March & Olsen (1972), called the garbage can model of decision making. In this model "choice opportunities" within an organisation are seen as "a garbage can into which various kinds of problems and solutions are dumped by participants as they are generated" (1972: 2). As Kingdon further elaborates this basic theory and adds – among others things – the notions of 'policy entrepreneurs' and 'window of opportunity', his theory is used here.

2.   Kingdon's theory has mainly explanatory power for a specific part of the decision making process. Its rather instrumental and situational focus leaves it insensitive to more structural and cultural circumstances that might equally influence decision making processes (a criticism expressed by Mucciaroni, 1992). Kingdon agreed with this criticism and later adapted his theory by stating certain institutional frameworks define decisions on moments outside the aforementioned 'policy windows'.

municipal division that comprises other units that also have surveillance and enforcement tasks – for instance the inspection agencies for the built environment or of environmental permits.

Finally, teams of municipal officers are locally – at the level of neighbourhoods and boroughs – embedded through contacts (and in many cases *contracts*, see below) in neighbourhood management. This local management decides, in close contact with the team coordinators of municipal officers, in which areas the municipal officers should work.

As said, such formal hierarchical layers can explain only to a limited extent how and why decisions are made in municipal disorder policing. More important is the way these various players reason and make priorities, their rationale when it comes to making decisions on disorder policing. In what follows three such 'logics' will be discussed. These are respectively political, managerial and frontline logic.[3]

2.1   *Power to the big players: deciding on disorder policing through political logic*

As pointed out in the previous chapter, decisions on disorder policing might start with a council debate between various political representatives. From a democratic perspective, one could also maintain that this is the way decisions *should* be made – supreme authority should be granted to democratic political decision making by the city council and the administration of mayor and aldermen (Rosenthal, 1996). In practice however, political decisions on municipal disorder policing take this classical form only to a limited extent. Despite the formal hierarchy described above, particular interests and incidents often appear to dominate political decision making. In this respect *political logic* takes several distinct forms.

Political attention
The more classical way of political decision making on municipal disorder policing can be found particularly during a series of formative moments. As described in chapter 5, the formation of city surveillance agencies was preceded by council debates. In several cases these debates incited by the abolishment of unemployment benefit schemes, centred on a 'call for surveillance' and the need for municipal officers who could 'make a difference'. Another occasion on which politically motivated decisions are made is with regard to issues of professionalisation. In the case of Rotterdam for example, the local Audit office published a critical evaluative report, stimulating important changes in the Rotterdam city surveillance agency (Rekenkamer Rotterdam, 2012). Likewise in The Hague, concern regarding professional standards and the way municipal officers collaborate with police officers led

---

3.   Important to note is that these 'logics' pertain to a way of thinking about disorder policing, and not to specific persons. Hence, managerial logic for instance is not limited to managers, but might also be found among frontline professionals and politicians.

to political attention and eventually spawned the formative policy plan *Handhaven op Haagse hoogte* ('Enforcement on a The Hague level').

In some cities the ideas of particular political key-players, such as aldermen or board members played a large role. Nijmegen provides an example of a city surveillance agency that draws a relatively large amount of political attention. Both in a council debate and through the efforts of a dedicated alderman of this city, Nijmegen's Bureau of Surveillance was established and its orientation qualified as being connected to notions of 'hosting', an approach of disorder policing with relatively little emphasis on law enforcement and more on reassurance and service provision (see also chapter 5).

In several cities this political attention for the city surveillance agencies continues after such formative moments. In Nijmegen the initial emphasis on hosting had to compete with subsequent political views. Municipal officers and their coordinators in Nijmegen point out that consecutive aldermen and mayors have different ideas about the outlook of municipal disorder policing. Nijmegen's frontline professionals and coordinators recount stories in which political interference can directly impact upon their work. In one and the same case one alderman might highlight strict enforcement, whereas the other sees things differently. Likewise, diverging political preferences are manifest in daily prioritising. For instance, when discussing whether citizens' reports should be responded to immediately. As one coordinator states,

> The [alderman] of public spaces says, 'take those reports seriously'. [The alderman] for mobility would say, 'Don't go there, we have to make it clear that people can solve it themselves'.

Thus, political notice for disorder policing is dependent on the individual ideas of one or a few of these political players, making this attention at times rather incidental, as it could probably change or disappear with the advent of other players.

Incident(al) policy
While such political interference could be seen as inherent in any policy process in which decision makers are in office for a limited amount of time, 'incidental concerns' also have a second, more literal meaning. In this case policy creation is not dependent on changing beliefs and views of the politicians involved, but of incidents in which specific problems come to the fore and specific policy is presented as a solution. Political decisions here must be understood as the result of the meeting of different 'streams', especially where the solution of new municipal officers is awaiting an appropriate problem, and this solution is pushed by specific policy entrepreneurs (Kingdon, 2014).

Crucial to understand the impact of incidents on the work of municipal officers is the realisation that they can be used for a wider range of tasks. Thus in recent years decision makers started regarding municipal officers as a proper solution to new problems. Often mayors play an important part in these decisions. As mayors are responsible for public safety in Dutch municipal administration, some of them see a large role in this respect for 'their' municipal enforcement officers. Consequently, these officers are seen as the 'mayor's tool' by some. Here safety indexes play a big role too. Eindhoven for instance, has long featured in the top-end of the AD-crime monitor (see also chapter 5). This induced the mayor to invest more in public safety measures, and likewise to ask more from the (*his own* – as some may say) municipal city surveillance agency, hence – at least partly – explaining the relatively large portion of public safety tasks done by Eindhoven's municipal officers.

However, in cities that feature less prominently in these indexes mayors are also increasingly prone to see their own municipal officers as a suitable solution to new issues and incidents, such as high incidences of burglaries or such divergent problems as disturbance caused by fireworks, street youth or issues particular for nightlife areas. Often lobbying by groups of residents and attention in local media play a large role here (see also chapter 8). Furthermore, this tendency is strengthened by the preferences of both municipal officers and police officers. Thus quite a few municipal officers and coordinators are eager to subscribe to more public safety tasks, keen on doing 'new things' and want to do more 'police-like work'. Such tasks give them a chance to prove they are a professional group that is capable of serious work and to shake off their past as alleged dysfunctional employees. In this respect, these players might be acting as specific policy entrepreneurs. At the same time, the police are withdrawing from minor disorder issues. According to many respondents in this study the police tend to extend the category of issues they consider as 'minor', and thus not theirs to address. In this respect it is telling that municipalities have kept the number of municipal officers on an equal level or even expanded it since the police reorganisation of 2013, irrespective of the widely felt urge for cutbacks (Terpstra, Foekens & Van Stokkom, 2015).

They say jump; you say how high
In network terms, the interests of decision makers, officers, officials and specific groups of residents are of importance in understanding this form of decision making. In that respect, various players form their own implicit network. It results in a precarious policy frame in which municipal officers are expected to respond to changing wishes.

A clear example of this is provided by the city surveillance agency in Utrecht. As a consequence of the large amount of incidental and changing assignments they get from political decision makers, this agency has changed part of its organisation into a flexible pool of municipal officers that is willing to live up to changing demands. These range from running night shifts in what is called the *Breedstraat area* (see chapter 8), to patrolling neighbourhoods to detect illegal fireworks, to preventative surveillance in neighbourhoods with high incidences of burglaries, car theft and car burglaries, bicycle theft or vandalism.[4]

According to some respondents, this political influence puts a lot of strain on the daily work of municipal officers. A coordinator words his frustration at the continuous pressure to respond to (political) requests – "they say jump; you say how high". In one particular case officers were requested to go to a recreational lake that got a lot of negative media attention as a result of fisticuffs and the harassment by a group of youngsters. The coordinator says,

> Everybody freaks out and yells for solutions that are not supported by everybody. 'Get it done!'
> And we always did, because we thought it was really important and we wanted to make a good
> impression. But after a while you can't keep jumping up. You meet your limitations.

This emphasis on responding to changing wishes and assignments implies that "choices have to be made," in the words of many respondents; quite a few priorities succumb to the abovementioned 'incidental policy'. An Eindhoven coordinator explains, "our enforcement apparatus is limited, so we have to make choices". In other cities, managers and coordinators assert that an agency that is merely allowed to implement changing demands and assignments – "running projects all the time" – makes it difficult to set up a structural form of disorder policing. Others say that these municipal officers are overwhelmed by the abundance of tasks – the amount of requests, assignments and demands is just too much, as a respondent in Utrecht states.

2.2   *Power to the figures: deciding on disorder through managerial logic*

Managerial thinking
It might first appear that political logic is the dominant rationale of decision making. When discussing local policy with managers and coordinators, they replicate their position in the municipal hierarchy and maintain they merely implement the policy made elsewhere.

However, on closer inspection these managers express a specific view of how disorder policy should be decided upon, representing a second dominant rationale. Managerial logic shows the influence of a set of specific views and practices, condensed in the belief that efficient management of diverse actors provides the best (most effective) solution to the problem of disorder (Pollitt, 1993). In fact, managers in municipal disorder policing often oppose political decision making by tapping into concepts that can be seen as part of the New Public Management wave. This specific notion of managerialism appears as an alternative to the centralised state model, lending bureaucrats technological self-governing capacity in the effective

---

4.   Known as the 'WAFV team' (the abbreviation refers to the Dutch words for these offences).

and efficient organisation of their tasks (Christensen, 2006). It uses terms derived from business and commerce as a response to alleged ineffective and bureaucratic public management. This has also permeated city surveillance agencies and impacts upon the role description of team coordinators and municipal officers themselves, albeit it in a specific interpretation. Instead of quasi markets, business models and competition, this thinking here implies an emphasis on (performance) measurement and the use of managerial tools.

Managerial thinking is not limited to senior managers of public safety departments, but can also be found in the accounts of various coordinators and even frontline professionals (see also chapter 7). Thus coordinators in city surveillance agencies might speak of themselves as 'contractors' and of others as 'clients' (for instance neighbourhood managers), of customers that 'pay for a job to be done', of the 'assignments' they have, the 'lists they have to keep to', the 'role they have been given', the 'product surveillance and enforcement' and the contracts they have with, for instance neighbourhood management. Likewise, these same coordinators state for their part that they are clients of other municipal units, for instance maintenance or street cleaning. A coordinator from Tilburg explains how he is in touch with the 'Agency for Public Maintenance'. He explains that a 'tender' had been made, and 'subcontractors' have been 'granted' the contract to clear rubbish. As such, the division of tasks is not limited to municipal officers executing assignments from others, but continues with their managers in their turn instructing others, being bound to others through 'contracts', or 'outsourcing' tasks to other agencies.

Managerial logic is most evident in the often heard reference to issues of 'monitoring', 'steering' and 'measuring'. Consequently, questions of how and where municipal officers are needed and – to a lesser extent – how to measure effects of municipal officers seem to preoccupy many managers and are mostly solved by reference to standards that are meant to objectify incivilities and disorder. These objective standards allow managers to control the work processes and the 'production' of their organisation (cf. Noordegraaf & Geuijen, 2011). The tendency to control is most evident in the use of three different managerial tools – quality of life scans, citizens' reports and registration systems.

Quality of life scans: rating the neighbourhood
The first of these often used managerial tools are known as 'quality of life scans' or 'neighbourhood monitors'. As the municipal city surveillance agencies legitimate themselves through addressing the most common annoyances of residents, they rely on these tools to manage their disorder policing efforts.

An important part of these scans and monitors are surveys. These are meant to get a better understanding of how residents perceive their neighbourhoods. In Nijmegen for instance, neighbourhood monitors are used to question residents on general issues of public safety and quality of life. Questions might entail "How do you value your neighbourhood?" but also: "Out of ten possible elements, what annoys you the most?" Likewise, The Hague has quality of life scans to measure residents' view on littering and what are bottlenecks and issues that could hamper their sense of well-being, providing residents with the possibility to rate their environment.

Although opinions on the efforts of municipal officers are not addressed directly in the surveys underlying these scans and monitors, their outcome does form an important input for decision making. As such, monitors and scans often form part of a more encompassing model for planning and control. These are indicators for target measurement meant to constantly monitor and define results (Noordegraaf & Geuijen, 2011). In Nijmegen for instance 'The Enforcement Cycle' is a managerial tool to ascertain the need for surveillance, and is informed by Nijmegen's neighbourhood monitors. Likewise, The Hague's scans are used as input for public safety and quality of life meetings on the level of boroughs, meant to supplement the citywide priorities for policing with local highlights. In yet other cases these scans and monitors are used as input for the 'enforcement meetings' between local neighbourhood managers, team coordinators of municipal officers and police officers.

In a few cases the professionalisation of scanning and monitoring has resulted in specialised municipal intelligence departments. These departments are concerned mainly with what are seen as public safety issues, such as youth groups, burglaries or carjacking, plotting maps with the highest levels of reports, complaints or the worst overall rating by residents. This is done by using, for instance colour codes and signal lights. As a municipal manager in Eindhoven states, they have "a sort of dashboard, with real time analyses," and "reports are plotted on maps". Likewise, signal lights changing from green to red indicate more attention is needed, the hottest areas being the hotspots where – among others things – the most municipal officers would be needed.

In some cases the outcomes of scans and monitors result in ratings. Although not each municipality commits itself exclusively to these figures, they do provide an additional managerial standard used to create a measurable goal – a performance target. The Hague for instance, has made it into a goal to upgrade the overall citizen's judgment for public space in the city from a 7 to an 8.[5] Likewise, managers in Nijmegen seem to commit themselves to the output of these monitors. "These neighbourhood and safety monitors will lead the way from now on. These will have to show if the approach works or not," a team coordinator says.

It appears that these indicators are one of the prime means to decide where municipal officers should be deployed. However, these are used but seldom to evaluate

---

5.   Gemeente Den Haag (2011). *Handhaven op Haagse hoogte: Beleidsplan voor de handhaving van de leefbaarheid van de openbare ruimte.* In the Netherlands report figures range from 1 to 10, with 1 being the lowest rating and 10 the highest.

the effect of municipal officers' efforts. Many coordinators and municipal managers highlight there are too many factors impacting upon these ratings to use them as such. Therefore such indicators are not used to account for municipal officers' actions *afterwards*, but merely as indications *in advance* of the areas where they would be most useful. As such, they may be seen as pre-performance indicators to determine targets and priorities.

Citizens' reports and complaints: sorting out the hotspots
A second tool that is often used in decision making consists of citizens' reports about disorder issues in their neighbourhood. Municipalities increasingly professionalised their information flow by setting up service agencies where citizens' reports are registered and linked to the right municipal department, for instance maintenance, traffic support or city surveillance.

Reporting has been further enabled by a nation-wide change in accessibility of municipal organisations through the establishment of customer support centres. These centres can be used by citizens to report their complaints and questions. Since 2005, Dutch municipalities have started to implement a special telephone number of 5 digits, starting with '14', and followed by the 3 digits of the city's area code.[6] The municipality of Rotterdam for instance, can thus be reached through '14010', the municipality of Utrecht through '14030', and so on.[7] In some cities it is made even easier to file complaints by technological innovations, such as the 'Better streets app' [*buiten beter app*] in Rotterdam.

As these agencies present themselves as the guardians against 'whatever annoys citizens the most', many managers state that residents' reports are taken highly seriously. Moreover, many (team) coordinators see these reports as important legitimation for the tasks of their officers. As a coordinator of the city surveillance agency in The Hague remarks,

> We now mark the locations of the reports we received from residents and our own observations; those are the [prime sources] for policy, those are the things we address the following year. [...] you can't tackle it all, so you might as well say, I've got several problem areas, and I'll give those areas extra attention.

In this respect, rather than paying attention to every single citizen report, these are collected and preferably used to get a better overview of those areas with the most issues, the hotspots. Such overviews can then be used for the planning and allocation of officers. Many coordinators appear to concentrate on *patterns* of reports, more than on individual reports. This ideal of a planned approach, reminiscent of

---

6.   Retrieved from: https://www.kinggemeenten.nl/sites/king/files/KING_factsheet_14.pdf.
7.   In 2014 93% of Dutch municipalities had introduced this service line (Van de Wijngaert, Ten Tije & Jansen 2014 "14+netnummer vanuit burgerperspectief" Centre for E-government studies Universiteit Twente).

problem oriented policing (see also chapter 2), is often contrasted with ticking off the reports they receive from citizens (*meldingen afhandelen*) – the reactive form of policing in which a municipal officer waits for new reports to which to react. "We have to wonder whether it is the task of the municipal officer to run after every single report," as one manager states.

Hence, municipal managers actively try to stimulate citizens to report more of what is bothering them, thus trying to improve their 'report-willingness' (*meldings-bereidheid*). A municipal area manager in The Hague calls these reports their 'mantra',

> That is our mantra. You send your blue where it's needed. If you make sure those residents react only when something's wrong, and you respond to that in the right way, then you antici-pate the demands of society. We do that here by emphasising, if there's something wrong, call 14070, so every week I can see exactly who called about what.

In some cases, special neighbourhood meetings with residents are organised. This can be done through projects, for instance through an increasingly popular citizen participation project called 'The neighbourhood governs' (*De buurt bestuurt*, cf. Schuilenburg, 2016).[8] In this project, first developed in Rotterdam, citizens can indicate what issues should be prioritised by police and municipal officers. In other cases, meetings are limited to one evening, but also bring issues to the fore that concern tasks for municipal officers. Although these meetings and participation projects serve numerous goals, managers of city surveillance agencies usually see them as means to collect more information from residents. In the short intermezzo at the end of this section a particular citizen participation project in Eindhoven is described (BOX 1).

Registration systems
A third managerial tool for decision making on the deployment of municipal officers concerns the use of work registration systems. Scans and monitors are used to indicate *in advance* what might be complaint hotspots or areas with a low overall rating, but managers of municipal officers use these instruments to demonstrate the effect *afterwards*.

Many team coordinators express uneasiness at the use of work registration and target numbers because managers appear to realise that issues as 'quality of life' or 'trust' (see also chapter 5) cannot be related in an unambiguous way to the numbers of fines and reports that are issued. Nevertheless, these function as a means to control municipal officers' activities. A coordinator at the Rotterdam city surveillance agency discusses his ambivalence,

---

8.   These projects are reminiscent of the CAPS project in Chicago (Skogan & Hartnett, 1997).

> You indicate the domain of law enforcement, so I want to know how many fines have been
> written. [Work registration in terms of] hours doesn't say that much. But the number of fines
> doesn't say it all either. However, I find a whole shift without a single fine hard to believe.

Managers may have a love-hate relationship with target numbers, but in fact do use these to account for their actions, to determine future investment of personnel and tasks and to scrutinise individual employees' actions. As such, tools that are meant to account for municipal officers retrospectively also predetermine their actions; often only those activities that can be measured and accounted for are seen as relevant (Pollitt, 1993).

Summing up the insights of this section, the managerialism in municipal disorder policing is not fundamentally different from that in other sectors of public policy (Noordegraaf, 2008; Pollitt, 1993). Here too, municipal managers dominate local policy and structure the planning of disorder policing by productivity systems of measuring and accountability (Pollitt, 1993).

Nevertheless, quality of life scans, citizens' reports and registration systems function as means of retrospective performance management only to a limited extent. They appear to have more relevance to providing managerial grip on future disorder policing, as 'pre-performance management'. As such, managers state it is hard to measure the concrete outcome of officers' activities. 'Quality of life' or residents' feelings of security are complex phenomena to which municipal officers can only contribute in a limited way, and municipal managers grapple with making sense of the outcome of officers' activities. Instead, they tend to focus on what can be measured and what provides a grip on their human resources, even though the relation between those indicators and the use of municipal officers is far from unambiguous.

This eagerness to control has at least two effects. On the one hand, municipal officers are allocated to those areas with low ratings by residents and many citizen reports without a clear idea of the effect of their activities. On the other hand, managers seem to prefer output to outcome. Hence, as numbers of reports and fines are measurable, work forms and activities that are related to these are given precedence over activities that are less measurable. It leads to a prominence of hotspot thinking and target numbers over general preventative surveillance or contacts with neighbourhood residents. In yet other words, the actions of municipal officers are not evaluated on their outcome in terms of enhanced quality of life or better ratings, but mostly on their output in terms of work registration and (sometimes) the number of fines.

BOX 1: Eindhoven's citizen participation as managerial tool for extra reports

Some cities actively design policy to enhance the willingness of residents to make reports. In Eindhoven for instance, residents of 'action neighbourhoods' are given a say in how municipal officers should be deployed by indicating at a neighbourhood community centre what should be the focus of these professionals. Eindhoven's municipal officers participating in this project have been dubbed 'attention fielders' (*aandachtsvelders*).

Professionals and managers both state this approach differs from reactive response to citizens' reports. "These people are wearing a uniform and are in touch with the public; they provide service," a neighbourhood manager states. Equally, professionals highlight their function as a 'contact point' in the neighbourhood, with an emphasis on 'service provision'. Because these officers are connected to these neighbourhoods they claim that it becomes easier to have a structural bond with residents. "You are bonding with those groups. You visit [neighbourhoods] regularly," an officer says. Residents know who these municipal officers are and know they can contact them to share their complaints with them, others claim. Conversely, municipal officers are satisfied with the possibility of making agreements with residents.

On closer inspection however, the initiative has also been encapsulated in managerial logic of planning and control. Residents' complaints that are collected at the neighbourhood centre are sent to the city surveillance agency where they are used to plan personnel deployment. As a result, municipal officers have a confined and fixed number of hours to respond to residents' reports and are but seldom present in their neighbourhood for more than one or a few hours; they are allowed to address these reports and then have to move on to their next chore. In addition, various workers are sent to the same neighbourhood to deal with the reported issues. This appears to have a negative impact on their (preventive) presence and the actual contact with residents. Moreover, according to several respondents the participation projects attract mostly only the small group of residents that already knows how to approach the municipality and do so regularly. Although many respondents state this project *does* enhance contact between municipal officers and neighbourhood residents, the officers are in the neighbourhood less than before and only a group of residents already known is involved.

As such, a project that claims to enhance the contact between individual citizens and municipal officers results in a more controlled work form with employees having to act more efficiently. "Now you have a couple of hours, whereas you used to have entire daily periods. And the citizen notices that," a municipal officer claims. A municipal neighbourhood manager expresses his criticism in the same fashion,

> What they should do when they are in the neighbourhood is address anything they come
> across [...] so go out without any predefined assignments, go to the community centre,
> pick up the signals and work on it. They shouldn't take them to the office, where these
> reports are planned into a schedule and are then dealt with four weeks later. It's hard to
> explain that to the residents.
>
> Hence this project appears to have goals reminiscent of community policing, in which
> the officers are strongly embedded in their neighbourhood and residents are involved
> in local decision making (see also chapter 2). In practice however, officers are still
> under a managerial grip. Here the resulting focus on reports as a means to predeter-
> mine the work of municipal officers becomes a goal in itself and clouds other, less
> measurable goals.

2.3   *Power to the professional: deciding on disorder through frontline logic*

The third and last rationale of decision making opposes the alleged objective
means of measurement and reporting so typical of managerial logic. In 'frontline
logic' municipal officers (and team coordinators) might even frustrate the designs
of senior managers. They have their own way of defining disorder policing, closely
in line with personal observations and experiences of disorder. Professionals of
various organisations come together and agree on how disorder should be policed,
thereby showing practice can also be a site of joint action, where decisions on
shared problems are made in close coordination between frontline professionals
and based on their own resources (Laws & Hajer, 2006).

From managerial to frontline logic
Many coordinators of municipal officers point out that instruments such as quality
of life monitors provide a limited perspective on "street reality". A respondent in
Rotterdam states there are all kinds of objective measurements to indicate the effect
of these officers, "you've got your absolute figures, you've got the public safety
monitor, and you've even got the AD crime monitor".[9] However, in his opinion
these indicators do not do justice to "what happens on the street", to the observations and experiences of municipal officers and to the various ways of policing that
might be effective but not measurable, he states.

In addition, respondents claim that residents' experiences of quality of life are
determined by a wide variety of factors; as a Utrecht respondent remarks, municipal officers are but one factor among many that could impact upon how residents
rate their neighbourhood. Moreover, local interests distort these scans, as a coordi-

---

9.   See also chapter 5.

nator of municipal officers in The Hague says when speaking of residents' desire to get rid of a 'coffeeshop' (soft drug outlet) in their neighbourhood,

> The only thing neighbours want is to get rid of that coffeeshop. That's their aim. So they'll ha-
> rass the municipality [with reports]. And if you ask them using a quality of life scan, 'what do
> you think of your living environment?' Those figures don't say that much.

Likewise, hesitations about the value of citizens' reports can be heard. A coordinator in Nijmegen for instance, states he is expected to send his officers to the neighbourhoods with the most reports: but in his opinion, those areas do not necessarily have the most problems. While talking about a relatively well-to-do neighbourhood, he remarks,

> Those are the areas with the real nags. In general highly educated people. So when they see an
> empty can on the street, they'll call us, saying, 'I'm paying taxes for this, come clean it'. [...] But
> don't you think there's too much capacity going to this area? If you compare that with [...] the
> really deprived neighbourhoods, what are you doing [in that other area]? Do we really have to
> respond to every report? Or could we say: 'why don't you pick up that empty can yourself?'[10]

Thus quite a few of these coordinators express unease about the ratio of these figures and performance indicators. If they are to decide where to send their officers, they prefer to use other indicators of disorder. In contrast with these tools for objective measurement, these team coordinators show more affinity with frontline work and the observations made there.

Prominence of observations and ad hoc plans
A first prominent characteristic of frontline logic, as opposed to managerial logic, is that decisions on disorder policing are based on professionals' observations. When it comes to issues that need to be addressed, those working on the street know best, many team coordinators maintain. Disorder and incivilities need to be determined by their information and contacts in the neighbourhood. Moreover, many of these coordinators have a background as frontline professionals themselves as municipal officers or police officers, and at times are eager to 'go out into the streets' themselves. The affinity with daily street work leads them to put a lot of confidence in the street knowledge of their workers, and letting those observations help define tasks and goals of municipal officers.

Sometimes this is supported by formal policy. The policy emphasis on holistic policing discussed in the previous chapter is an example of formal policy that

---

10.   Although this quote illustrates an aversion of basing decisions on reports, it might equally be inter-
      preted in other terms. The coordinator quoted here also points out how he ideally pictures the
      tasks of his municipal officers or the 'responsiblisation' of citizens, a theme that will be discussed
      more extensively in chapter 7 and the conclusions.

acknowledges frontline observations. Thus, in some municipalities officers are specifically asked to 'keep their eyes open' and to work 'holistically', implying officers are expected to address issues that reach beyond the chores they are assigned that day.[11] A coordinator says about his workers,

> So they're doing parking control and they see some rubbish, dumped illegally, or a lamp post that's broken, then they dealt with that right away. In that sense it's a holistic way of working.

In many cases however, there is but little policy to support this prominence of observations by frontline professionals.

Secondly, this often implies plans – hardly to be called 'policy' – are made pragmatically and locally, often in collaboration (or networks) with local coordinators of different organisations involved. In these cases, different coordinators agree on their pragmatic approach of local issues and collaboratively develop an idea of what needs to be done – "creating solutions together," as a coordinator in Tilburg puts it. By contacts, based on personal acquaintance, decisions are made. As such, they speak of "the things they can do for each other", of "communication" and "short lines" (direct relations), sometimes because professionals and coordinators have known each other for a long time, and 'speak the same language'. These are specific networks of professionals who decide among themselves how they should deal with disorder policing. Moreover, in several cases senior managers validate their yearly plans with the local neighbourhood managers, even though these managers formally contract municipal officers for specific tasks and numbers of hours. A team coordinator in Rotterdam for instance, explains the central department of Public Safety merely "steers on a meta-level," whereas "the real tuning of operational activities is [done] by the area coordinator as link between [requests from the] borough and the execution by municipal officers".

These team coordinators usually refrain from making statements about what would be the overarching goal or the legitimacy of disorder policing. We are "making happen what needs to happen," as one of them expresses it. Yet they have a large amount of influence on local decisions on disorder policing. A team coordinator from Utrecht explains how plans are made in practice,

> I am the pivot of [those plans]. I receive input from 15 different stakeholders. And that's how I decide on my policy and the employment of my officers. My people deliver input, residents' reports, housing corporations, the agency of maintenance, the Public Safety department, the neighbourhood community centre, the police, the neighbourhood police officer, youth work, street coaches. Those are all partners and I refer to them in my daily employment of workers.

---

11. Hence, apart from being policy that is geared at citizens' expectation (as discussed in the previous chapter), policy that emphasises 'holistic policing' may equally be seen as a valuation of frontline logic discussed here.

As such, coordinators do not rule out scans and monitors, but merely use them as input for their meetings with other frontline coordinators and as a supplement to the observations and signals of their own workers.

Again, municipal policy in some cases is especially designed to support these networks. In Eindhoven for example, the municipality designed a position entitled 'attention fielder' – municipal officers who are assigned to certain neighbourhoods, and are meant to stay in close contact with designated areas, their residents and local partners. Likewise, in Utrecht some of the municipal officers are 'neighbour-hood municipal officers' who have the responsibility for their own specific neigh-bourhood. In Nijmegen the function of 'networker' has been developed to stay in close contact with residents and shop owners, and in Rotterdam new policy is also aimed at the local embedding of municipal officers. In most cases however, it seems up to frontline workers themselves whether they invest in their network or see it as their responsibility to stay in touch with other professionals (see also the next chapter for their views on this matter). In the next box an example of such frontline logic and the ensuing close collaboration between municipal officers and police officers is discussed.

BOX 2: Collaboration in Nijmegen city centre

An obvious case of how frontline logic works can be found in Nijmegen's city centre. In this area police officers and municipal officers work closely together. Two elements characterise their collaboration. First of all, the cooperation between municipal officers and police officers in Nijmegen's centre area is characterized by the large number of requests for municipal officers submitted by the local police team. Put simply, this team lacks the capacity to deal with all issues in this area. This leads some police offi-cers to see the Nijmegen city surveillance agency as a 'police extension'. Municipal officers in the Nijmegen centre assist the police with issues such as reporting shoplift-ers or incivilities caused by loitering youth. Most notably these municipal officers also address, fine and arrest certain 'notorious disorderly persons', a group of homeless people that stay in a nearby shelter. A municipal officer speaks about these tasks,

> Previously, if I were to find someone passed out with a beer, I'd think, 'Am I qualified, can I do something?' I would have called the police. Now, I say, this behaviour is disturb-ing, I don't want it here. And I know this guy, I know why he does this, I can help him get on his feet. That is something we worked on the last couple of years.

The involvement of municipal officers causes a large 'grey area' of tasks between police and municipal officers, and difficulty in indicating what are the boundaries of their work, as indicated by a coordinator – "you might run into this or that," but, he continues, the assistance of the Nijmegen city surveillance agency happens in a "self-evident" way,

It's not a conscious choice that we fill up some kind of gap. It just happens self-evidently.
And that's what we work for, so the citizens get the feeling this is a nice place to reside,
work and live.

"Common sense," he states, "helps do the right thing in coordination with the police".
A second characteristic of their cooperation is the support of municipal officers by the
police. This is based both on practical preconditions and on personal acquaintance.
Municipal officers have their own room in the police station for making reports after
arrests and police officers brief them three times a week. Thus both occupational
groups are well aware of their respective activities in the centre. To a certain extent,
privacy sensitive information is shared as well. However, these agreements are not the
result of top-down or managerial interference. Likewise legal arrangements appear to
play a minor role. These agreements have a pragmatic character in which personal
acquaintance seems to play an important role. A constable states he generally sends an
email with questions or warnings, for example the description of a shop lifter. "It's all
public order, and public safety," he states, "nothing inferior". Thus for him cooperation is highly satisfactory,

If I ask them, can you go see if Johnny is sleeping somewhere on a porch, I wouldn't have
to check it, because they will do it. Also because they find it important themselves. And
the boys in our team would do the same thing.

A Nijmegen neighbourhood manager adds that "the police and city surveillance
agency have found each other" in the centre of Nijmegen, and that most police officers
in the centre would see a municipal officer as "one of them". Another policeman
defines them as "pals", "colleagues" and additional "hands and feet". As such, these
frontline police officers' clear and vocal need for support and the willingness of the
municipal officers to grant the police's requests, appear to be very important. The
facilities provided and the smooth handling in the event of an arrest all contribute to
positive cooperation.

3   TENSIONS AND CONFLICTS

Having discussed the three different 'logics' that define local decision making on
disorder policing, it might appear these relate to neatly distinguishable realms,
each with its own particular network. However, 'logics' do not operate in isolation
and multiple tensions and conflicts can be observed between them. As already
briefly noted, managerial tendencies to objectify disorder could clash with professionals' preferences based on their daily observations. Conversely, senior managers in central policy departments at times express frustration at the headstrong
local coordinators and professionals that go about their own business, and make

their own policy plans. Likewise, the incidental political interference with the work of municipal officers could cause strain and frustration.

Thus this chapter underscores that conflicts and tensions are not limited to the formal decision making process in the political arena (Compston, 2009; Rhodes, 1997; Rhodes, 2006; Rosenthal, 1996). Before moving to the conclusions of this chapter, the two most prominent conflicts are highlighted here – the complaint that municipal officers are acting too much as managerial extensions, and the difficulty of policing under political pressure.

Policing the figures?

A regular complaint about municipal officers by partners such as neighbourhood managers or police officers is that they are focused too much on their own tasks and merely address those issues they are asked to by their own management.[12] They are too much 'inward' oriented and apparently have a narrow model of the resident/consumer as "a bundle of preferences waiting to be satisfied" (Pollitt, 1993: 125). In the opinion of these partners, municipal officers are basically just 'policing the figures'.

This is partly due to the fact that tasks are split up and divided over numerous organisations. This leads to a problem that is often referred to as 'compartmentalisation' (Dutch: *verkokering*). Dealing with disorder is not the responsibility of municipal officers alone. A civil servant in Utrecht for instance, observes this is a common problem in the area where she works. Various professionals work within the confines of their own organisation and are reluctant or unable to share their experiences with other professionals. "We collect loads of information. The city surveillance agency collects information, street coaches collect information, youth work, housing corporations," she states, "but little to nothing happens with it". This could lead to a situation in which frontline professionals appear to be locked up in the goals of their own respective organisations. Thus often municipal officers work in isolation, without using the opportunities to "deliver their street information," as a respondent in Tilburg words it.[13]

Another reason is that the focus of municipal officers on their own assignments and their lack of interaction with other professionals is strengthened by specific

---

12. This reproach shows the 'logics' discussed here are not connected to specific persons, but indicate a way of deciding. As such, managerial logic might also be embraced by frontline professionals, and – conversely – frontline logic might be subscribed to by coordinators or managers.

13. In this respect, the fruitful collaborations described under frontline logic are but one side of the story. As networks have become essential aspects of the implementation and creation of policy, collaboration between various actors is of vital importance. As indicated by the examples given here such cooperation might involve professionals from "widely differing backgrounds, with markedly distinct value preferences" (Laws & Hajer, 2006: 414). Hence, cooperation might become vulnerable, where "[e]xpectations of reciprocity suddenly seem thin in the face of conflicts rooted in distinct histories and organizational identities that must continually be adapted to one another and a volatile environment" (*ibid.*).

characteristics of municipal officers and their agencies. One of these is the apparent tendency of some city surveillance agencies to increasingly work on a flexible basis. Through the flexible use of work force, sending municipal officers to various neighbourhoods depending on changing wishes and reports, the embedding of municipal officers in neighbourhoods is further hampered (as discussed under political logic). In addition, many respondents maintain municipal officers' unwillingness to look beyond the confines of their reports and figures, is exacerbated by what may be called their 'trained incapacity': "that state of affairs whereby one's very abilities can function as blindnesses" (Burke, 1984: 7). Thus often complaints about municipal officers merely 'policing the figures' directly involve their professional standards. Uncritically embracing assignments and a narrow approach are seen as aspects of a profession that is still in progress (see also chapters 7, 9 and 10). As an example, a neighbourhood manager recounts the interaction between municipal officers and residents during neighbourhood meetings, pointing out that municipal officers often think and talk about their work in strict bureaucratic divisions that do not match residents' experiences,

> It's kind of funny [when they talk about their work], they put it in formal terms […] And then you see some people look [puzzled], Often [these officers] speak in internal language […] everything is covered in this formal sauce. You see that people don't understand it 'And then he reports it in the system…and that's transferred'. And then you get an explanation of the whole procedure. It makes us laugh sometimes […] Residents just don't understand who is responsible for what in public spaces.

Thus, the tendency to follow up on requests and orders often causes frustration of partners. They claim many municipal officers are stuck in managerial logic, are focussed too much on their own assignments and are alienated from actual neighbourhood problems.

This conflict points out that the managerialist tendencies of some city surveillance agencies lead to a remarkable paradox. Although these managers and officers claim they structure processes in such a way as to live up to residents' wishes efficiently, in practice they are seen by many as alienated from neighbourhood residents because of their managerial view of reality. This is a criticism that is found more often with regard to managerialism (Pollitt, 1993).

Hotspots and special interests: municipal disorder policing under political pressure

A second recurring conflict is related to the unease with political decisions. Although some officers might be eager to show themselves as serious officers in particular problem-ridden areas, many other coordinators and officers state that the political demands for continually changing and increasing tasks hamper their regular work, so that many managers prefer political decision makers to be kept at a distance (see also: Self, 2000, in: Christensen, 2006).

Neighbourhood managers for instance, sometimes point out that politically motivated deployment of municipal officers is not in accordance with their perception of neighbourhood issues. Political decisions appear to be preoccupied with the popular images of certain areas, for instance 'priority neighbourhoods' or other areas with a longstanding image of being problem ridden. Thus some hotspots are determined as structurally needing a lot of investment, whereas in reality those areas have changed for the better. As an illustration, a neighbourhood manager points out how political decision makers perceive street youth in his area,

> In the past there have been a couple of serious incidents that remain at the centre of attention, a continuous political pressure to deal with it, involving the police, youth services, whereas things have really changed for the better. It became a lot safer and not only because there are fewer incidents, also in the perception of safety by residents. But you still have to deal with the after effects, the image of this area […] and political decision makers are still guided by that image.

This is most notable in the case of particular 'hot' public safety issues. Street youth hanging around for instance, is one of those hotly debated political issues, "there is an administrative ambition breathing down our neck," a central municipal manager admits, pushing them to demand more investment of municipal officers on those issues, away from physical disorder issues. Conversely, this disproportional focus on those neighbourhoods with a bad image might entail these neighbourhoods are being "cosseted to death," as a Nijmegen neighbourhood manager remarks, and areas that are in need of more attention are neglected.

This appears to be an issue that is typical of local governments. Due to the proximity of city surveillance agencies to political decision making, plans for surveillance and law enforcement could change according to political preferences, without the previous plans being sufficiently implemented. Therefore, some notice that political interference makes the work of municipal officers a lot more difficult when compared to that of police officers. A police officer in The Hague for instance, claims the police "are less dependent on how politicians regard us," whereas the municipal organisation "needs to weigh everything carefully" (cf. Van Stokkom & Foekens, 2015). Therefore, these respondents claim political attention in itself is not the problem, but rather the lack of consistency, the divergent visions of subsequent politicians, and – sometimes – the tendency to uncritically pay attention to whatever annoys residents the most.

4   CONCLUSION

In this chapter local decision making on disorder policing was scrutinised. First of all, the general approach to local decision making was introduced. This chapter and the chapters that follow are informed by theories of policy networks, street level bureaucracy and policy as the result of 'organised anarchy'. In section 2, three 'logics' were unfolded through which decisions on disorder policing are realised. Through describing political, managerial and frontline logic, it was shown that many different actors have influence, but none of them has decisive power in deciding on disorder policing in practice.

In the description of the first, political logic, it was observed that decision making might be determined by political interests. In part, this concerns a process in which decisions on disorder policing are made during council debates and by mayors and aldermen. However, in many cases politically based decisions on disorder policing are made in more precarious ways, depending on the preferences of particular aldermen or mayors. In other cases political interference with municipal officers might be fairly direct, stimulated by acute problems and incidents. Important to understand this interference is the discovery of municipal officers as a solution to problems of public safety. Often the term 'mayor's tool' is used to understand this top-down interference with local policy. This process is strengthened by municipal officers' and coordinators' eagerness to prove themselves as policing professionals and the withdrawal of the traditional police from minor disorder issues. It turns city surveillance agencies into flexibly employable pools of officers that 'jump' at any request coming from the top. This change is looked upon critically by some, not least by managers who see their control of municipal officers overruled by the whims of political decision makers.

In the second, managerial logic, senior municipal managers determine what kinds of disorder problems should be addressed and how this should be done, using various means of measurement. Managerial logic shows the influence of a new public management discourse of contracting and performance management and the eagerness to control production. It leads to an emphasis on hotspots and reports. Nevertheless, managers are hesitant to use these means of measurement to hold municipal officers accountable. As such, quality of life indexes and citizens' reports are merely the dominant managerial tools through which disorder is comprehended. However, the use of these tools could imply less measurable goals disappear in the eagerness to 'police the figures'. Moreover, the complaints of professionals of other organisations about some municipal officers being caught up in managerial logic point to a remarkable paradox. In their eagerness to respond efficiently to residents' reports and ratings, in practice municipal officers appear to be alienated from the very residents they hold in such high regard.

The third, professional logic can be contrasted with this logic as one in which disorder is actively defined as the result of pragmatic frontline considerations in local networks. In this case the most important decision makers are team coordinators, frontline professionals and partners – such as neighbourhood managers and police officers. These frontline decision makers often determine disorder policing, irrespective of what senior managers have indicated. Hence performance is not a mechanical application of rules and standards, but a continuous response to positions and relations as one would find these in concrete situations (Hartman & Tops, 2005). In this respect, it is also logic that is hard to pin down. Considerations of higher goals are hard to find among frontline professionals and coordinators who 'have found each other' and 'do what needs to be done' in a more pragmatic way.

These three 'logics' of decision making, as well as the tensions between them will provide the groundwork for the following two chapters. In the next chapter it will be shown that these ways of decision-making have a notable impact on the views of frontline professionals. Chapter 8 will further elaborate how these different 'logics' interact in practice by discussing two case studies.

Introduction

One of the most prominent ideas informing the previous chapter was the notion that practitioners' views are unlikely to represent formal policy goals. Chapter 6 showed that frontline professionals often form their own sort of network with other practitioners, decide on disorder policing in their own manner and often oppose managerial framings of disorder. The ensuing frontline logic was characterised as a pragmatic and ad hoc way of making decisions. This rationale depends on the quality of contacts within networks, the direct and personal relations with other frontline professionals who speak the 'same language'.

This 'meso level' description of frontline logic was meant to specify the structure of local policy making. As such, it did not go into detail on the specific interests, views and routines of municipal officers themselves. Like many frontline workers in policing professions, municipal officers have a high degree of discretionary autonomy – a large say in their everyday work (Bervoets, 2013; Eikenaar & Van Stokkom, 2014; Moors & Bervoets, 2013). They can and must decide in individual cases when they issue a fine, when they merely report or intervene, in what way they approach citizens. Likewise, they have to consider how to cope with demands, how to report on their tasks or when and how to consult other frontline professionals. In this respect, frontline professionals' views could be in accordance with frontline logic described before, but municipal officers might equally subscribe to a managerial or political logic.

This chapter deals with these micro-level views of municipal officers (sub question D). It does so by taking their views as a point of departure and scrutinising what frontline professionals value the most in their work. Hence sections 1 and 2 discuss their ideas about responsibilities on the one hand (section 1) and contact with non-compliant citizens in practice on the other (section 2). These sections show that municipal officers' views vary widely, even within the accounts of individual municipal officers. The third section will be reserved for a reflection on these variations, showing that some views bring to mind how police officers approach their work, but that certain contrasts and dilemmas are characteristic for this occupational group. Section 4 concludes this chapter.

1   MUNICIPAL OFFICERS ON THEIR RESPONSIBILITIES

The ideas of municipal officers show much similarity with those of regular police officers (cf. Muir, 1977; Reiner, 2010; see further section 3 below). This might be related to the fact that municipal officers have a role in society that partly resembles that of the police. Municipal officers are also subject to demands for law enforcement, even though they lack the police's status as the ultimate authority that can be called upon when force is needed (cf. Bittner, 1970). Moreover, like the police, municipal officers have a range of options to deal with these demands; they have various options for supplying policing services and enforcement is but one of these.

Although this basic distinction in *demand* and *supply* is too rigid to capture all ideas of municipal officers, it does lie at the basis of this and the next section.[1] Hence for an important part, this first section deals with how officers look upon the demands that are made on them. However, instead of merely discussing municipal officers' ideas about explicit demands, this section discusses how professionals' view their responsibilities in general. The second section zooms in on their views on the contact with non-compliant citizens, thereby providing more insight into what they see as the appropriate 'supply' to problems of disorder.

1.1   *Addressing annoyances*

In the interviews with municipal officers' the responsibility of dealing with citizens' 'minor annoyances' plays a prominent role. Hence, this notion runs from policy goals (chapter 5), to managerial decisions (chapter 6), to the practice of frontline professionals.[2]

A municipal officer for instance, states the same issues are "a thorn in the eye everywhere," such as illegally parked trailers, dog litter and household waste. Likewise, many of his colleagues take it for granted that citizens call the municipality about what annoys them most, especially because the police are reluctant to address these issues. These professionals state that annoyances are reported to the municipality, not to the police and that they are the authority that has to respond to them. A municipal officer from Eindhoven summarises residents' vision of his work,

---

1.   This distinction is made by Bittner in his analysis of the police's role in society (Bittner, 1970; Brodeur, 2007).
2.   The term 'minor annoyances' has a somewhat controversial nature. It is used repeatedly by both policymakers and professionals as an umbrella term for all those rule infringements that seem to bother citizens most and that largely define their work (as will become clear in this section). However, the addition 'minor' suggests these are trivialities that do not deserve too much attention. This is in contrast to their position at the top of neighbourhoods' lists of annoyances. Hence, trivial as they might be on first inspection, they are leading in what bothers neighbourhood residents the most.

These residents say [...] 'We don't see the police anymore, [...] but we don't need to call them. Those guys from the municipal department are here too and they work at it too. [...] they're not a bad choice'.

Likewise, a Nijmegen municipal officer pats himself on the back: "citizens say you'd better call the municipal department, they'll make sure it's done". An officer from Eindhoven states municipal officers "have more time to dedicate to citizens" (see also chapter 9). Thus the concept of 'minor annoyances' (*kleine ergernissen*) is very much part of these professionals' language, appearing as the prime legitimation for their efforts. Even more strongly, some municipal officers regard themselves as the extension of citizens' wishes. "The citizen wants more surveillance [...] that can never be enough, so it's good we are here," an officer from Nijmegen remarks. "It is important to deliver a good service," as one of his colleagues from Utrecht states. In that respect, not only reported annoyances determine their orientation: some municipal officers think that all residents' complaints should get their attention.

As a result, the notion of 'service provision' is often heard in professionals' accounts of their work. Here this appears to imply citizens are depicted as 'consumers'. "First and foremost we are there for the people, we are service providers," a municipal enforcement officer from Eindhoven states. In some accounts this is mixed with the new public management concepts introduced in the previous chapter, as is shown by another officer in Eindhoven,

So you have a little chat and after a while you'll ask them, 'Is there any news, are there any complaints'. And also, 'How can we do things better?' That's the surveillance product, a little piece of quality; we all have to contribute to that. Quality is also about asking people how we can make things better.

Many of these municipal officers proudly claim they are more visible than police officers. They know how to deal with issues of disorder in such ways that citizens see that something is done about it and that disorder is dealt with swiftly (see also chapter 9). As in the case of the managers discussed in chapter 6, 'annoyances' function as a mantra for many municipal officers.

Between acting as confidants and responding to reports
On closer inspection it appears that this discourse of minor annoyances and 'service provision' provides a lot of room for interpretation. For a part, municipal officers see it as their task to get in touch with neighbourhood residents, actively trying to find out what might be bothering them. Officers sometimes leave their phone number behind with those citizens who report most frequently, or visit neighbourhood meetings and citizens' participation projects to make sure residents know who they are and where to file their reports. Some professionals even see

themselves as *confidants*, officials who can be entrusted with reports without having to fear repercussions. They see it as their task to be approachable for residents,

> People know they can trust me. If a man at number 8 says something about a man at number 20,
> then that stays between the man at number 8 and me. I wouldn't go to number 20 to tell them
> what they are saying about him. You are also a confidant, you have a bond with these people,
> and you have to be discrete.

Occasionally, these officers state that they are also there to give people a safer feeling: "people like it when they see a uniform," a municipal officer states – although most municipal officers do not seem to be too enamoured by this type of reassurance policing (see also chapter 8).

Other officers are equally focused on minor annoyances, but see themselves less obliged to have direct contact with residents: residents' wishes are reflected in the tasks they get from their management. Thus, as opposed to the municipal officers who see themselves as confidants, others attach more value to the managerial systems discussed in the previous chapter. These municipal officers put a fairly strong emphasis on the implementation of assignments they get from their management: they do what they are told to and attend those areas from which the numbers of reports are highest. In that respect, municipal officers highlight they respond to clear expectations.

   These officers emphasise the importance of responding adequately, and some even tend to compare their agencies with emergency services, even though they do not receive emergency calls. "Citizens call the municipality for minor annoyances, as they would call the fire brigade in case of fire," as one officer puts it. Consequently, professionals define their work primarily as reactively responding to reports – albeit with less urgency than the police. A municipal officer points out how this works in practice,

> On the west side of town you have a lot of reports, but on the North side next to none. […] This
> afternoon I'll be in that North part, but after half an hour or so I'll go back to the West side
> again, to tackle the reports there.

Although this does not mean municipal officers tick of their reports uncritically – on occasion they point out they get in touch with the complainant – the initial complaint report seems to weigh heavily: "we are a municipal authority, and everything is reported and we have to respond to those reports constantly," a municipal officer in Tilburg claims.

   This attitude is most notable in the reference to 'hotspots' by municipal officers: those areas (blocks or neighbourhoods) that show a pattern with a high rate of complaint reports are the areas that receive most attention. Although these hotspots are determined by coordinators and managers, municipal officers also seem inclined to prioritise those areas. "We send our people to the hotspots with most complaints," a Utrecht officer says.

In this respect, municipal officers' views on responsibilities are in line with the managerial assignments they get. Making plans, consulting others in the neighbourhood might draw the attention away from these complaint hotspots. Many municipal officers show themselves loyal to the assignments they get. As a municipal officer from Tilburg states, they should not make too many complicated plans: "we don't need a plan, just get it done". A Rotterdam municipal officer simply states, after being asked about newly developed policy on establishing networks, "I don't know anything about those things, they are lost on me. You know, I'm alright with things as they are, as long as I've got my job".

1.2   *Expanding responsibilities*

Evidently residents' reports largely dictate professional ideas about what is demanded of them. However, that does not exclude other notions of responsibilities.

Criticising citizens' demands

On occasion – and contrary to the adherence to minor annoyances and complaints described earlier – in practice municipal officers experience various reasons to nuance the reports to which they are asked to respond. Sometimes there is quite a simple reason to do so, a professional from Eindhoven explains,

> You would be surprised of what people are reporting, for instance a pile of sand. The weirdest things. Some bricks that are lying around. You know, the thing is, citizens don't talk to each other anymore. If my neighbour leaves her dustbin on our drive for two days, then I ring her bell, 'hey neighbour, we put the bin back around the house, ok?' But people stopped doing that, so now they call us for all these things.

These municipal officers consider citizens to be highly demanding. Irrespective of the present efforts by authorities, they keep claiming more investment by both police and municipality. Like the municipal officer from Eindhoven quoted above, more of his colleagues point to an ever-growing range of complaints that are filed with the municipality, and like this officer, other professionals also observe citizens are increasingly reluctant to address each other.

In response to these demanding citizens, officers point out there is a clear distinction between realistic and unrealistic complaints. Some of these insistent citizens are felt to be unreasonable by municipal officers. Consequently, officers try to counter citizens' demands, even to inform neighbourhood residents of what can be seen as 'real incivilities'. Sometimes they address complaining citizens directly and confront them with their 'irrational' wishes.

Moreover, officers lament the lack of willingness among citizens to address one another and the lack of respect shown to them by citizens. These residents merely want their complaint to be addressed, and refuse to speak to others themselves. An officer from Eindhoven expresses her frustration at the thought that she and her colleagues are complying with citizens' wishes, but barely receive any gratitude for their efforts,

> We used to be scared when the police drove through our street. But that's bygone times. It doesn't matter if they're small or behind a walking frame [...] Citizens just want their problems to be solved, from small to large, they report them and they want them to be solved.

This entails a core dilemma in the work of these municipal officers. They have to find a balance between the focus on annoyances and the irrationality of residents' wishes they experience in practice. This points to the limits of complying with residents' demands. Although in many respects the work of municipal officers appears to revolve around a near consumerist vision of citizens (see also chapter 5), and officers claim they are there to address any and all reports, they also appear to get tired of constantly responding to these reports. This dilemma will be addressed more extensively at the end of this chapter.

Broader perspectives: 'co-creational policing' and 'street policing'

Officers who refuse to embrace the reports and demands of citizens uncritically often air alternative views on responsibilities. Instead of defining their work in terms of top-down assignments and reports, these officers attach more value to what was in the previous chapter called their own frontline logic. This generally takes two different forms.

First of all, some municipal officers are convinced of the need to solve problems jointly with other professionals. As described in the previous chapter, these officers form an occupational group that is surrounded by other governmental and non-governmental partners who are in some way equally focussed on residents' concerns – municipal maintenance personnel, community police officers, social workers, municipal neighbourhood managers and partners from welfare and educational institutions.

On occasion, municipal officers state it is of vital importance to collaborate with these other professionals. "It is not only reports," a municipal officer from Tilburg states, "but networking as well". For example, because their work starts where others stop, as a municipal officer in Eindhoven explains,

An example is parking issues. The police ignore those, and citizen are increasingly annoyed, because people have two or three cars these days, so it gets fuller and people start parking on the pavement. Then we are asked to do something about it. But keep in mind it has been tolerated for years by the police. We can't just rigorously wipe the streets clean of cars, so we are always in touch with the community police officer about these things, how we should do this.

In other cases this tendency to 'co-creation' might prevail because these professionals experience a certain level of ownership of their neighbourhood, deem themselves to be responsible because they know the neighbourhood, its residents, and their problems,

We are the points of reference. If something goes wrong, I've got the feeling I can be held personally accountable. That may sound heavy, but it is *my* neighbourhood, my hood, and employees working in that hood have to keep it running.

To get things done, they emphasise it is of importance to approach these partners, to stay in close contact with them, not least because the range of local network partners in many cases is quite large. Municipal officers state that they only have a small 'piece of the pie' and that it takes a lot of coordinative investment to make sure all these different partners do not work in their own bubble (see also the criticism expressed at the end of chapter 6). Thus sometimes municipal officers see their responsibilities as part of a network of partners, working together to address issues of disorder.

Second, narrowly defined demands might also be opposed by officers due to an emphasis on their own observations. Resembling the policy for holistic approaches described in chapters 5 and 6, the officers who are convinced of this broader perspective state it is of importance 'to take everything into account' in their everyday work. They consider themselves to be "street rats," as a municipal officer from Eindhoven puts it. Some even emphasise they are on the streets much more than police officers (see also chapter 9). These professionals advocate a routine that may be called 'street policing' – an approach of disorder that emphasises what happens 'on the street', in the interactions with residents, non-compliant citizens and other professionals.

Although some cities might develop particular policies for this form of policing (see chapter 5), the question whether municipal officers work in this way largely depends on their personal views. In this respect, many municipal officers claim it is their responsibility to address any and all disorder. "If I drive along the Schubert street, and I see a big pile of rubbish bags next to the container, I can't just ignore that," an officer in Eindhoven states.

Remarkably, the question whether or not municipal officers have a broad view of disorder again gives rise to reflections on professional standards. In section 3 of the previous chapter it was pointed out that many partners believe that municipal officers have a narrow view of their work and that this is related to their lack of professional skills. In contrast, municipal officers themselves stress that they have evolved from less professional city wardens in the 1990s. These former city wardens here seem to fulfil the function of a chimera, of the unprofessional predecessors that gave present-day municipal officers their reputation of 'good-for-nothings', having little understanding of what needs to be done to address quality of life and public safety issues. Many municipal officers emphasise that now they have a 'broad view', that they are capable of dealing with a wide range of enforcement tasks. Sometimes they say their tasks have expanded and thus became more interesting. More often however they rationalise their broad view as a result of their presence on the streets. "You should not look too narrowly," a municipal officer expresses this view, not least because of the image of them held by 'the citizen'. "They should see we are dedicated," an officer from Nijmegen states. "Show that we address everything and that you can deal with anything".

To sum up, this section about municipal officers' ideas of responsibilities shows that their views are rich in diversity and contradictions. 'Minor annoyances' might largely determine their work, but the generic nature of that concept generates many different interpretations – contact with residents, focusing on top-down assignments, coordinating action with professional partners, or an opinion that should involve any form of disorder in the everyday line of work. Evidently some of these differences are a result of differences in policy. However, more often they seem grounded in views that are characteristic for street-level bureaucrats, and should be seen as the personal allegiance, for instance to managerial assignments (managerial logic), or conversely, the belief in the direct relations with partners or the preference for street level signalling and addressing any issue they come across (frontline logic). This interpretation in terms of street-level routines will be addressed in section 3.

2   MUNICIPAL OFFICERS ON NON-COMPLIANT CITIZENS

As said before, municipal officers' accounts of their work are characterised by a recurrent (implicit) distinction between views about responsibilities on the one hand and the approach to non-compliant citizens on the other hand. After having discussed officers' views on their responsibilities, this section now deals with their approach to disorder and disorderly behaviour itself – the non-compliant citizens.

2.1   *Decent treatment*

If minor annoyances dominate much of municipal officers' accounts of their responsibilities, then the word *bejegening* is one of the recurring terms in their view of how to deal with non-compliant citizens. This notion refers to how municipal officers approach offenders, somewhat unsatisfactorily translated in English as 'decent treatment'.

In Dutch, *bejegening* can have different explanations. It can refer to the (formal) requirements of interaction between officers and non-compliant residents, conveying the demand offenders should in any case be addressed in a respectable and reasonable manner. The 'decent treatment' in the accounts of these officers appears to combine this requirement of reasonable interaction with citizens, with subtle, yet allegedly vital aspects of person to person interaction. Many officers even see this as the core of their work.

The municipal department of Eindhoven provides a good example of employees highlighting this form of 'decent treatment' of offenders. One of them explains *bejegening* in these terms,

> I have learned to [make myself small] in certain circumstances. Anybody can fan the flames, but [making yourself small] to get someone to your level, so a decent conversation is possible isn't all that easy.

Officers repeatedly state that "fining is a last resort". They keep saying, "our mouth is our only weapon", or "we have to solve problems by talking". They seem very aware of their limited powers, but also stress the necessity of approaching every situation through their conversational skills and often with the intention of solving problems by talking. One of these Eindhoven officers points this out,

> You can only do this job if you like people. In fact, we are communication experts; we are busy communicating all day. Our work consists for eighty percent of psychology, constantly interacting. So you could march through the city like a bunch of tough guys, [or] just go into those neighbourhoods in a relaxed way and do what you have to. And that occasionally involves being strict, but I prefer that other side.

Key in this emphasis on *bejegening* is the ability to explain the reasons why someone is wrong. Thus, the capability to explain the situation or knowing "how to sell the fine," as one officer has it, is vital. The interviews with frontline professionals are rich with anecdotes of how they managed to solve issues by explaining to people they were crossing a line, and thereby preventing escalation.

The reasons that these professionals emphasise verbal abilities are partly caused by their limited coercive means (see chapter 1). However, this is but part of the explanation. More often, municipal officers stress various forms of what in chapter 5 was called 'behavioural compliance'; the officers that highlight this approach claim to regulate behaviour in public space by explaining what those addressed are doing that is wrong. Enforcement, so they claim, can and should be done by many more means than just issuing fines if it is to have a structural effect.

Thus, these officers believe behaviour can be changed for the better with 'decent treatment'. Professionals describe their work in terms of basic normative correction: they explain why a rule is there, why dog litter annoys people, or why cycling in pedestrian areas is not appreciated, for the simple reason nobody else does. An officer in Eindhoven points this out,

> You can fine a 14 year old, but you can also ask him, 'Why are you doing that, do you think that's smart? Look at those people' […] 'Oh, I've been kind of stupid'. Then I say, 'See, I think it's more important that you get it.' So this way you get more things done than with a fine.

In addition, some of them claim, people are simply ignorant: you cannot blame them for violating the rules.

Many of the officers who emphasise 'decent treatment' of offenders, also claim it is of importance to be familiar in a neighbourhood. In this case these officers want to be able to stay in touch with those who *cause* incivilities, such as residents who repeatedly place their trailer on the pavement, who refuse to put their dog on a leash or youngsters who keep coming back to spots where they were asked to stay away. They want to be able to act conditionally in respect to these 'uncivil characters', by warning first before fining. An approach that is only possible when they are known in neighbourhoods, they claim.

2.2   *Contextual judgment*

The emphasis on verbal skills results in a view of disorder policing as a personalised interaction with a strong emphasis on 'decent treatment', seen here as effective communication between officer and non-compliant citizen. The chief reason for this emphasis seems to be that the goal of a change of behaviour is deemed to be more important than strict enforcement of these rules.

In the narratives of municipal officers, this accent is often related to another notion – an understanding of the circumstances of an offence. Municipal officers seem to infer that any structural change of behaviour demands a certain level of empathy. As such, many municipal officers who stress behavioural change note the importance of the context of a rule infringement.

Obvious as it might be for any policing profession, it is remarkable how often this basic notion of contextual judgment is highlighted by municipal officers. Even more, its most common denominator 'discretionary autonomy' has also gained a firm foothold in the language of these professionals. "Every minute is another case," a municipal officer in Eindhoven states.

Officers legitimate this idea of contextual judging in different ways. The type of neighbourhood might dictate their approach, they claim. A residential neighbour-hood is in need of a different approach than the city centre, a municipal officer in Eindhoven explains: with neighbourhood residents one can make an agreement, whereas the temporary visitors deserve a stricter approach. Often the need for con-textual judgment and an emphasis on being consistent and thorough in fining are combined in one account. Many professionals experience this as the core dilemma of their profession.

An additional reason for taking context into consideration might be that some municipal officers see themselves as "the city's business card"; municipal officers claim they are less "brief in discussions", "less harsh than the police" and are able to "cool things down," for instance because they claim they want people "to have a pleasant feeling". On several occasions they express reluctance to fine in the reali-sation this might scare people off. "The police are much stricter, but we are also the city's business card. People need to enjoy their stay here, you want them to come back," a municipal officer in Utrecht explains.

Thus these officers are willing to take into account a wide array of reasons why a fine is not suitable, for empathic reasons (a non-compliant citizen might have dif-ferent reasons for not following the rules), pragmatic reasons (a fine does not always provide the best solution in a given situation) or for the reason these offi-cers do not see themselves as mere enforcement officers, but as 'hosts', as the wel-coming committee of the city centre.

2.3   Consistent enforcement

A final commonly heard view of disorder policing among municipal officers appears to stand in stark contrast to this last approach: the tendency to focus on consistent enforcement. Again there appear to be several reasons why municipal officers embrace such an approach.

First, the urge to fine consistently for rule infringements often directly follows from an unconditional adherence to the complaint hotspots in municipal officers' beats. Put simply, municipal officers see reports on minor annoyances as their prime responsibility, and as these minor annoyances are structured in a pattern of hotspots, it seems evident to employ a consistently repressive approach in these areas. Thus, officers respond to demands by offering what they can in terms of fin-ing. A municipal officer from Tilburg for instance, even expands the concept of 'hotspot' to mean more than just a location. "A hotspot means we really focus on some infringements. [...] some things are really not allowed, we fine for those things right away".[3] In this respect, a strict approach to rule infringements is the

---

3.   This professional probably mistakenly expands 'hotspot' to mean more than a geographically
      defined area designated for intensified policing. Nevertheless, this quotation is illustrative for the
      embrace of strict enforcement that follows a close allegiance to assignments.

simple result of adhering to demands, adapting policing responses directly to the demands these officers receive (see also chapter 10).

A second frequently heard legitimation for consistent fining is rooted in behavioural assumptions about the effect of fining. Zero tolerance policing allegedly conveys a symbolical message. It helps to convince other residents they should not litter, put their rubbish outside too early or should put their dog on a leash. Municipal officers assume their actions will not go unnoticed and residents tell each other about them. Repression in terms of consistently fining would have a general preventative, psychological effect of deterring others from showing the same disorderly behaviour. "You can tell that fining has an effect, people talk about it," as a municipal officer says.

Third, embracing strict law enforcement might again be rooted in a somewhat resigned and cynical worldview, albeit here in terms of a loss of respect for basic norms. Officers often think the only way to prevent people from disregarding these norms, is by deterrence: conveying the message disorderly behaviour will not be tolerated. A municipal officer from Utrecht speaks of a structural normative decline, in Dutch commonly referred to with the peculiar term *verhuftering*, the 'loutisation of society',

> The other day one of the fines we issued was for a pub-crawler who kicked and tore a rubbish bag. On purpose […]. This loutisation of society is a normal thing. I said, 'What if they do this on your doorstep?' 'Yeh, that stuff happens, it happens daily, will be cleaned the next day,' [he responded].

What these municipal officers indicate here is that people are incorrigible, but their behaviour can be controlled by influencing their choices: if the chance of a fine increases – for example for not cleaning your dog's litter – people might do it by themselves. In some cases this idea of incorrigibility is attached to specific 'target groups' and municipal officers make an explicit division between honest, compliant citizens on the one hand and those groups needing policing on the other hand (this target group policing is addressed in the box below and in the next chapter).

Finally, tendencies to consistent enforcement are strengthened by (implicit) considerations about municipal officer's authority and the wish to be 'taken seriously'. As a municipal officer, so they state, you want to project a consistent attitude. It would impact negatively upon your image if leniency in one case is alternated with strictness in the other. Thus many municipal officers are content with a strict approach for reasons of clarity. Members of a specific group of municipal officers for instance, who oppose lenient approaches to street youth (see chapter 8), emphasise that consistent enforcement of street youth is a lot clearer,

> I like it. At the beginning we were really searching. [...] Are we supposed to get in touch with
> these youngsters, or do we just go out to observe? Now I can say, we are youth enforcement
> officers; we have to go the repressive way.

As a result, municipal officers can often be heard wishing for more powers, so they can enforce rules consistently and do not lose credibility in the eyes of neighbourhood residents. Also, some maintain, the citizens want it. "You are in uniform, it is expected of you," an officer states (see further chapter 9 for officers' considerations on their powers).

In summary, frontline professionals defend consistent enforcement on varying grounds, ranging from a focus on hotspot areas, the assumption that it would convince other residents to comply, to the wish to be taken seriously.

Although the contrast to the previous approach with its emphasis on explaining rules and trying to structurally change behaviour for the better seems great, the overlap in these two ideas is in fact quite large. Both approaches to rule infringements are basically about situational control of misbehaviour. The difference lies merely in what is seen as the most effective way to do so: by trying to influence the reasoning of offenders or by giving disincentives. As an officer from Nijmegen states, "it's all about behaviour. And behaviour becomes a habit, and we want to curb those habits".

BOX 3: Target group policing

An example of consistent fining by municipal officers is provided by the growing role these officers have with regard to 'disorderly persons'. Municipal officers in an increasing number of cases are assigned the policing of designated target groups. These are groups of repeat offenders (or 'repeat rule infringers') whose presence and/or behaviour appear to distress residents and for which the regular police cannot realise sufficient capacity.

Although municipal officers were previously merely allowed to report to the police about the whereabouts of these groups, they are getting increasingly more responsibilities in target group policing, such as fining, deterring or even arresting them so they can be subjected to restraining orders. Examples in this study are a group of municipal officers in the centre of Nijmegen who deal with clients from a nearby shelter for homeless people (see also the box in the previous section), the night-time policing of drug related issues in the city centre of Utrecht and youth enforcement officers in Rotterdam.

Especially in the latter cases, officers ground their approach in ideas about 'deviant characters'. These 'characters' – mostly street youth, homeless people, drug users and drug dealers – by their appearance and their function in the street scene are defined as targets, as 'police property' (Reiner, 2010). Here too professionals evince a somewhat cynical view as they are convinced of the incorrigible nature of this group of perpetrators. Thus, although there are gradations, the basic view of these groups is evident: these are 'junkies and drunkies', street youth who hang around, incorrigible characters that bother innocent bystanders and neighbourhood residents and need to be fined or deterred. A municipal officer who operates on nightshifts in the city centre of Utrecht words it as such,

> Those folks from the nuthouse, they all hang around here. They also walk through my street, walking around like zombies. Then I wonder, why do you set these folks free? Others really think it's bad the way we deal with them. They think they should be allowed to be like this. Until they pee over their front door. Or that they drop their pants, [showing it] to people, women, children, whatever.

Again the somewhat cynical stance on incorrigibility can be heard among these professionals. Most youth enforcement officers, for instance, are convinced of this harsh stance. Preventive action, support, 'giving youngsters chances': it does not work. They had their chance, this youth enforcement officer tells me about street youth in his neighbourhood,

> Those kids don't accept a thing. [Previously] we used to send them to others if we saw any issues. And we were putting a lot of energy in one group. But after a while you find out they don't take their chances. Then we were told to go repressive. [...] Those kids get crazier too. I had a 12-year old with a sexual offence the other day.

The next chapter deals more extensively with two of the cases briefly mentioned here, showing there is more to these views than the personal opinions of the officers involved.

3   MUNICIPAL OFFICERS AND POLICE OFFICERS

The findings in this chapter show that municipal officers are subject to a large variety of demands and incentives, resulting in various tensions, contradictions and even dilemmas. The most prominent of these is the contrast between an emphasis on the wishes of citizens on the one hand and expectations of consistent law enforcement on the other hand. As a result, municipal officers for instance, might see it as their responsibility to be present for the citizen (so that they can address their annoyances), but it is this same citizen who might be prone to parking his car on the pavement or unleashing his dog where he is not allowed to do so. Another tension concerns that between a demand to take assignments seriously and the context of specific rule infringements. Thus, officers might be dedicated to consistent enforcement in hotspots, whereas in practice they might experience a moral conflict when they notice someone who broke the rules within the confines of this hotspot can hardly be blamed for this.

Neither these tensions, nor officers' responses to them are wholly unique to the frontline practice of municipal disorder policing. In fact, all street-level bureaucrats experience dilemmas in their work and develop routines and coping mechanisms to deal with them (Lipsky, 2010). In this respect, the views described here might be a way of legitimating the street-level routines that municipal officers have developed to deal with high demands (Lipsky, 2010). An emphasis on assignments and work rules for instance, might be a defence against a plethora of demands coming from citizens, partners, colleagues and coordinators. Defining work as merely 'responding to reports' in this respect could actually be meant to limit responsibilities, and protect municipal officers from other demands (Lipsky, 2010: 149). Opposed to this, other views expressed by municipal officers may be seen as forms of non-compliance with assignments and managerial expectations (*ibid.*: 17). Hence, the emphasis on 'street policing' and 'co-creational policing' might be seen as the way municipal officers legitimate a routine that gives prominence to their own observations and to the requests from other professionals.

In addition, the similarities between the beliefs of municipal officers and those of police officers are particularly striking. Many of the descriptions here resemble the various types of professionals described in classic ethnographic studies on police. Hence, some of the core characteristics of police culture described by Reiner (2010) can be found in the accounts of municipal officers described above. For instance, the way many police officers appear to look upon their work with a "sense of a mission" (Reiner, 2010: 119) somewhat resembles how municipal officers see themselves as the last professionals who are willing to pay attention to citizens' complaints about annoyances. Likewise, the closely connected cynicism – "the despair felt that the morality which the police officer adheres to is being eroded on all sides" (*ibid.*: 120) – appears to be in accordance with the resigned and cynical views held by some of the municipal officers quoted above. In addition, the emphasis on consistent enforcement echoes with what Reiner calls 'the new centurion', 'responding to reports' may be compared to the 'uniform carrier' and 'co-creational policing' has aspects of what Reiner calls the 'professional' (and what Muir calls 'the reciprocator'; cf. Muir, 1977; Reiner, 2010).[4]

Likewise, the categories used by municipal officers seem in accordance with previous police research. Although "simplifying their clientele and environment" (Lipsky, 2010: xii) is again a common trait of street-level bureaucrats in general, these categories also have a remarkable resemblance to those used by police officers. The idea of 'police property' – "low-status, powerless groups whom the dominant majority see as problematic or distasteful" (Reiner, 2010: 123) – for instance

---

4.   As well as the divisions of numerous other authors, as Reiner himself remarks in his comprehensive work on police culture (Reiner, 2010).

seems to coincide with what was observed here in the case of 'target group policing'. Equally, municipal officers often subscribe to a rather pragmatic or even
opportunistic standpoint, for instance in addressing whatever they come across
during their beats (as described under 'street policing'). This stance resembles the
"conceptual conservatism", notable among police officers, with their "pragmatic
short-termism" and aversion to "analytic approaches" (*ibid*: 132).[5]

Nevertheless, the range of views of municipal officers is not strictly comparable to
those of police officers. In fact, and as stated above, municipal officers tend to highlight notable differences with the police and consciously create an image of their
own occupational group, while contrasting this with a 'police culture'.[6] For
instance, unlike what Reiner (2010) says about American police officers and Terpstra & Schaap (2013) about Dutch police officers, municipal officers claim to be less
prone to action, thrill and sensation.[7] Furthermore, seeing complaining citizens as
'rubbish', as some police officers appear to do (Reiner, 2010) is at odds with municipal officers' alleged dedication to residents' annoyances. Also, they claim to be
less macho than police officers and the often heard emphasis on 'decent treatment'
also seems to contrast with the "sexual boasting and horseplay" that characterises
the views of some police officers (Reiner, 2010: 128).[8] In contrast to the police,
municipal officers would say, they are more patient.

   Furthermore, the specific combination of being utterly dedicated to citizens'
reports (at least, allegedly more than the police) and being focused on law enforcement in other cases, seems to entail more of a contradiction for municipal officers
than it does for police officers. Municipal officers' uncritical ways of addressing
citizens' annoyances might lead to conflicts with professional standards, as has
been noted above. Moreover, there are additional reasons why municipal officers
might emphasise strict law enforcement more than the police do. Among these are
the dominance of hotspot thinking, the lack of options for more structural solutions
to disorder due to their limited powers, and the fact consistent enforcement in their
case adds self-efficacy to their vulnerable occupational pride and the 'proof' they
have developed into a type of officer that needs to be taken seriously.[9] These points
will be addressed more extensively in chapters 9 and 10.

---

5. This standpoint appears to be more typical for American police officers, than for Dutch police offi-
    cers. Terpstra & Schaap (2013) note that Dutch police officers tend less to such 'anti-intellectual
    pragmatism'.
6. This will be addressed more extensively in chapter 9.
7. In chapter 8 it is shown that the views of some municipal officers are at odds with this self-image.
8. Again Terpstra & Schaap (2013) observe such machismo might be of less relevance for the culture
    of Dutch police officers.
9. See also Thumala, Goold and Loader (2011) for a comparable quest for legitimating strategies
    found among private security officers.

4   CONCLUSION

This chapter discussed how municipal officers look upon their work. By discussing their views on responsibilities and on non-compliant citizens it showed the practice of municipal officers is highly diverse, containing strongly contrasting beliefs and perspectives. Nevertheless, several characteristics appear to be dominant.

The first section showed the notion of 'annoyances' has found its way into the discourse of municipal officers. Having the status of a guiding principle through which they legitimate their work, it also proves to be a principle with a number of differences in interpretation. Some officers maintain these annoyances are best ascertained in close contact with neighbourhood residents, actively getting in touch to find out what is bothering them. Others see the objective complaint reports that are processed by their municipal colleagues as proper reflection of these annoyances: they prefer to keep close to these reports, ticking off the hotspots with the most complaints.

Although this orientation on citizens' wishes is the predominant concept in officers' accounts, other officers deem their tasks to consist of more than these annoyances and put demands in a broader frame. They actively oppose what they see as nagging residents and loathe citizens' reluctance to solve issues themselves. Instead, these professionals might see themselves as part of a more encompassing group of professionals who are occupied with neighbourhood problems and annoyances – 'co-creational policing'. Others highlight a more pragmatic stance on responsibilities: they see themselves as frontline professionals who are confronted with a wide range of violations in their daily work on the streets. Any and all of these they see as part of their responsibilities. Thus, their view of responsibilities may best be described as 'street policing'.

In the second section of this chapter, the views of municipal officers were further scrutinised in their approach to non-compliant citizens. Again, the differences seem great. Most officers highlighted the importance of 'decent treatment' [*bejegening*] in their day to day contacts with people who do not comply with the rules. They express an almost psychological take on interaction and the assets of developing subtle and nuanced verbal abilities. Mostly these officers do this as it will enlarge the chances for more structural behavioural compliance. Closely related to this, these professionals note the importance of taking the context of rule infringement into consideration. Acting conditionally is the consequence of this idea: fining happens only when agreements made earlier or warnings are disregarded. Again, whatever could promote behavioural compliance seems to determine their interventions. Lastly, a sizeable group of officers highlights consistent enforcement. On the surface this approach seems to contrast with the other approaches, but although they do so for different reasons – including a dedication to hotspots and an eagerness to project authority – considerations about the behavioural effect of consistently fining also plays a large role. In box 3, consistent enforcement was equally associated with 'target group policing'. Officers who are occupied with such forms of policing deem consistent enforcement suitable when it comes to designated groups of regular perpetrators.

The chapter ended by comparing municipal officers' work views with those of police officers. This section started by observing that municipal officers' beliefs might be meant to support their street-level routines. In addition, similarities with police officers' views were described. Like police officers, many municipal officers seem to imbue their work with something of a mission, at times hold cynical views and appear to use categorisations, often with a sense of pragmatism. Nevertheless, despite these similarities, municipal officers emphasize views that are unique for their profession. Moreover, the tension between 'service provision' and 'law enforcement' appears to be more apparent for these officers.

Looking back upon this analysis, this chapter is at odds with the image of this occupational group as it is sketched elsewhere.[10] Instead of insecure and hesitant wardens with few powers and a lack of professional standards – as some still seem to believe is the case – these municipal officers show a remarkable self-consciousness when it comes to their work. Put simply, they clearly claim to know what they are doing.

Diverse as their views might be, they are still clearly defined by two prominent characteristics. One is the tendency to highlight citizens' minor annoyances as legitimation for their work. A specific, almost consumerist view of citizens as customers defines many of the opinions of municipal officers.[11] The second prominent characteristic is the pragmatism of these officers, focusing on those spots with most complaints and preferring any approach that might be effective in regulating anti-social behaviour. These characteristics might well be strengthened by managerial thinking discussed in the previous chapter. In the concluding chapter these aspects are reflected on more extensively.

---

10. See for instance the reports of local Audit offices mentioned in chapter 1.
11. Although this emphasis on citizens' concerns may also be partly rhetorical. In this respect, this chapter did not deal with the question to what extent officers' daily work is in accordance with ideals about 'citizen oriented policing'. The next chapter discusses some tensions between different views of officers as they express them in interviews or on the streets.

In the preceding chapters various dimensions of municipal disorder policing have been discussed – national developments in chapter 5, local decisions on disorder policing in chapter 6 and the beliefs of individual municipal officers in chapter 7. In this chapter these dimensions recur in the study of two specific cases of municipal disorder policing.

A general reason to single out two cases is that the dimensions discussed so far influence each other in practice. The tasks and activities of municipal officers are often influenced by both political preferences and managerial aspirations. For instance, a political urge to address specific forms of disorder might lead to more emphasis on target group policing. Likewise, if political decision makers have indicated residents' estimation of some neighbourhoods has to go up from a 7 to an 8, managers attach more value to quality of life monitors in deciding where to send their officers. Hence the various dimensions discussed separately earlier, mutually influence each other. Therefore to better understand how different actors on different levels might interact, a more comprehensive approach is needed, for which case studies provide the best opportunity (Swanborn, 2010).

In addition, this chapter deals with two *specific* forms of municipal disorder policing – a team of youth enforcement officers in Rotterdam and municipal officers in Utrecht who are policing issues that are related to drug trading and homelessness. These cases were selected for various reasons. First these policies provide an opportunity to study the practice of hotspot policing, one of the dominant forms of municipal disorder policing, as should be clear from the preceding chapters. Another reason to select these cases is that they show how political logic works in this domain. This political decision making deserves greater research focus, all the more because the previous chapters dealt predominantly with managerial and frontline 'logics'. Lastly, studying these cases provides an opportunity to scrutinise target group policing, a form of disorder policing that borders on police work and as such provides an insight into how municipal disorder policing might develop in the near future.

This chapter is structured in five sections. In the first section the two cases are described, as well as the impetus to policy changes, showing how changes in local political decision making, residents' reporting and incidents play a large role in defining the problem. Next, section 2 shows the importance of managerial interference. Policy changes are also the result of managerial ambitions and wishes. Following Cohen, March & Olsen (1972) and Kingdon (2014), these sections underscore that a new policy will be viable only when certain problem definitions correspond with proposed, often already existing, solutions. In addition, this section discusses how managerial control over local policy has increased. In section 3, the effects of policy changes on the daily work of municipal officers are discussed, pointing to an increased emphasis on information gathering and on deterring 'target groups'. Section 4 discusses professionals' experiences and views, indicating several tensions between these experiences and strict assignments. In the final section, the findings of this chapter are summed up.

1   POLICY CHANGES: INCIDENTS, POLITICS AND ANGRY RESIDENTS

Chapter 5 showed that municipal officers in general have a limited set of tasks that mostly concern physical disorder issues, such as littering or parking violations. The cases in this chapter show that municipal officers deal with different tasks. In particular circumstances municipal officers are given responsibility for particular hot issues, involving heavier tasks with more responsibilities, more risks and (often) involving more powers. In these cases the impetus for these new policies cannot be understood without taking the context of civic unrest and political interests into account.

Policing street youth: street coaches and youth enforcement officers in Rotterdam

The first of these hot issues discussed here are incivilities caused by street youth. In recent years the Netherlands has seen an increasing concern over anti-social behaviour of youth in public spaces and many interventions and new professions have been developed to deal with this issue of 'youth hanging around' (Dutch: *hangjongeren*). Likewise, city surveillance agencies are increasingly willing to accept tasks that are related to street youth, even though these issues were initially seen as phenomena too complex and even dangerous for municipal officers to deal with.[1]

The municipality of Rotterdam is one of the forerunners in using its municipal officers for street youth. In 2011 this municipality saw the introduction of a project entitled *street coaches* in which municipal officers were given special tasks regard-

---

1.   For more extensive discussions on national developments in thinking about street youth, see for instance Koemans (2011) and Martineau (2006).

ing street youth.[2] Remarkably, this project was established long after problems with street youth had been recognised by the city council. Hence the reasons for introducing these street coaches initially had little to do with political attention, but more with available funding and managerial opportunism.

Following a continuous (national) debate on anti-social behaviour by Moroccan street youth, the national government provided new grants for local governments to address these issues. These funding opportunities were warmly welcomed especially by the staff of the city surveillance agency. These grants provided this agency with an opportunity to counter a negative image sparked by the critical conclusions of an Audit report about municipal officers and their lack of professional standards (see chapter 5). New street coaches could function as images for a new type of professional, locally embedded and capable of nuanced judgment. The police's reluctance to become further involved with street youth and heavy cutbacks for local youth work provided further incentive for the Rotterdam city surveillance agency to bolster this role. Furthermore, installing *municipal* workers (instead of private contractors) for the specific goal of addressing the trouble caused by street youth would enable the Rotterdam administration to manage and steer their *own* officers.

Thus these street coaches would assume an in-between-position as 'extra hands and feet', between the purely preventative approach of youth workers and strict enforcement by the police. Moreover, the efforts of the Rotterdam city surveillance agency to change their image triggered a particular approach, highlighting group behaviour, youth culture and the specific circumstances of street youth.

Although the conditions for these new street coaches seemed to be good, their function description as 'street pedagogues' did not last long. In fact, the involvement of Rotterdam's city surveillance agency with youth did increase, but their approach changed considerably. At the end of 2014 it was decided that the number of municipal officers allocated for dealing with street youth would be increased to 25. Their names however, changed from 'street coaches' to 'youth enforcement officers'.

On the surface this change seems to be political. With a newly elected city council the approach to street youth became more focused on strict enforcement, reflected in the title of the recent youth policy programme, loosely translated as *The threatening stick*.[3] In addition, the most recent alderman responsible for Public Safety made dealing with anti-social youth a more prominent goal. As a senior manager states,

---

2.   The term 'street coach' is originally an intervention designed in Amsterdam. In recent years this professional has been introduced in many other Dutch municipalities, often with different goals and tasks. As opposed to the case discussed here, mostly private contractors are hired for this function (Loef, Schaafsma & Hilhorst, 2012).

3.   Gemeente Rotterdam (2015). *Stok achter de deur*.

> [The alderman] is keen on repression. 'Care? Assistance? Whatever. I want to make those neigh-
> bourhoods safer again. All that trouble experienced by residents, I don't want it,'[he says]. So
> it's seen much more from the residents' perspectives and less so from what youngsters might
> think.

In addition, public safety issues as such appear to have a large electoral draw, as several respondents emphasise. Thus council members would probably be more eager to pay attention to residents' reports that concern such issues. In Rotterdam this seems connected to the popularity of one particular political party – *Leefbaar Rotterdam*. This party, holding the most seats in the city council and part of the coalition at the time of research, is mentioned by many as an example of a political party that is susceptible to neighbourhood residents that directly report their worries to them. It was this party that seems to have been responsible for a new approach to street youth.

Moreover, mayor and aldermen in Rotterdam are prone to address public safety issues with special attention for the experiences of residents. In Rotterdam it seems something of a tradition to address public safety issues quickly and 'hands on' (even before the much discussed 'regime change'; cf. Tops, 2007). More recently, political decision makers tend to 'descend into neighbourhoods'; in staged meetings the mayor or the alderman for Public Safety meet residents of those areas considered to be 'hot', to listen to their grievances and to address alleged dysfunctional professionals on the spot. Rotterdam has invented several means to improve the connection between mayor/aldermen and neighbourhoods with pressing issues, such as a 'Core team' (Dutch: *kernteam*) and the 'Steering group safety in the neighbourhood' (Dutch: *stuurgroep veilig in de wijk*). A senior municipal manager tells about these innovations,

> The alderman wants to feel the problems in the neighbourhood better, really to descend on the
> neighbourhood, talk to people, what is your problem and how can we solve it. Then a lot of
> different interests start to play a role.

In the 'Steering group public safety in the neighbourhood' residents meet the mayor, the chief prosecutor, the police chief, an alderman and the head of the municipal department of Public Safety. These officials then address the most pressing issues more quickly and without the alleged slowness of the bureaucratic system.

These interventions tend to speed up the pace of measures being taken, respondents state. Some would go as far as saying this is a typical change in political prioritising these days. A municipal manager sees it as the *Pavlov reaction* of modern day decision makers. "It is always assumed that what a resident says is true, and needs to be taken seriously". This shift in prioritising, he adds, seems irrespective of political beliefs of the mayor himself, but is characteristic for the change in decision making as such. Most importantly, by putting residents' concerns at the centre of attention the policy concerning street youth changed. As such, it provided one of the circumstances that contributed to the shift from street coaches to youth enforcement officers.

Dealing with drug related issues, homelessness and nightlife in Utrecht

The impetus for the policy changes in Rotterdam shows a lot of similarity with the changes elsewhere. The second case in this chapter is drawn from the city centre of Utrecht. In the *Breedstraat* neighbourhood a group of municipal officers has been dealing with issues of drug trade, homelessness and nightlife in the centre of that city.

This area is particularly problem ridden. It contains a street with prostitution, several coffeeshops (soft drugs outlets), a shelter for homeless people and a high concentration of bars and nightlife locations. Many disorder issues had been mounting in this area for several years. A civil servant characterises this neighbourhood.

> Why did things in the Breedstraat area appear to get out of hand? Not because we had most
> trouble, but because it was all concentrated in a very small area. Utrecht has a very fragile and
> small inner city centre. The Breedstraat area became some sort of a meeting point [of problems].
> Also because the area around the central station, another meeting point, was redeveloped. So all
> of it ended up in this area. And it is a hard neighbourhood due to all the nooks and crannies.

Most of these issues were related to the use and trade of drugs. In response the municipality had been taking measures since 2008, measures such as street management to stimulate economic development and physical adaptations of public places to make the area less attractive for loitering drug dealers and users. In 2010 the mayor of Utrecht introduced area restraining orders for the individuals causing most trouble in this part of the city.

However, these measures were deemed to be insufficient. Distress among residents kept mounting. Despite earlier interventions, residents' complaints grew dramatically between 2009 and 2011. In the course of 2012, and under great pressure from the city council and mayor, a set of additional measures was introduced. These ranged from the involvement of municipal officers for extra surveillance, extra camera surveillance, closer surveillance by the police of drug dealers and users and the involvement of public health partners for closer monitoring of inhabitants of the hostels for homeless people. In addition, in 2012 the mayor appointed the area as a 'public safety risk area', enabling organised stop-and-search actions by the police.

Thus the involvement of Utrecht's city surveillance agency in the course of 2012 should be seen as part of a wider municipal effort to restore order in this part of town, through intensified surveillance, contributing to the fining of a group of repeat offenders (referred to as 'target group members') to help issue area restraining orders and (eventually) to walk night shifts.

Like Rotterdam, the influence of a group of neighbourhood residents is vital to understand these changes in policy. This group had been reporting on incivilities since around the turn of the century, trying to increase pressure on Utrecht's mayor, aldermen and council. A plethora of letters, signed petitions, manifestos and even problem analyses sent to the city council conveyed the message that the measures being taken by the municipality were not satisfactory, stating politicians and city council were merely fighting the symptoms. Hence the same group of residents kept asking for more measures to address the troubles in this area. Eventually this continued pressure led to the staging of a 'Council information evening' (*Raadsinformatie Avond*), initiated by council members to obtain more information from neighbourhood residents.

During that evening a sense of political urgency developed. A neighbourhood manager recounts that evening as something of a turning point. "Very heavy, with residents and shop owners standing up on the benches, yelling how bad things were". It provided a clear occasion for upset neighbourhood residents to voice their frustrations. This made members of the city council acknowledge the sense of urgency that residents were experiencing, as a police constable recounts.

> Someone from the childcare was there, telling stories about parents and kids being confronted with junkies. Entrepreneurs made their point about junkies hanging around in front of their doors. Residents who were not amused about the junkies on their doorsteps. These things never got priority before.

The worries of residents voiced (or shouted) on this particular evening caught the attention. A few days later all representatives of Utrecht's political parties signed a resolution asking the mayor and aldermen to intervene with extra measures.

Hence, this case can also be seen as an illustration of policy established through the close contact between neighbourhood residents and the city council. "These residents are in close contact with the city council […] personal acquaintance works best," a municipal manager states. These 'shorter lines' might also be established by the ability of residents to organise themselves. Utrecht has 'neighbourhood councils' for instance. In the case of the Breedstraat area this council seems highly active, well-organised and well-acquainted with both political representatives and civil servants. A civil servant tells about his contact with one of these neighbourhood residents, Mr. Z.

It happened quite often, on our department someone would say now and then, 'guys, we need to look this and that up, Mr. Z. has rung again'. He was a bit the pain in the neck for the munici-pality. But he did know how to get his point across. He knows how to do that, is educated, and doesn't accept simple answers. He keeps asking questions, in a charming, but in a nagging way [...] He also asked me to help him. So I advised him [...] I spoke openly with these people, because I think a citizen has a right to that. [...] I told him you can defend yourself as a neigh-bourhood, to meet your opponent legally well-founded, for instance by setting up a foundation. So they did.

In addition, as in Rotterdam, the proximity between mayor, aldermen and these neighbourhood residents has changed. The same respondent explains the mayor of that time was keen on visiting neighbourhoods to become informed about the issues there: "We went there to ask, what is going on, what do you think should happen to improve things here". As in Rotterdam, Utrecht's respective mayors seemed increasingly willing to listen to 'the citizens' and take their concerns seri-ously.

2   MANAGERIAL INTERESTS

Both cases suggest that a combination of incidents, increased pressure by residents and the willingness of politicians to respond to them are the main contributors to policy change. However, these new initiatives cannot be understood without the role of municipal managers; those players appear to be the ones who truly enabled and initiated these new approaches of disorder.

Managerial interests and ambitions

In the case of the street coaches, initial plans were largely drafted and implemented by a local manager for the policies on street youth. These local managers were part of Rotterdam's boroughs, administrative units with their own elected council. Thus the initial projects for street coaches were the responsibility of local managers, largely independent of political interference. Civil servants decided how and where to develop this project, in close accordance with the designated borough for this pilot scheme, Delfshaven.[4] As a result, this first borough had ample room to experiment with the new approach, whereas other boroughs had no street coaches.

However, senior (and central) municipal managers increasingly considered the differences between boroughs as undesirable. They had little insight in how the issues with street youth were tackled and what exactly worked in these local poli-cies. Put simply, the city central department of Public Safety wanted to have more

---

4.   Delfshaven was an area that was qualified as one of the 'Focus neighbourhoods Moroccans', one of the 'Youth attention neighbourhoods', one of the 'focus neighbourhoods with Safety issues', and one of the 'focus neighbourhoods with Social issues' (Bouziane & El Hadioui, 2012).

grip on how street youth was dealt with.[5] This demand was obviously increased by political pressure, but a vital moment in achieving this came from outside Rotterdam when boroughs as administrative units were abolished by the national government in 2014.[6] This change in organisational structure provided a chance to strengthen the grip on local policy. In the case of local youth policy it implied a more direct link between central senior managers and local managers dealing with youth issues. Consequently, the local managers in youth approach became 'experts on neighbourhood safety' who were directly accountable to the central department of Public Safety. A manager points out that this led to a better overview and more hold on what was happening in Rotterdam's boroughs with regard to youth,

> The mayor, the head of police and the public prosecutor now know exactly what youth groups we have […] and with the disappearance of the boroughs, the central Directorate is responsible. We have a better overview, and we report more often to the city council.

In addition, the larger role for central management contributed to the shift to youth enforcement officers. These new officers would get a stricter task description, and their role in helping to downscale the city's youth hotspots would have to become clearer. This led to a more distinct and more controllable division of tasks among frontline professionals, in which the municipal officers would get the piece of the pie that merely concerns law enforcement, whereas the elements of youth policy concerning 'risk factors' such as early school drop-outs or domestic violence were defined as belonging to other professional domains. The same manager says,

> We tried to make the policy programme more repressive and to get rid of care and assistance. Now it's only about surveillance in public places […] Locally it might be a bit more complicated now, but I think it's more pure.

Some respondents state that a street coach who is also enforcing rules would cause "confusion with the audience". It is easier to "draw one line," as a senior manager points out.[7]

Several changes coincided and combined for this change in policy, for another solution for the same problem to surface. As a result, new youth enforcement offi-

---

5.   As such, the street coach projects may well have ended due to a lack of insight into their effect. See also Eikenaar & Van Stokkom (2014) for a more extensive discussion of this criticism on street coaches.
6.   Apart from Rotterdam, the city of Amsterdam also had boroughs. From 2014 these are no longer political entities, but merely administrative commissions (*bestuurscommissies*; cf. Van Ostaaijen, 2013).
7.   Another development that might have also influenced the decision to discard the term 'street coach' – although hard to actually prove – is the influential criticism of street coaches in a study of municipal quality of life policy (Lub, 2013). Hence, the change to the term 'youth enforcement officers' might also have a semantic ground.

cers are less in touch with residents, fine more often and are less keen on getting in touch with youngsters preventively. The changed approach will be discussed more thoroughly in sections 3 and 4 below.

In Utrecht the convergence of political and managerial 'logics' also played a large role, as the political urge was also augmented by managerial ambitions and wishes.

Acknowledging the sense of urgency among a group of residents of the Breedstraat area, Utrecht's mayor at the time seemed inclined to look for a manageable group of officers that would be willing to run extra surveillance shifts. Especially since – as in Rotterdam – the police refused to be the sole party responsible for intensified surveillance. Going even further, claiming to have insufficient capacity, the police demanded extra effort from the municipality. This support was provided by Utrecht's municipal officers.

Most importantly however, the ambitions of the city surveillance agency itself pushed for the involvement of municipal officers. In fact, the management of Utrecht's city surveillance agency took the initiative. One of their managers was quite vocal about his ambitions. "I said, mayor, if you think we won't be able to pull this off. Well, I will only try harder". This agency did not merely execute the mayor's decision, but showed assertiveness in the design, establishment and implementation of the new approach.

These developments resulted in a tougher profile for Utrecht's municipal officers' involvement in this project. More 'firm' officers were attracted from other teams. "You need people who know how to do these things," a team coordinator states. At first, this involvement of workers happened on a voluntary basis, but eventually all officers with a '*BOA* – qualification' were supposed to be involved with these shifts.[8] The extra surveillance of this area started with dayshifts. Gradually, after resolving several organisational hindrances, shifts on Thursday and Friday night were introduced. Tasks mainly concerned uniformed presence, fining alcohol possession and consumption, dealing with street prostitution and reporting on issues for which they were not allowed to fine, such as dealing drugs. This implied that municipal officers were mainly policing 'target group members', such as drug dealers, homeless people and/or drug addicts. In addition, these officers were supposed to assist with the area restraining orders by consistently fining target group members.

The two cases – the youth enforcement officers and the municipal officers in the Breedstraat – area show how several 'logics' interact in the decision to involve municipal officers for new tasks; both political priorities and managerial ambitions play a large role. Thus in Rotterdam the general changes in youth policy were as

---

8.   See chapter 1 for an explanation of this qualification.

much a result of the (partly) self-imposed proximity of mayor and aldermen to specific neighbourhoods / residents, as of a wish for stricter management and control. In Utrecht such factors likewise contributed to new policy for municipal officers: pressure by a group of residents, municipal officers' willingness to take on new tasks, the high ambitions of the city surveillance agency and the reluctance on the side of the police to be the sole party responsible. In the words of Kingdon (2014), political priorities and new problem definitions provided a window of opportunity for specific civil servants to launch their solutions. Most notably, in both cases it led to stricter enforcement, an emphasis on 'target group policing' and a tough approach of (potential) offenders.

It is important to note that the coalition between political and managerial actors does not mean that they necessarily agree. Bearing in mind what has been said in chapter 6, some (local) managers could feel overruled and frustrated when other solutions are side-lined. Likewise, they might see these processes as implying unfair outcomes. "There is at least as much trouble [in another neighbourhood], and maybe even more. I can't explain the amount of energy for this neighbourhood, only because it's a political wish," a local manager points out. In this respect, the influence of reports of a specific group of residents plays too large a role in the eyes of some civil servants: other areas would deserve at least the same amount of policing. Due to, for instance a lack of fruitful contacts with the city council or less willingness to report on behalf of residents, these areas do not get the same amount of attention and lack the intensive approach. As one senior manager puts it, referring to a specific square,

> [This square] has been designated as a problem area for years, but in our analysis of statistics and in our contact with our colleagues it always had a low score. However, a lot of people who live there are [well acquainted with] political players and know how to get their problem on the agenda. And it was one of these locations with a lot of *Leefbaar Rotterdam* voters, who had those contacts […], and who know how to get their point across.

Here the clash of managerial logic with an eagerness to control and measure processes (and products) with political short-term and emotional thinking is evident. Nevertheless, the general tendency to embrace strategic thinking in terms of hotspots is undeniable. This has a great impact on the organisation of these projects in general and frontline work in particular.

Tightening control

A notable effect of the enhanced role of managers is more control: a greater emphasis on general measurement, more top-down control of frontline professionals and the introduction of local safety managers who need to account to their senior managers.

First of all, the heightened attention for the issues described above has led to tighter control and measurement of local policy. In Rotterdam senior managers introduced clearer and more measurable goals, for instance to diminish the number of so called 'youth hotspots' from 15 to 4, and the number of citizens' complaint reports by 25%.[9] In Utrecht extra measurements have been introduced to assess the level of incivilities in the Breedstraat area. In 2009 a baseline survey was held, followed by extensive surveys in 2011, 2012 and 2014, and the involvement of a consultancy bureau in 2013, evaluating the measures taken until that time, mainly by interviews with professionals. In the municipalities' own surveys residents, shop owners and passers-by were questioned, the traffic monitored and police reports scrutinised.

Second, tighter control has led to a stricter role for professionals. In Rotterdam's case various organisations have long since been involved.[10] Previously, these professionals were all coordinated by the borough's own manager youth approach.[11] With the introduction of a special model, called the 'cappuccino model', the department of Public Safety tried to specify and divide the respective roles of these partners more strictly in several consecutive steps. These steps go from mild and benevolent approaches to stricter enforcement (referred to as *opplussen*, 'scaling up'), representing the different layers of a 'cappuccino'. Local youth work, organising leisure activities, can be scaled up to the flexible and ambulatory urban team of youth workers for hotspots [*Stedelijk Team Jongerenwerk*] focusing exclusively on incivilities. Next, youth enforcement officers can be sent in if the powers of youth workers are seen as insufficient, especially if the groups involved are classified as 'anti-social' or 'causing hindrance'. The last step consists of the police, mostly if youth groups are classified as criminal. Although the Directorate Public Safety already introduced this model before street coaches were replaced by youth enforcement officers, the emphasis on this approach became stronger. The respective tasks of the different partners involved have been distributed more distinctly, with a clear role for each partner to play. Contact with reporting citizens for instance, is now a responsibility for youth workers, and youth enforcement officers are merely allowed to deal with the incivilities themselves, not with those who report it. In comparison, the collaboration in Utrecht's Breedstraat area seems less

---

9. Policy programme *Stok achter de deur*. The department of Public Safety appoints hotspots by considering the answers to questions in the safety index that address local residents' feelings of insecurity, and by grouping three categories of figures on objective public safety derived from the police registration system: residency of juvenile suspects for various offences, locations of offences committed by juvenile offenders and 'incidents youth incivilities' as reported to or observed by the police.
10. Different types of youth workers, 'square coaches', the police's youth sergeant, the neighbourhood police officer, 'neighbourhood fathers', regular municipal officers, street coaches / youth enforcement officers, at times professionals from housing corporations and 'city marines'.
11. This municipal manager was responsible for assembling reports from partners and for the so-called *Beke list*. Together with a local police officer and youth worker this manager assessed the youth groups in the borough as to whether they are 'anti-social', 'causing hindrance' or 'criminal'.

strictly structured, although control also became tighter. Regular briefings of municipal officers by the police and meetings between police, municipal officers, public health professionals and the neighbourhood manager were introduced. To monitor and develop the new approach a policy team of various partners held regular meetings during part of the project's running time.

A third element showing that senior managers exert more grip is the introduction of local managers who are directly accountable to their central managers. In Utrecht a municipal safety manager has the predominant role among all partners involved. This manager is in touch with all relevant partners, and is the lynchpin between decision makers, the police, the department Public Safety, professionals who have to follow these orders and a consultative group of neighbourhood residents. In the case of the Breedstraat area it is partly to the credit of this manager that the preconditions for the involvement of municipal officers were met (cf. Eikenaar & Van Stokkom, 2014). In Rotterdam the relatively new function of the 'neighbourhood safety expert' fulfils this role, albeit mainly through closer steering of frontline professionals.[12] These new managers develop strategic plans, specify the roles of all the professionals involved, chair meetings where partners share information on individual youngsters, evaluate several goals and sub-goals in that plan and – most importantly – have to account directly to the senior managers of the Directorate Public Safety using their strategic plans as "the guideline we have to account to," as a public safety manager states, "followed by an evaluation to see what we accomplished and what are the bottlenecks". As such, these public safety managers seem to have more influence on what the municipal officers do than their own team coordinators.

With a characteristic example of NPM speech, one of these team coordinators emphasises that the city surveillance agency merely implements the policy made elsewhere,

> The market demands it, the department of Public Safety. There are more and more situations where rules are broken, where other ways of approaching, de-escalating, the preventive approaches apparently are not seen as effective anymore, and then we are sent in.

As such, political and managerial 'logics' seem to strengthen each other: council, mayor and/or aldermen might demand more central control and municipal managers provide the means for control. As those politically involved tend to grant senior managers a more prominent role, they tighten control: all frontline profes-

---

12. As opposed to Utrecht, contact with political decision makers is a responsibility of senior managers in Rotterdam.

sionals are mainly meant to play a well-defined role and to show that public safety issues are addressed by the municipality.[13]

3   DAILY WORK: STRICT ROLE DEFINITIONS

In the cases described here, expectations are fairly clearly defined. With quite a lot of political pressure, a strong, top-down emphasis on hotspots and the eagerness to address these, municipal officers get strict assignments and know what is expected of them. This raises questions about the impact on their daily work.

In this section it is first pointed out that municipal officers' daily work is defined by a strict task description. This results in a particular focus on information and on an emphasis on deterring 'target group members'. In the next section, section 4, municipal officers' own ideas are analysed.

Collecting and sharing information

A first characteristic of municipal officers' clearly defined role is a particular focus on information, underscoring their specific position in the network of partners. In Rotterdam for instance, youth enforcement officers spend a lot of time collecting information about youngsters and sharing it with partners. Whereas the street coaches were often seen as falling short in this respect (cf. Eikenaar & Van Stokkom, 2014), youth enforcement officers spend a great deal of time with what they call 'drawing youngsters out of anonymity'. This means mainly obtaining information about individual youngsters at the hotspots, asking for their IDs and documenting their whereabouts and possible misbehaviour.

Moreover, the youth enforcement officers use this information in a different way than the former street coaches. Whereas street coaches emphasised the circumstances of a youngster and tried to gain their confidence, youth enforcement officers are less interested in such matters. Background information is generally not collected to know more about the youngsters' circumstances, or to show them opportunities for care or assistance. These officers stress they are only interested in such information to 'use' it: to reprimand them when they are on the streets when they should be in school, *or* to be able to threaten them with exclusion from the activities of youth work when they cause trouble. A youth enforcement officer points out how he sees his role in this respect,

---

13. As noted in the first section, political and managerial logic are not always in line. In Rotterdam for instance, second thoughts can be heard when it concerns the distribution of scarce resources. Although managers state they have been able to identify the most troubled areas, some of them particularly find it hard to draw full attention to what they see as the *real* objective hotspots, especially in the case of a hotly debated subject as incivilities caused by street youth. The requests for enforcement officers are seldom totally unjustified, a senior manager says, but youth is not the main problem in every case.

> To get to know a [youngster's] background story, you need to gain his confidence. That's a task
> for youth work, not for us. If you get into a situation that demands a fine, you'll lose that confi-
> dence again. So it's no use to gain it in the first place. [...] On an individual level, we don't [get
> really acquainted]

Also in the case of Utrecht's Breedstraat area the focus on information seems to have become stronger. Here too, the role of municipal officers with regard to this information is predefined. Initially, these officers met the police in their briefings to share information on the 'target group members', for example about who has an area restraining order. Utrecht's municipal officers had access to a police file with all 'suspects' and relevant information.

This sharing of information happens mainly with one thing in mind – to rid the streets of these target group members. Moreover, professionals from public health care and the shelters for homeless people were also involved for this reason. Thus at the height of the coordinated efforts, police, municipal officers and field workers in healthcare met every two weeks coordinated by the neighbourhood safety manager, exchanged more information about who causes trouble so that this could be transferred from 'blue' to 'white'. This gave a better overview of the 'target groups' and how to control them better. As a civil servant states, "you can also limit trouble by taking people out of that situation, confine them and place them in halfway houses". When the issues caused by these target group members diminished after several years, the various organisations involved stopped their close collaboration. The absence of issues in public spaces meant information collection and sharing was no longer seen as important.

Thus the frontline work of municipal officers is for an important part about collecting information and using it for fighting the anti-social behaviour of street youth or removing target groups from the streets.[14] Whether youngsters or homeless people were referred to care or social assistance by officers "totally depends on [individual professionals]," in the words of a Utrecht municipal officer. In general however, they do not appear to see it as their assignment to think of ways to address the problem other than by law enforcement. An officer in Rotterdam indicates their assignments leave no room for doubt, "Our task is just to monitor anti-social behaviour in the hotspot-areas".

Deterring target group members

This leads to the second aspect of the work of municipal officers. On their shifts these officers focus largely on hotspots, as these are the areas where most target

---

14. There was insufficient room to investigate whether the approach to 'target group members'
     changed all together. It would have required a more thorough study of the approach of – for
     instance – youth work or health care.

group members are likely to be found.[15] Patrolling these hotspots, officers deter and fine their target groups, following them around, almost in a game-like manner. Municipal officers compare the relation with their 'target groups' to a 'cat-and-mouse' game or a 'harassing contest'. An observation in Rotterdam –

> We approach four Moroccan boys. It is a windy and cool evening. The officers told me in advance that the streets might well be empty on days like these, but we encounter plenty of youths hanging around. This is the third hotspot we visit; a secluded, small courtyard, surrounded by three and four story residential buildings. The boys are standing on the other side of the park, among a broken garbage can and some litter. We approach them peddling on our bicycles. Three immediately walk away upon seeing us, one stays put. He responds snappily, without being addressed. "I can stand here, I am waiting for my sister," he says, looking grimly at the officers. He loiters around the bench. One of the officers waits until the boy saunters away. As this is a hotspot, the officer tells me later, he would certainly have fined him if they had more back-up. With just two enforcement officers and no idea as to whether the police could be here soon, he decided to avoid the risk of a fight and to send the boys off.

In each of the hotspots certain areas are prioritised – hotspot locations. During their shifts the youth enforcement officers constantly visit these streets, squares or parks, travelling around, mostly by bicycle if the weather permits it.

Although some respondents want youth enforcement officers to use their powers more often, these officers themselves claim they fine a lot more than their predecessors, the street coaches. They state that loitering in doorways, urinating in public or smoking weed are frequently fined. In this respect, their limited powers do not stop them from addressing youths for more offences than those for which they are authorized, such as the use of soft drugs. In these cases an officer points out, they look for ways to express it as 'anti-social behaviour' (*overlast*),

> Smoking weed is tolerated in the Netherlands, but not in a shopping centre or close to a playground. Then it's anti-social behaviour [*overlast*]. Especially when residents reported it. Such things are mostly known to us and the police, but you have to delineate it clearly, or it will be dismissed.

This application of their limited mandate is not uncommon. Officers also stretch their mandate to address loitering in other, non-public places, such as the hallways of flats where some youngsters take refuge during bad weather. Although not a public space, officers scan and visit these spots using keys provided for them by the housing associations.

---

15. For the case of Rotterdam it must be noted there might be considerable differences between neighbourhoods, depending on the preferences of Experts Neighbourhood Safety or individual youth enforcement officers. For these case studies I have only been able to join shifts in two boroughs.

As a result youngsters are constantly deterred, and youth enforcement officers follow them, for instance in the staircases of these flats, "It's hard to catch those youngsters in those flats. They know them really well and might escape through the fire-escape on the other side".

This idea of hotspot policing and deterring target groups, can also be noted in Utrecht's Breedstraat area. Although Utrecht's city centre and its problems with drug dealers and drug users are of a different nature, there are important similarities in the ways that these problems are addressed by municipal officers in both cities. While talking to two municipal officers about their work, they assure me they know how to deal with these target groups,

> "It works just by being present". He points at one side of the table. "If these guys walk here, I would stand there," moving his finger to the other side. "If they proceed, you cycle along with them. Nice and easy. They will go crazy".

As in Rotterdam, deterring and sometimes fining target group members are the dominant approaches at hotspots. Here too, their presence seems largely dictated by these target groups. Put simply, they follow them around. As an officer states, "We'll see who wins the harassment contest".

Utrecht's municipal officers also have limited powers. Like their colleagues in Rotterdam, they look for other ways to address, deter or fine target groups. Again, the most notable example is their approach to drug use. Although these officers are not mandated to fine for violations of the Opium Act, they have found innovative ways of dealing with loitering drug dealers and users. Two officers explain how this works,

> A: If you are a dealer, and I can't fine you for your drugs, but you are cycling on the pavement, I'll give you one for that. Just don't hang around here. Get out of here. [And] if you're annoying enough, I'll give you one [at night too]. I can decide for myself when to write a fine. But I can't do anything that concerns the Opium Act. I can't confiscate a spliff. A police officer can.
> B: We look for the right way of fixing them up with a fine.
> A: We can make it really hard for them, so it won't be interesting for them to loiter around.

The repeat offenders – "our little friends," as some officers call them – appear to be well acquainted with the municipal officers. One officer even claims that they know when officers are on patrol and when they are inside for a break, "they don't take any risks". One of the effects is the moving of 'target groups' to other areas. Municipal officers speak of a displacement effect. On their shifts officers can be seen to adapt to the changed situation and the Breedstraat area is now a minor part of a much larger area in the city centre where these enforcement officers are asked to patrol.

4   VIEWS AND EXPERIENCES OF FRONTLINE WORKERS

Approving of tough strategies?

As is apparent from the previous section, both in the Breedstraat case and in the case of the youth enforcement officers in Rotterdam the work of municipal officers is dominated by close monitoring of target groups and a strict approach to these people. Especially the approach by youth enforcement officers is a far cry from the street coach approach. It raises the question of how officers themselves qualify and experience this stricter approach.

At first sight, municipal officers seem satisfied with a more repressive, and in their opinion, clearer approach. In Utrecht for instance, most municipal officers are convinced that a tough zero tolerance approach works, both with regard to the target groups and the designated area. An officer says that area restraining orders were needed to keep things 'liveable'. "Increasing numbers of those people were coming, it was piling up". They are also keen to apply the rules decreed as 'zero tolerance' in designated areas concerning, for example alcohol, even when someone is not necessarily seen as part of the target group. The 'public safety risk area' appointed by the mayor is sufficient legitimation in these cases, for example to drive any sleeping individuals out of the station hall or to fine anyone with an opened beer bottle, target group or not, as was apparent during observations.

However, on closer observation professionals do express doubts and even discontent with the demands made by their management or political decision makers, for example because their assignments do not provide them with enough work to do, they do not see their activities as meaningful, or they experience unease with the strict approach of target groups. As noted in chapter 6, their ideas may be antithetic to the wishes of politicians or managers. Again, the two cases provide useful opportunities for studying such conflicts.

Bored with their work

In both cases, the strong emphasis on hotspots and target group members entails municipal officers having to patrol these areas and look for designated individuals, even when the chances are slim that there is "anything to be found," in the words of an officer.

During observations at times these officers appear somewhat purposeless. In Rotterdam, due to a fixed work schedule municipal officers also have to go out when youngsters are not or scarcely on the streets, for instance during winter or during day time. Although the officers occupy themselves during these shifts with asking around about possible issues at local businesses, at times they are actively searching for extra work. In Utrecht confrontations with the original target group have diminished considerably. Dealers, users and homeless people have largely disappeared from the streets, according to municipal officers' stories and what can be observed during their shifts.

As a result, in both cases municipal officers sometimes have trouble filling their shifts satisfactorily. This apparent idleness causes discontent among some of them, especially since they say they are prone to action, preferring confrontations, sometimes even in different neighbourhoods – "always being in the same neighbourhood causes boredom, it becomes a drag," as one of the youth enforcement officers says. In Utrecht new hotspots and new tasks are not always considered to be too interesting either. During one of the shifts for instance, officers have to observe whether eating places without a permit have customers inside

> We hold still at the end of the street. We meet the other couple here. They have checked the other side of this street. Officer A. sighs, looks from under his helmet at the other municipal officers. "Any news on your side?" he asks. "Nothing," officer B. responds. "It's dead as a doornail here," A. says. "Let's go back to the city centre, there's a funfair there and a lot more to do".

Thus with each other these officers express action-eagerness, highlighting their quest for confrontations and lamenting the lack of activity.[16] It would be too easy however, to see these officers as purely action-prone.

Unease

In fact, and as opposed to being keen on action and chasing target groups, at times officers also express unease with their strict assignments. Many officers combine opposing views in their work. Apart from the apparent urge for action, they seem to approach their assignments with more than mere zero tolerance thinking or cynicism about the alleged malevolence of their target group members, sometimes showing sincere involvement (cf. Björk, 2008). The same applies to their stories of fining. Although many of the officers highlight that they fine more, in the shifts with municipal officers I seldom saw them actually use these powers. Their interaction with target groups or with residents might have a different tone than what they say that they do, illustrating the difference between a canteen culture and a street culture, in which the latter shows more nuances and less bragging (cf. Waddington, 1999).

This also causes conflict with assignments that tell them merely to deter and fine their target groups. In Rotterdam some of the youth enforcement officers acknowledge many youngsters do not have a lot of room to go to in this neighbourhood. They also voice nuanced and relatively compassionate ideas about these youngsters,

---

16. Terpstra (2012) noticed comparable sentiments amongst municipal officers in his study of private security officers who are employed as municipal officers in two Dutch municipalities.

Often it's minor, cheeky behaviour of older boys. They often come from large families and they
have nowhere to go. So we don't really want to remove them, we just want them to cause no
trouble. No littering, no noise, no urinating in public.

In some cases this leads to observations by enforcement officers themselves about
their work being mainly about the symptom and less so about what could help
these youngsters.

The municipal officers in Utrecht's Breedstraat area also have more nuanced
ideas than their harsh approach would suggest. When joining them on their shifts,
it turned out municipal officers often oscillate between different views. Convinced
of the strict approach to regular perpetrators as they seem to be, they also question
the relevance of the approach to these people, especially when it comes to the area
restraining orders. A lot of the target group members, such as the homeless people,
cannot afford to pay the fines, they state, and will only be chased into nearby
neighbourhoods. An officer adds, "and sometimes you have the troublemakers
who live in those neighbourhoods. What do you do with those? You can't send
them away everywhere".

Nevertheless, these relatively nuanced perspectives are often overshadowed by
their assignments. Consequently, some lament there is so little use made of the
frontline knowledge these professionals could provide. Something that is also
hampered by systems of accounting, so it seems: everything revolves around the
question whether contacts yield enough information and this information can be
used for close tracking and policing of individuals.

Enlarging responsibilities

In other cases the criticism of limited assignments is expressed in deeds instead of
verbal discontent: some municipal officers actively stretch the limits of their work.
Not only by creatively applying their powers for a wider array of offences, but also
by looking for new tasks. Youth enforcement officers for instance, can be seen to
enter shopping centres to watch out for shoplifters, or to get in touch with the
police to ask if they can assist them. In Utrecht municipal officers now actively deal
with pub-crawlers and have started to regulate the taxi area at night.

It is hard to determine what causes such assertiveness. Part of it might be related to the action eagerness described above. However, a form of 'professional
imperialism' could also have explanatory power here: officers tend to expand their
work outside their designated assignments, incorporating more and more work in
a bid to add value to their occupation. In Utrecht for instance, apart from merely
keeping themselves busy, officers sometimes hope that by adding streets to their
surveillance rounds, their managers might acknowledge their observations of new
incivilities. "We're hoping they add this part to our rounds. If you find something
there, it might turn into a pattern and become part of the regular nightshifts," one

officer says. Or as another officer says about the taxi areas, "You're moving around anyway, maybe we can have some significance for those issues too". Again, their particular background as former city-wardens wanting to prove themselves as serious policing officers seems crucial in this respect. In terms of the previous chapter, the *supply* of these actively patrolling officers creates its own *demand*.

Ambivalence towards citizens reporting

A last testimony to a disagreement with assignments is the officers' ambivalence towards citizens' complaint reports. These citizens have reported issues that are temporary or confined to a few moments a week, according to municipal officers' experiences, but still these reports have given neighbourhood managers and politicians the occasion to designate these areas as 'hotspots'. Consequently, officers feel that the requests for their presence in these areas are informed by reassuring complaining residents, by a need for mere symbolical presence. According to some municipal officers in Utrecht the same applies to the area restraining orders that are issued to target group members,

> Those area restraining orders are mainly for the outside world, to show we are dealing with it. But you have to do it in another way if you want to solve that problem. Now it's mostly PR, you're doing it for the citizen who is complaining and is bothered by it.

In the eyes of the officers themselves, this symbolical presence has a rather low relevance. As a result, they seem reluctant to visit some of these hotspots. They simply want to keep themselves occupied and useful, but reassuring complaining citizens is not perceived as meaningful. As an officer in Utrecht states, the council is at a large distance from what is actually happening on the streets. Moreover, these opinions show that in practice officers' ideas do not always match with officers' emphasis on minor annoyances discussed in chapter 7.

The downsides of political logic are particularly evident in these cases. Professionals and some of their coordinators get tired of political interference with their work, being dragged around to different hotspots. Especially Utrecht's city surveillance agency appears to have become a victim of its own success, as a coordinator states. As with the Rotterdam youth enforcement officers, these officers are increasingly seen as a flexibly employable policing force that can be used to quickly respond to the areas that are seen as urgent (see also chapter 6).

Consequently, other neighbourhoods suffer from this political cramp and eagerness, several municipal officers state, "We used to have maybe 25 people in the neighbourhood, now you should be happy if it's two. There are so many projects now". Thus Utrecht's city surveillance agency has changed, according to many respondents, from a de-centralised organisation with neighbourhood teams and close contact with other professionals around the city, into a flexible pool of municipal officers, housed in a central building. "You occasionally get into those neighbourhoods," one of them says, "but it's so big, so you just go from one report to the next". In this respect, at times both professionals and coordinators see themselves as victims of political populism and incident-related policies culminating in a disproportionate emphasis on certain areas and certain reports.

5   CONCLUSIONS

This chapter showed that municipal disorder policing is the result of various interacting factors. Previous chapters already indicated that this profession is as much the result of political preferences and municipal ambitions as it is of managerial and frontline logic. In addition to those insights, this chapter illustrated that these influences might mutually strengthen each other. This is particularly evident in the strict enforcement approach towards target groups in the case studies that informed this chapter.

Initially, new municipal policy to tackle anti-social behaviour was triggered by changes in political attention. More specifically, the eagerness of mayors and aldermen to 'listen to the citizen' led to more pressure to address disorder. In Rotterdam's case, this partly explains why the earlier street coaches were replaced by youth enforcement officers. Their introduction as a solution was supported by a new eagerness for 'acting out' and showing who owns the streets (Garland 2001). Likewise, in Utrecht's case, initially the municipal officers in the city centre were a political response to reporting citizens. In fact, only after the much discussed resident meeting where "residents were standing up on the benches to yell how bad it all was," were municipal officers introduced as a solution to the problem.

However, this political focus can only partially explain why municipal officers were assigned to these tasks. This policy change was enabled as the result of managers who saw these new problem definitions as a good opportunity to launch their solutions (Kingdon, 2014). Thus policy changes also reflect managerial ambitions and wishes for more control. Furthermore, these political and managerial preferences led to a tighter control of local policy: means of measurement are positioned more prominently and the work of officers is made more accountable to municipal managers. At times the pressure of these decisions turns the daily work of municipal officers into a straitjacket of firm enforcement. Officers are engaged in collecting information, policing hotspots and deterrence of target group members. As such, these officers seem at least partly loyal to these assignments and they seem content with the clear, zero-tolerance approach towards these target groups. Moreover, their limited powers do not seem to hold them back in this respect.

Nevertheless, different stakeholders do not always agree. Managers might express frustration at the political constraints and eagerness to constantly listen to angry residents. In addition, particularly the experiences and ideas of frontline professionals often conflict with political and managerial expectations. For instance, at times these professionals have boring days. However, this should not lead to the conclusion that municipal officers necessarily want more target groups to chase. In fact some of them express unease about the policy of deterring these target groups. It might not be the most sustainable solution to the problem. In yet other cases, municipal officers are dissatisfied with their responsibilities. They often look for extra work and incorporate new-found tasks in their daily routines. Finally, professionals are ambivalent about politicians' inclination to rely on citizens' reports. Often they see politicians as detached from "the reality on the streets".

In summary, whereas municipal officers might have a large range of strategies and approaches at their disposal, one may wonder if these alternatives will be used when assignments predetermine officers' action as strictly as described here (Bervoets, 2013; chapter 7). The point may even be made that officers in these cases are 'kept small', derogating their evolving professional standards by forcing them to keep to strict assignments and hotspots. In addition, the tendency of these professionals to fulfil more tasks than those to which they are assigned and their urge for action and confrontations raises questions about the limitations of municipal disorder policing in relation to police work. This theme will be discussed in the next chapter.

MUNICIPAL OFFICERS, POLICE OFFICERS AND
THEIR WORK DOMAINS

1   INTRODUCTION

The work of municipal officers cannot be understood without taking developments
in police work and organisation into account. This applies to all levels of analysis
used here. On a macro level, the initial development of municipal disorder policing
must partly be understood as a response to changes in police policies and forces.
Next, local decisions on disorder policing depend on collaboration with the police
and their local priorities, as was noted in chapter 6. In addition, municipal officers'
views are reminiscent of how police officers deal with their work. In this respect,
they can even be seen as realizing a part of the police's role in society. Finally, the
previous chapter illustrated how the involvement of municipal officers in new
tasks is dependent on the police's position in specific cases. This close dependency
demands a more comprehensive approach to the relation between these two occupational groups, a discussion that provides further insight in how the division
between their respective work domains is seen.

   This chapter provides such a discussion, albeit not in terms of a clear-cut overview of the essential characteristics and tasks of both occupations. Instead, the
growth of municipal disorder policing and its relation to the police are seen as
depending on these professions as 'social actors'. This Weberian inspired approach
regards occupations as "collectively conscious groups" with their own shared
beliefs and specific interests (Macdonald, 1995: 27; Van der Krogt, 1981). Hence not
only do divisions of task differ factually between municipalities, the views on this
division are also part of collective beliefs and subject to the strategies of the occupational groups involved. As such, this chapter challenges a functionalist approach
in which occupational domains are seen as stationary situations or defined by "stable and fixed characteristics" (Macdonald, 1995: 8).

   In what follows the views on the work domains of municipal officers and police
officers will be discussed in two consecutive steps. In the second section, some theoretical notions are briefly explored. The same section introduces three types of
argumentations that are used in the debate on work domains – fundamental, economic and hierarchical argumentations. These modes of reasoning inform four
positions about the differences between the two occupations in the third section.

Two of these positions point out that there is a strict division between the work domains of police and municipal officers (3.1 and 3.2) and in two positions the two occupational groups are seen as closely related (3.3 and 3.4). The final section comprises of an overview and a short reflection on these findings.[1]

2   ARGUMENTATIONS IN OCCUPATIONAL STRIFE

The descriptions by both municipal and police officers to define occupational domains are in no way neutral characterisations. Instead, these descriptions are part of a constant strife over "the boundaries of [these] domains and the membership who belong within them" (Macdonald, 1995: 8). In this respect, the relation between different policing occupations is reminiscent of the strife and negotiation between other professions that also operate in a field with shared or closely related goals – such as medicine or law. As with these professions, the division of a general (policing) function over various professions ('plural policing') implies that occupations are constantly (re)defining, securing or improving their position (Larson, 1977; Macdonald, 1995). This has been so from the very outset of municipal disorder policing. When the first city wardens were introduced, they entered an existing occupational domain, a social order in which police had been the predominant occupation and in which new professions would have to "strive to gain autonomy" (Macdonald, 1995: 8). In the words of Larson (1977), municipal officers have been involved in a *professional project*, attempting to wrest control of their occupational domain, thereby defining the social reality of that domain.

   Taking this idea of a professional project as point of departure, this chapter aims at unveiling how various players take up positions in this project. Hence this chapter provides both an overview of various positions on the division between police officers and municipal officers and also scrutinises the arguments that are used to support these. In doing so, the analysis builds on sociological approaches of professions elaborated by Macdonald (1995), Larson (1977) and Freidson (2001). Especially Freidson's influential work *Professionalism – the third logic* (2001) provides support in clarifying different positions. Freidson conceives of professionalism as a third logic, in contradistinction to that of the market and the state, offering a rich description of the ideal-typical elements of that logic. He sees the ideology of professionalism as the "primary tool available to disciplines for gaining the political and economic resources needed to establish and maintain their status" (*ibid.*: 105).

---

1.   This chapter is about rhetoric and less so about what police and municipal officers actually do in practice. This deserves to be mentioned as there could be considerable differences between the two. Police officers' discourse for instance, might tend to bravado, action and machismo, whereas in practice their approach shows more nuanced strategies (Reiner, 2010; Waddington, 2008; see also chapter 8).

However, through a less ideal-typical and more empirical analysis, this examination shows that positions are not only supported by this independent third logic
of professionalism. In fact, various players use arguments that also touch on economic considerations about scarcity ('market thinking') or bureaucratic considerations about hierarchy ('state-centred thinking'). These different argumentations are
combined and creatively used by players to legitimate the distinction between the
two occupations in ways that best meet their interests.

Three argumentations

Hence, a first step in clarifying the debate on the respective work domains of
municipal and police officers' is to shed light on what type of arguments are used
by municipal officers, police officers, and their managers and coordinators.[2] Three
types are discussed here – fundamental, economic and hierarchical argumentations.

Firstly, fundamental arguments about what is real police work and what is real
municipal surveillance work highlight the alleged core aspects of both occupational domains. As such, these arguments might appeal to transcendent values that
imbue tasks of these officers with a higher goal (Freidson, 2001). On the one hand,
such arguments are used by police representatives, for instance in their focus on
core tasks. Moreover, their emphasis on such core tasks has certain consequences
for the way how they see the tasks of municipal officers. The work of municipal
officers is defined in the slipstream of this dominant occupation as assisting the
police and helping police officers to spend more time and energy on their proper
tasks by taking alleged improper tasks of their shoulders. On the other hand,
municipal officers, coordinators and managers have developed their own view of
what are *their* fundamental core tasks, often in defence of an alleged tendency of
police forces to increasingly transfer tasks to city surveillance agencies. These arguments are in line with what Freidson (2001: 56) calls an occupational division of
labour in which one occupation defines its position in relation to other occupations
on grounds of the content of its expertise.

In contrast with this reasoning, a second argument is of a less fundamental and
more pragmatic nature. In this case, doing police work is looked upon more in an
economic sense as a product that may be provided by various suppliers. Thus, the
distinction between both occupations might be informed by a sort of free market
thinking of unconstrained competition over policing work (Freidson 2001: 46).
Likewise, it is a form of reasoning that is used to support different positions. Thus,
some might fully embrace this free competition over policing work, as will be

2.   For this chapter interviews with various respondents have been used, both from municipal city
     surveillance agencies and from the police organisation and working in various levels of both
     organisations. This variety was of importance to assure an encompassing overview of the perspec-
     tives on this hotly debated issue.

made more evident in the third position below. Others, endorse an economic approach to policing more instrumentally, for instance to support their view that police officers are too expensive to use them for minor disorder or for basic surveillance. These tasks can thus be easily outsourced to others. Hence, the argument here differs from the fundamental arguments described above: there is little fundamental difference between various policing officers, and "the division of labour can be very fluid," without too many constraints or concerns over professional standards or differences between the occupations involved (Freidson, 2001: 47).

A third and final argumentation about the differences between the two occupations involves considerations about professional status and positions in the hierarchy of law enforcement occupations. Although not fully coinciding with it, this line of argumentation is related to what Freidson (2001) calls the bureaucratic division of labour, implying "the organization of positions is pyramidal, establishing clear lines of authority leading up to the ultimate executive officer" (Freidson, 2001: 49). Many police respondents in particular use arguments that stress such a hierarchical division between police officers and municipal officers, the latter being subordinate to the former, both in powers and in professional status. They highlight for instance, that they can be distinguished from municipal officers through a claim on the monopoly on violence. These arguments provoke much dispute: the professional standards and the reputation of municipal officers are a constant source for strife and debate. Some of these disputes pertain to the legal differences between police officers and municipal officers. As described in chapter 1, most municipal officers are formally enacted as *BOAs*, 'Special Investigative Officers', implying they have the legal authority to write administrative fines or administrative penal orders for a limited set of rule infringements. This implies municipal officers may have coercive means at their disposal, such as pepper spray, a baton and handcuffs. However, these specific powers are looked upon differently and used to bolster various views. Some maintain municipal law enforcement is characterised by deficient professional standards: these officers would lack capacity, skills, expertise and knowledge. Others claim the professionalism of municipal officers has developed notably, and these officers have developed into a fairly professional policing body. Obviously such differences in views on (legal) competences result in different views about the respective occupational domains.

3   DIVISION BETWEEN MUNICIPAL OFFICERS AND POLICE OFFICERS: FOUR
         POSITIONS

The views about the differences between municipal and police officers and their work domains are informed by the three types of argumentations outlined above, combining them in various ways. In what follows, this is further elaborated by describing four positions.

3.1   *Strict division: police core tasks and 'catching crooks'*

One of the most frequently heard statements about what distinguishes police officers from municipal officers is that the police have the legal mandate for criminal
investigation and is there to address serious crime. This statement is more than a
somewhat obligatory, bureaucratic task description that would be agreed upon by
everyone. It is commonly used rhetorically to indicate such a domain is not only
the police's *ultimate*, but also their *main* responsibility: they should devote their
attention to 'catching crooks' (Van Stokkom, 2010). In fact, that statement is used
by respondents to fundamentally oppose other tasks and lies at the basis of the
inclination to transfer other problems, such as everyday annoyances and minor
issues of disorder, to other organisations. Many respondents express these
thoughts, such as this police officer,

> The real bastards, that's what we're here for. All the other hassle, quarrels between neighbours,
> parking on the pavement, a police officer may involve it in his daily shift now and then, but it
> should not be his main task.

However, quite a few municipal officers share the same thought, as a municipal
officer in Eindhoven says,

> Of course, the police don't deal with household waste. They have to deal with domestic vio-
> lence, that sort of things. If your neighbour is beating up his wife, you call the police, not the
> city surveillance agency.

Although respondents who support this view might acknowledge that minor disorder tops the list of the most important annoyances of neighbourhood residents,
they maintain that the involvement of the police with these problems is not an
issue, because it does not belong to their core occupation of 'catching crooks'. A
senior police officer for instance, concedes dog dirt is of no concern to the police.
"Dog dirt has no place in our vocabulary whatsoever. For us it's no problem".

This position – mainly based on fundamental arguments – is often voiced to
emphasise the distinctive nature of police work. The notion of 'catching crooks' is
utilised to further rhetorically absolve the responsibilities of the police from minor
issues. Some respondents would say for instance, that the one-on-one contact with
ordinary neighbourhood residents is not a police responsibility either. Police work
is misunderstood, a police chief thinks, if people feel the police should spend more
time with them. "Dear Madam, if a police officer spends a full hour having coffee
with you, something is terribly wrong," he adds.

Furthermore, this emblematic task designation is used to give meaning to what
the police have been doing wrong in the past. Thus, it was a mistake for the police

to be ever focussed on minor disorder or issues other than serious crime. A municipal manager explains this,

> Police have always been doing things that don't belong to their core business. They would say: 'if we don't do this, nobody will'. So you could say, municipal officers are now doing the tasks that were inappropriately done by the police before.

Many policemen are quite vocal on this matter too,

> Year after year, we have let the neighbourhood constable spread leaflets door to door. With all due respect, but a constable or a police officer should be catching crooks, not spreading brochures. That's something someone else should do.

Although this position is characterised by fundamental arguments, this same idea is often framed in more economic terms too. Patrolling public places, policing minor disorder and uniformed presence are all seen as a waste of precious police capacity. A chief police constable says,

> I'm really happy we are beyond that point of old fashioned thinking. That we don't send four officers to a funfair. It's so useless. Maybe the general public likes to see us there, but I rather put my people there were they are needed, assuming that others, and especially municipalities, will think about how to solve this.

With regard to municipal officers this view implies that they are the ones that are expected to deal with minor issues. The most commonly heard classification to distinguish the two occupations in this respect, is that between 'quality of life' and 'public safety': municipal officers should focus on issues of the former, whereas the police is responsible for the latter.[3]

In addition, many of the respondents who are convinced of the police as 'crook catchers' use hierarchical arguments. They see police work as inherently different from municipal officers' work, defending police work as a special, distinctive job, and police officers as a carefully selected elite. Often this lower position of municipal officers in the law enforcement hierarchy is supported by invoking the legal distinction between the two types of officers: *BOAs* have fewer powers than police officers. Remarkably, the 'monopoly on violence' is also invoked to bolster this view. Many police officers claim they are the only ones allowed to use violence, therewith wilfully overlooking the range of coercive means at the disposal of municipal officers.

---

3.   Remarkably, other studies show that police officers often predominantly use 'serious crime' as the denominator of their work, thereby equally designating 'public safety tasks' as the responsibility of other authorities (Van Stokkom & Foekens, 2015).

Also the reputation and history of city wardens appears to have a large impact. "They haven't got enough quality there," a police officer states when asked if municipal officers can be compared to police officers. Some respondents question whether municipal officers are sufficiently trainable. Can they learn how to deal with youth gangs, a manager wonders,

> I bet there are some that are fit for these trainings, but there are a lot there that will have a tremendous difficulty trying to grasp the material. And then they will have to be able to apply it in practice as well.

Another neighbourhood manager adds, "If out of ten, two are capable, it would be a lot". Although some municipal officers are only too happy to do so, this should be seen as an unwelcome development. You need to keep a close eye on it, according to a police officer. The same applies to the contact with homeless people and alcoholics, as a police officer in Eindhoven states, "These are tough guys, tried and tested, if you send in these officers, you send them wet behind the ears. You need a solid, experienced neighbourhood police officer here, to give these guys sufficient counterbalance".

In summary, these respondents point out that municipal officers should be doing substantially different work – a form of disorder policing designated for non-police officers alone, for fundamental and economic, as well as hierarchical arguments. These also enable police officers to designate the police as a specialised occupation that is essentially different from municipal disorder policing. Police officers here capitalise on their status as a *core discipline*, that "bear[s] on issues of widespread interest and deep concerns on the part of the general population [and that] address[es] perennial problems that are of great importance to most of humanity" (Freidson, 2001: 161). This status is further accentuated rhetorically by police representatives. This is not only done to defend their unique status as a profession, to claim a "monopoly" over their discipline (*ibid.*: 199) or to strive for recognition of their work as 'crook catchers', but also to ward off other tasks. Consequently, municipal officers are presented as operating in a universe that exists parallel to that of police work, with little overlap between the two occupations.

3.2   *Strict division: municipal core tasks and 'quality of life' policing*

This emphasis on a sharp distinction between police and municipal officers is also expressed from the municipal point of view. Some municipal officers also use an argument of 'core tasks' and show the same tendency to highlight the unique characteristics of their work to rhetorically create a quintessential prototype of municipal disorder policing. Again fundamental arguments dominate this position.

The idea that municipal officers should do less police-like work forms the basis of this position. Performing tasks that are discarded by the police distracts from the municipal core tasks, these respondents state. If municipal officers were to perform heavier duties at all, it is only because they claim more work than is justified by their expertise and professional level. As a result, municipal officers are seen as an addition to the police at the most, with an independent line of work; they are a separate policing force with its own responsibilities.

One way of highlighting these essential characteristics is by contrasting them to previous tasks that are seen as work of a bygone time. The previous city wardens and their tasks have an important role in this respect, as they are seen as the type of officers that their recent successors are said to have left behind. As opposed to these city wardens – officers who are generally depicted as having a lack of power and a bad reputation – new municipal officers are capable of fining, have more powers and know better how to address non-compliant citizens. They know how to 'make a difference',

> You used to have those wardens, and they would walk through the city, and say: 'Sir or madam, would you please get off your bike here?' Then [citizens] would tell you to get lost, and there was nothing you could do. Now you can fine those people.[4]

These respondents stress the city surveillance agencies have been able to develop an independent working style, with their own approach and justification that is mainly associated with 'quality of life' issues. As explained in chapter 5, the Dutch term *leefbaarheid* originates in the seventies, but was introduced into municipal public safety policy in the 1990s. It seems sensible that municipalities use their own (new) personnel to control the issues that qualify as such, for instance dog litter, rubbish or parking hindrances.

In some cities such distinctive characteristics of municipal officers are specifically contrasted to police work. This is particularly common in the city of The Hague. The surveillance agency of this city has been reorganised thoroughly, implying a reorientation on its priorities of physical disorder (see chapter 5) and the decision to house The Hague's municipal officers at the city's police stations. Furthermore, police constables have been assigned as team coordinators. At the time of research this caused a lot of consternation among the workers. The idea of being managed by police constables led to the re-emergence of an old fear of regressing to "the police's postmen" (see chapter 5). As a result, many of The Hague's municipal officers opposed the transition vehemently by reference to the fear their priorities would be overrun.

The ensuing defence of municipal priorities and the maintenance of a strict distinction between municipal surveillance work and police work takes several forms. One of these is by highlighting the amount of their own work. "What we are doing right now is more than enough," a municipal officer says. Another way of defend-

---

4.   See also chapter 5.

ing municipal work is by fully defining it as concerning quality of life issues. Public safety issues are for the police to deal with. Another remarkable example of this allegiance to quality of life tasks is how street youth are looked upon. Although The Hague's municipal officers do seem to have a task in this respect, they highlight that they are only willing to deal with street youth as far as the trouble they cause can be seen as – again – quality of life issues. A municipal coordinator explains how this might work,

> When you come in parks where young people are causing a big mess, but who are in no way criminal, you could step up to these kids, have a chat, show your face. [So youngsters know that] these are the people that deal with quality of life. [They realise] 'Municipal officers can also fine us because we do not clean up our mess'.

For this reason – and not only in The Hague – many municipal officers oppose the expansion of powers and equipment. Such extra coercive powers are not needed, they state, when enforcing rules that concern dog dirt, for instance.

In effect, these respondents oppose the all too opportunistic reasoning of the police. Police forces might be short of human resources, but this should not lead to the use of equally scarce municipal officers for what are basically *police* priorities. Thus, representatives in municipal disorder policing seem to defend the boundaries of their domain by highlighting the fundamental status of their own occupation, and their own transcendental values of quality of life tasks (Freidson, 2001). In addition, they appear to oppose police respondents' stress on hierarchy and subservience. Instead, these municipal respondents highlight municipal disorder policing has developed into a parallel occupation, with its own distinct domain and related tasks. Remarkably, their legal status as 'Special Investigative Officers' is not seen by them as underwriting their subordinate position in the law enforcement hierarchy, but as proof of municipal officers being a professional group of policing officers that needs to be taken seriously. Thus like police officers, municipal officers draw their own boundaries, also based on fundamental and hierarchical grounds, albeit in their case as part of a new discipline that needs to defend itself against dominant police thinking (Freidson, 2001: 202).

Hence both police officers and municipal officers highlight their respective core tasks – 'catching crooks' or 'dealing with quality of life'. Both maintain there is a strict distinction between the two occupations, albeit for different reasons and with different interests. Police stay true to their mantra of catching crooks in order to legitimate their priorities and to define their occupation as a special profession that deals with perennial problems for which they deserve recognition. Municipal officers, for their part, are loyal to quality of life issues in order to reject police tasks and equally to underscore the uniqueness and professionalism of their occupation.

In effect, both sides of this perceived division in policing tasks are characterised by their obstinacy in holding on to these (mainly) principled definitions.

3.3   *No strict division: towards a new municipal police?*

The third and fourth positions oppose these strict divisions as they are less concerned with the principles of the distinction between the 'real police' and other enforcement officers. The third position is generally characterised by pragmatic, economic reasoning. Consequently, the respondents taking this position are convinced that the replacement of police work by municipal officers can go much further than has been mentioned before.

The rhetorical device of 'catching crooks' enables police officers to define many different tasks as 'minor', and thus as non-police work. Whereas the police officers described before might highlight the uniqueness of their work, others creatively appropriate the notion of 'quality of life' to designate some of their original responsibilities as municipal work. Municipal officers in Utrecht and Nijmegen for instance, often deal with homeless people. Especially in Nijmegen, as several respondents emphasise, this is done by defining these issues as 'quality of life', and therefore as not a police responsibility.

Other respondents are even more flexible about this sharing of tasks, and seem to fully embrace a distribution of tasks that is based on free market thinking (Freidson, 2001). They highlight for instance, that traffic controls keep the police from fighting real crime. "It's a shame to use capacity for things like that. Other people can do that," a police constable says. A manager adds, "maybe cheaper sounds a bit condescending, but it does play a role". Police capacity is stretched, he adds, and expertise should be reserved for areas where this is really needed. In some cases, the responsibilities of municipal officers are stretched further. A police team manager explains,

> First of all, we as the police tackle the upper segment, violence, burglaries, muggings, robberies and emergency calls. But there is a lot in between, from fraud to ordinary theft, shoplifting, pickpockets, we don't do that anymore, we don't have the time anymore […] I want the city surveillance agency and the police to get closer to each other in general. Now the municipality is only doing the lower part, and the police is only occupied with the upper segment, and there is a gap in between.

Consequently, the division of tasks between the police and the municipal city surveillance agencies is based mainly on economic thinking. Some literally speak of a 'market'. For instance a policeman says,

Public safety is a market, and if I were mayor […], I would start approaching the problem differently, and say: 'Ok, I've got a problem, but I don't have to call the police right away, maybe I
can solve this with municipal officers or private security officers'.

These respondents are less concerned with the principles of their profession than
those quoted in the previous sections. They simply state that the police have no
monopoly over police-like work, and thus counter occupational divisions of labour
in which police monopolise this specific domain (Freidson, 2001). For this matter,
the most important question in their view is whether municipal officers can also be
employed for 'heavier duties'. A Utrecht police officer for example, sees municipal
officers as a big advantage. The police is there to deal with "structural problems,"
he states, and they can transfer (*wegzetten*) the responsibility for impromptu incidents to the municipal city surveillance agency. Others even say that there is no
predefined limit, other than "that the municipality should not be working on the
criminal justice side of police work," as a police constable states. "All the things
that happen on a daily basis and are handled by the police could equally be dealt
with by municipal officers," such as the enforcement of traffic laws, minor traffic
violations and traffic controls, he adds. "All the hot stuff where no crime is
involved," is how an alderman puts it.

   Others see mainly opportunities for the temporary employment of municipal
officers. An employee of the city surveillance agency in The Hague mentions
escorting a demonstration and surveillance during concerts. In addition, several
people suggest municipal officers can also run night shifts, such as those done by
Utrecht's municipal officers described in the previous chapter. Another example is
using municipal officers more as the "eyes and ears" of the police. Some suggest
this can not only be done in the case of an increase in burglaries, but even for certain aspects of criminal investigation. "If a particular property needs to be
watched, a municipal officer could do that too, assuming he has been trained properly," a police officer in Tilburg says. In addition, neighbourhood work as it is tra-
ditionally done by local police officers can partially be adopted by municipal officers. A police officer calls this 'maintenance'. "A relatively quiet district can be covered easily by other enforcement officers as well, such as municipal officers, or
even private security […] You can have them do some general work, patrolling,
talking to residents". A Tilburg policy-maker even sees municipal officers eventually as "the lynchpin with neighbourhood citizen platforms, citizen councils,
neighbourhood councils. Much, much more as an equal counterpart of the neighbourhood police officer".

   As such, some respondents are proponents of a more radical replacement of
police work by municipal officers. The only criterion is that they are well-trained.
"If people are trained and screened well, it doesn't really matter if they work for
the police or the municipality," a respondent says. Likewise, powers and equipment can be expanded. A police officer states, "So that they are trained in such a

fashion they are allowed to do more than they do now". In principle, there is no objection to increase municipal officers' powers and thus to expand the domain in which these officers operate as replacement for the police. Some would connect these ambitions with the term 'municipal police'. A manager from the city of Tilburg says, "Don't be so rigid about that dog litter". These officers could do so much more, but they are simply neglected by their partners due to prejudice about their professional level, or because municipal officers themselves are too modest.

Hence, this plural policing position is also embraced with reference to other types of arguments mentioned above. Some municipal officers seem eager for more tasks to prove themselves as fully professional policing officers in contrast to previous city wardens. As such, occupational pride and a need for recognition might have conflicting effects. Instead of an obstinate allegiance to 'quality of life' core tasks, defending the fragility of their newfound occupational identity, officers here aim for more tasks as a way to prove themselves and to shed the past, or as part of a preference to do work with a tougher and more serious reputation (see chapter 8). Previous chapters have shown plenty of examples of municipal officers who appear to be ready for more tasks (see for instance chapters 7 and 8). In fact, for many of them the legal possibilities given to BOAs are seen as limitations, hindering a further expansion of municipal officers' tasks. They loathe their limited powers, such as this municipal officer in Tilburg,

> We can now fine people for dogs. But often we see people sitting in their cars calling while driving. Then I'm itching to do something. Here, in the city centre, I'm waiting for the traffic lights sometimes, loads of people ignore those red signs. It really annoys me.

Often they can be heard to lament the alleged negative impact this has on the authority they have among the public. Another officer also relates how he is passed while waiting at a red light – "people just pass you by, laughing". In addition, some police officers believe that municipal officers can deal with a wider range of issues because this enables police officers to do other things. As such, the first position and this position seem alike, with the difference that police officers in this case are less concerned about the principle of the limits of their profession.

This view on respective work domains indicates how municipal officers and police officers agree on an expansion of municipal officers' tasks, while using different arguments. The cases of Rotterdam and Utrecht, as described in the previous chapter, provide good examples of this. In both cities police officers, who claim that they have too much to do, are welcoming eager municipal officers who are willing to prove themselves and both sides of the divide form a temporary coalition. In contrast to the previous positions, this agreement between different officers seems to be informed more by pragmatism, than by an obstinate allegiance to 'traditional' tasks. In this case, municipal officers and police officers are seen as a part of the same policing family and tasks can and should be transferred more easily from one organisation to the other.

3.4   *No strict division: the police should do all disorder policing*

The fourth and final position discussed here also refrains from drawing a strict distinction between both occupations. However, instead of seeing municipal officers as suitable for a wider variety of police tasks, it holds the view that it is the police that should do more. Consequently, respondents in support of this position see the policing of minor disorder as a traditional police responsibility that has unfortunately been ceded to others. This unique view of the division between the two professions can be found among a relatively small group of police officers.

These officers claim the introduction of municipal officers is due to doubtful and regrettable choices made by the police in the past; doubtful, because the advent of municipal officers impacts negatively on police officers' own position in neighbourhoods and on the legitimacy of the police. This view taps into both fundamental and hierarchical argumentations about designated tasks for specific professions. A police officer in Nijmegen for example, points out how he used to do these supposedly minor tasks, but was constrained to let them go,

> We haven't been doing this part of the police job for a long, long time, because we didn't have the time for it, and also because some of my colleagues see it as inferior work. But when I was a neighbourhood police officer [...] and I constantly had trouble with some rubbish bag, torn apart [...], I would go through it too [in search of an address], because I wanted to catch that jackass. So in that sense, these guys are replacing us here.

Respondents who subscribe to this idea are often concerned about the pluralisation of policing. A coordinator of a city surveillance agency states,

> That which the police leave behind, will be automatically seen as a job for municipal officers. [...] So eventually you'll get the reinvention of the municipal police. And maybe the VNG[5] says they don't want it, but they don't put their money where their mouth is. And the same goes for the minister, saying: 'police, focus on criminal investigation and a tough approach'. This is happening right now. And in practice, it can't be reversed anymore.

A policeman states that many of his colleagues are acting too much on the principle of core tasks. The reason the police would not want to deal with minor forms of disorder is caused by rigidity – the refusal to be managed by municipalities. "Because I deal with murder and homicide, not with those shitty rubbish bags," he summarises the ideas of his colleagues.

---

5.   VNG stands for *Vereniging van Nederlandse Gemeenten*: the association of Dutch municipalities.

These respondents state that this stance leads to a loss of the police's connection with everyday life in neighbourhoods and of police legitimacy in the eyes of citizens. "Criminal investigation is important, sure, but what happens in those neighbourhoods has basically to do with matters of quality of life," a civil servant from Nijmegen states. As such, many of these officers do not really see the difference between quality of life and public safety issues; these matters are closely related, at least in the eyes of neighbourhood residents. Likewise, some think any form of law enforcement should be done solely by the police, as they not only know best how to address people, but to keep all forms of enforcement in one organisation also prevents differences in performance.

As a result, municipal officers are looked upon in somewhat ambiguous ways. On the one hand, the need for municipal officers is regretted, as it is police work they are doing. As such, they are seen as a second best solution. "It would not worry me if all of these municipal officers were policemen," a municipal manager adds. Others argue the police should also be out on the streets for general surveillance and should equally be approachable for neighbourhood residents. On the other hand, many applaud the fact that at least there are officers who are willing to concern themselves with these forms of disorder.

The same ambiguity can be heard in more economic arguments. The money for municipal officers would be better spent on the police, a police officer states, but unfortunately the budgets in his city are just not allocated in such a way,

> They should've had a decent conversation with the police organisation. If they would've told [the police], 'here's [a large amount of money]', of course the police would have said, 'yes please, of course we will deal with those issues too'.

In addition, people who defend this position state that municipal officers may do the things from which the police have drifted away. As a Nijmegen police officer puts it: "If the police do not live up to the citizens' expectations, you should be happy with anything that can support you".

These respondents express the view that the police should be very cautious not to lose more credibility by a further withdrawal from public spaces. The police should also be visible and – among other things – focus on general surveillance in public spaces. "That entails walking beats, going around, cycle through the neighbourhood," a municipal official from Nijmegen states. Moreover, "a good police officer should have a feeling for his neighbourhood," as a manager at The Hague's city surveillance agency puts it. Therefore, surveillance in public spaces can never be fully outsourced to municipal officials. A manager in the same city says, "You have to get to know your neighbourhood. [...] Get a feel for the area. Go there, walk around and visit those places".

Thus, although these respondents see municipal officers as a somewhat regrettable supplement to the police, they acknowledge the plural policing reality of a shared domain of surveillance and law enforcement in public spaces.[6] In other words, they long for a traditional police profile as monopolistic guardians of law and order, but at the same time see municipal officers as 'junior partners', or as part of the same policing family.[7] Respondents expressing this view are mostly experienced neighbourhood police officers who have witnessed the various changes in the police organisation and prioritisation.

4   CONCLUSIONS

This chapter started with the observation that the relations between regular police officers and municipal officers play a vital role on all levels of analysis discussed hitherto, demanding a more comprehensive discussion. In what followed, occupations have been discussed as actors instead of stable functionalist domains that actively engage in defining respective tasks and strife over domains and responsibilities (Larson, 1977; Macdonald, 1995). To understand the dynamics of this strife and negotiation, three different types of argumentation were introduced in the second section and related to three different perspectives on divisions of labour as they are proposed by Freidson (2001).

   In the extensive third section four positions were discussed. Two of these stress the unique characteristics and values of the respective occupations, one by repeating the mantra that the police should be catching crooks, the other by stressing municipal officers are just there for quality of life issues. In contrast to this, the third and fourth positions highlight the common ground of the two occupations. The third position sees the division between the police and municipal officers as highly flexible and maintains that municipal officers should perform more police-like work, whereas the fourth also acknowledges the similarities, but wants police officers to deal with all disorder issues.

In conclusion, this chapter has shown that perspectives on the work domains of municipal and police officers, for an important part, depend on the struggle between a dominant occupation and the 'newcomer'.

   Another way of seeing the hitherto discussed positions is by highlighting them either as protective or as expansive positions. In this respect, the first two positions can be characterised as being protective, defending a strict division between the two occupational groups, often with reference to alleged distinctive characteristics and mostly based on fundamental arguments. In these positions, respondents dig in their heels, holding on to the characteristics of their occupations. As such, the professionalism described here differs from frontline logic in chapter 6. Frontline

---

6.   This same position can be found among Dutch mayors. Although they are generally content with 'their own personnel' (see also chapter 6), these mayors generally seem to think the work of these municipal officers should be done by police officers (Terpstra, Foekens & Van Stokkom, 2015).

7.   The notion of 'junior partners' is elsewhere used for private security officers (Button, 2002).

logic as a specific mode of local decision making gives prominence to practical knowledge, the 'short lines' between various professionals and has a highly pragmatic nature. By contrast, the dominance of an occupational division of labour discussed here refers to the emphasis on unique professional and transcendental values, implying social closure (Freidson, 2001), instead of the rapprochement discussed in chapter 6. In this respect, the police occupation still seems to exert a claim of privilege, which "consists in holding a monopoly over the exclusive right to perform a particular kind of work in the marketplace" (Freidson, 2001: 198).

Whereas Freidson understands this monopoly (or 'social closure') mainly in relation to consumers, the above text suggests social closure might well apply also to the distinction *between* these two occupations. As such, both occupations are involved in their own *professional project* (Larson, 1977). However, this process is not necessarily negative. Following Freidson, one could also see this formation of boundaries serving the formation of "a body of formal knowledge and skill, or discipline" (*ibid.*: 202), and "social closure is vital for the work of professions to survive as distinct disciplines" (*ibid.*). In yet other words, the attachment to such transcendent values as 'catching crooks' or 'quality of life tasks' gives these occupations meaning and justifies their position and independence.

As opposed to this, the third and fourth positions are generally informed by a view that proposes a more expansive stance. Highlighting the shared ground between both types of officers, the possibility of a more market driven distribution of tasks is explored. In the third position this results in the belief of proactively employing municipal officers for more police-like work. The fourth position adds to this expansive view, albeit in this case proposing to let police deal with more disorder issues.[8] For one thing, such expansive positions seem to be more susceptible to outside demands and make it easier to adapt policing supply to such demands. Again following Freidson's analysis of professionalism, these expansive positions might mean that the formation and strengthening of an independent body of knowledge is hampered. Likewise, replicating what police officers holding the fourth position have said, it appears that the profound division of policing tasks and other policing occupations could impact negatively on their legitimacy as a distinct discipline.

In this respect, both the protective and the expansive positions have their own particular down-sides. Professions that are self-absorbed with their own tasks could fail to acknowledge outside needs. In other words, a strong inward focus on their own professional project overlooks the consequences of a further division of policing, a full retreat of the police to core tasks and a strict and somewhat artificial allegiance to quality of life tasks by municipal officers. In contrast to this, the last two positions invite other reflections. An overt eagerness to take on more and more tasks could hamper professional work performance and the development of an

---

8.   This position brings to mind one of the scenario's presented by Van Stokkom and Foekens (2015).

independent profession. Striving for ever new responsibilities might stand in the way of structural training and practice, and the acquirement of a "body of shared knowledge" (Abbott, 1988). This latter consideration is all the more relevant as the third position described here might well become the most dominant one. The developments in municipal disorder policing point to a likely further replacement of police officers by municipal officers on tasks such as dealing with night life, street youth, a large range of traffic offences, and intensified contacts with citizens (see also Van Stokkom & Foekens, 2015).

CONCLUSIONS

The aim of this study was to develop a better understanding of Dutch municipal disorder policing in its societal, organisational and professional context. By adopting a multi-level approach and involving diverse stakeholders, the resulting impression is that of a fragmented occupation that is subject to various interests and expectations. For one part it is the canvas upon which societal changes are projected; for instance, a growth in feelings of insecurity, or ideas about the erosion of collective norms. For another part, it might be the battle ground of local stakeholders as diverse as managers, frontline professionals and politicians, each with their own views, interests and ways of decision making. For yet another part, it is one of the prime areas in which changes in policing come to the surface and various ideas about policing are made manifest.

This concluding chapter reveals dominant factors and perspectives by discussing and reflecting on the findings. This is done in four consecutive sections. Section 1 serves as an overview of the most important findings and as an introduction to the sections that follow. In section 2 these findings are discussed in depth – the concluding thoughts on dominant developments in municipal disorder policing. Next, section 3 further reflects on these conclusions by referring back to several sociological interpretations that were presented in chapter 3. The last section offers a final discussion.

1   FINDINGS: AN OVERVIEW

The development of municipal disorder policing

Municipal disorder policing is a relatively new profession with a short, specific history that has a large impact on contemporary goals and views. Chapter 5 described this development. The first forms of municipal disorder policing in the Netherlands should be seen as part of a nation-wide focus on crime prevention. At the end of the 1980s, city wardens were introduced after the Roethof Committee had urged a new approach to the high level of petty crime in Dutch society. Reducing the opportunities for such crimes was a then dominant approach and thus these first wardens were mainly employed as basic uniformed surveillance, as guardians to reduce the opportunities for vandalism, bicycle theft, shop lifting, etcetera.

The popularity of situational crime prevention in policy is but one of the factors that explains how city wardens developed. The rapid spread of projects for city wardens in the 1990's is as much the result of the availability of unemployment arrangements. Hence, the wish for 'more eyes on the streets' appeared to be at least as important as providing unemployed people with a job. However, the prominence of these work reintegration goals hindered a clear definition of disorder policing goals. At the same time, the wardens' subordination to the police hampered their own unambiguous occupational identity; city wardens were simply often employed to do surveillance chores that the police deemed unworthy of their attention.

A first substantial change in early municipal disorder policing came in the first years of the 21st century. In all municipalities in this study wardens were merged into new city surveillance agencies and the emphasis in municipal disorder policing shifted to firmer and tougher forms of law enforcement – 'making a difference' by imposing sanctions. This shift in approach, to a certain extent, can be attributed to a national political urge for strict enforcement and less leniency. Other factors which contributed to this shift concerned new ways of measuring citizens' annoyances and feelings of insecurity, and the Dutch police's tendency to focus on 'core tasks'. At the same time, the budget cuts for unemployment benefit schemes forced municipalities to discuss the financing of city wardens. These developments contributed to the establishment of municipal city surveillance agencies and a beginning was made to attract new officers who were expected to fine (known as *BOAs*). The emphasis on law enforcement and the quest for occupational pride and a new occupational identity developed hand in hand.

In recent years these enforcement ambitions have been tempered. The city surveillance agencies have reconsidered their tasks and strategies. By and large this has led to a (re)orientation on issues of physical disorder, such as littering, unleashed dogs or parking violations. In addition, and in contrast to the strict targets of fining of the preceding years, behavioural compliance has come to determine disorder policing approaches. Finally, all municipal departments have turned to some form of citizen oriented policing, implying that 'minor annoyances' and residents' concerns are given prominence in the work of municipal officers.

Local decision making

In chapter 6 the analysis shifted to a meso level, thereby showing that disorder policing developments are as much the result of municipal policies and local stakeholders as of national policies. Three different 'logics' determine decision making at this municipal level.

First, decisions might be the result of political interests in disorder policing. On the one hand a classic form of political decision making generally concerns specific formative moments with regard to city surveillance agencies. On the other hand, political decisions on disorder policing at times are stimulated by close contact between the local administration and particular citizen groups. Likewise, the special interests of mayors in 'their own' enforcement workers play a large role here, especially where the police tend to withdraw from minor disorder issues. Such political interference often defines the work of municipal officers as a flexibly employable form of disorder policing.

Second, local decisions might also be under the strong influence of managerial logic. Senior managers in particular decide on disorder policing by using various means of measurement that allow them to objectify disorder issues, such as quality of life monitors or residents' reports. At the same time these managers appear to realize that citizens' opinions about quality of life are but to a limited extent related to the deployment of municipal officers. Thus, they do not use monitors and reports as performance measurement in retrospect, but as 'pre performance measurement' to select the hotspots where officers are probably most useful. This way of thinking is not confined to managers. Some municipal officers are equally dedicated to such figures and reports.

Finally, decisions might also be the result of frontline logic when disorder policing is decided upon through everyday insights and ideas of municipal officers and their operational coordinators. Instead of embracing top-down assignments, frontline professionals might equally highlight the worth of their own observations, or their contacts with residents and other frontline professionals. Obviously, such frontline notions could lead to conflicts with stakeholders who attach more value to the measurable output mentioned above.

These different approaches to which problems should be tackled and how, result in conflicts and tensions between stakeholders. For instance, municipal officers' dedication to formal assignments and citizens' reports might lead to frustration among partners who see this managerial approach as detached from neighbourhood realities. Equally, managers and frontline professionals criticize political interference as it draws attention away from their own assessments.

Views of professionals

Chapter 7 further scrutinised the ideas of municipal officers. Their reflections may be divided into two segments – what they see as their prime responsibilities and what they see as the most appropriate approach to disorderly behaviour.

Regarding their responsibilities, certain notions are strongly represented in any and all reflections of municipal officers. The most prominent of these is the idea of citizens' annoyances. However, the explanation of how these annoyances should inform their work differs widely among officers. This results in large differences in work style. Some directly interact with residents to find out what bothers them the most, whereas others embrace managerial assignments. Some look for coordination and collaboration with other neighbourhood professionals about these issues ('co-creational neighbourhood policing'), and yet others have a broader perspective, picking up any issue of disorder they come across during their shifts (referred to here as 'street policing').

This divergence also applies to officers' views on non-compliant citizens. Most officers see a respectable and decent treatment (*bejegening*) of non-compliant citizens as highly important. Some expand this to the context of a rule infringement; not every infringement deserves the same response. In this respect the notion of 'discretionary autonomy' plays a prominent part in the discourse of these professionals. Yet other professionals are more prone to consistent law enforcement, and for different reasons. They might value their assignments, might believe consistent fining sends a clear message that certain behaviour will not be tolerated, or they believe strict law enforcement is the only answer for certain 'target groups'.[1]

To sum up, municipal officers have developed into a new profession and have learned to determine their chief responsibilities and the best approaches to non-compliant citizens. Although these officers are typical street level bureaucrats whose diversity of views brings to mind the variety in approaches of regular police officers, some elements appear to be characteristic for their work. The most prominent of these is the combination of a focus on residents' concerns and the occasional (but unmistakable) urge for strict enforcement, and the conflicts that could arise between these two views.

Hotspots

After having discussed municipal disorder policing on various levels, chapter 8 presented two case studies that show how various 'logics' of local decision making could reinforce each other. In two cases of policing 'target groups' – street youth in the first case, and drug dealers, drug users and homeless people in the second case – new municipal policy was shown to be the result of various factors. Not only did the political focus on the grievances of a group of residents play a large role, also coordinators' ambitions to display the vigour of their officers, a managerial focus on control and measurement, and the refusal of the police to increase their efforts were of vital importance.

As a result, frontline professionals are more tightly controlled and steered, both through measurement tools, stricter role definitions and more subject to the authority of municipal managers. This confines their work, for an important part, to hotspots and the deterring of the 'target group members' they find there.

---

1.   A category that is comparable to what Reiner (2010) calls 'police property'.

Although quite a few professionals agree with this harsh approach to target groups, frontline professionals' experiences and views also conflict with their assignments, ranging from sheer boredom at the sight of empty hotspots, to frustration at the assignments they get, to unease about the policy of strict enforcement. As such, these cases show that the variety of work styles and professionals' views discussed in chapter 7 are under pressure in these new policies.

Strife over work domains

The final empirical chapter 9 dealt with the relations between police officers and municipal officers. It showed that municipal officers' emphasis on specific aspects of their work is also greatly dependent on how they perceive their relations with the regular police. This chapter showed that these two occupations do not have stable, well-defined work domains, but that municipal officers and police officers strive about definitions of goals and (core) tasks, and thereby disorder policing itself.

Four positions in this strife were discerned, either highlighting the differences or the similarities between the two occupations. On the one hand, both municipal and police officers are prone to defend the uniqueness of their own profession by highlighting respective core tasks – 'catching crooks' in the case of police officers (position 1) and 'quality of life issues' in the case of municipal officers (position 2). On the other hand, two other positions maintain a broader view of their respective tasks. A third position thus sees municipal officers as capable of performing more police-like work, whereas a fourth position maintains (conversely) that the police should actually do all disorder policing.

2   A NEW PROFESSION DEALING WITH DISORDER

Throughout these findings several characteristics of municipal disorder policing stand out. First of all, the goals of city surveillance agencies and the work carried out by municipal officers, for an important part, can be seen as typical for a newly evolving profession. In that respect, municipal officers are still developing their own professional domain and have to cope with the reputation of alleged unprofessional predecessors. These aspects will be discussed in more detail in subsection 1. Second, Dutch municipalities shape disorder policing with a clear preference for specific goals and strategies. These are discussed in subsections 2, 3, and 4.

2.1   *A new profession and its quest for organised autonomy*

The initial decision to involve long term unemployed people for surveillance tasks has cast a long shadow over municipal disorder policing, if not in professional deficiencies, then in reputation. The early city wardens were generally only hired for their uniformed presence, and work reintegration was more important than public safety goals. Lacking a history as a surveillance profession and an associated "body of shared knowledge" (Abbott, 1988), these officers could hardly be called a profession at all. It is this image that set the stage for the phases to come. Municipal officers' values and preferences up to this day are haunted by the reputation of 'living dolls' and 'uniformed road barriers'. Consequently, policies emphasising more and tougher law enforcement at the beginning of the 2000s were not only the result of political demands. Municipal managers' urge to make a complete break with the past and to prove the usefulness of the new municipal agencies should not be overlooked as reasons to claim more powers and effectuate enforcement strategies.

Thus dominant views in the practice of municipal disorder policing, for an important part, can be understood as the result of a new occupation's striving for organised autonomy (chapter 9; Freidson, 1971). These officers, their managers and coordinators have had to carve out their own habitat in the policing domain, prove themselves to be a valuable policing occupation and combat a negative reputation. The resulting self-awareness and occupational pride impact heavily on this new profession and how it has professionalised over the years. Moreover, successive phases in the development of municipal disorder policing can also be seen through this lens of an evolving new profession. If the urge to 'make a difference' can be explained as part of a self-assertive shedding of the past, the subsequent emphasis on behavioural compliance for its part can be seen as countering the reputation of 'fine-hunting officers'.

This process of an evolving occupational identity can also be framed in terms of *supply* and *demand* (chapter 7; see also Bittner, 1970). Those involved in municipal disorder policing became increasingly aware that they could decide autonomously on their supply of policing without merely focussing on external demands of citizens reporting disorder. As such, municipal disorder policing became more of a proper profession over the years, a new occupational group in which officers developed their own professional habitat, using their own knowledge and expertise in response to citizens' demands (Freidson, 2001).

However, this growing consciousness of independence as a new policing profession cannot be considered as a uniform and evolutionary succession of different stages. The preceding chapters discussed several practices that show that professional autonomy played only a minor role (and even was given up) or – by contrast – was given an exaggerated role. On the one hand, cases have been discussed in which disorder policing is uncritically defined by the demands of citizens. In these cases officers are forced to comply with requests by citizens as consumers without further consideration. Chapters 6 and 8 provided examples of cases of hotspot policing in which officers' judgment was overruled by managerial and political decision makers and officers were simply expected to respond to citizens' wishes.[2] On the other hand, municipal officers might be strongly focused on their own internal concerns and disregard external demands. Officers and coordinators at times are still keen to prove that they are a valuable profession. It can partly explain the tendency to look for new, police-like tasks (chapters 8 and 9), and the tendency to claim typical municipal surveillance work in contrast to the domain of the regular police.

In effect, municipal disorder policing can only be understood as part of a professional project in which the use of a specific discourse also functions to provide autonomy to occupations (Larson, 1977, see also chapter 9). As such, terms such as *leefbaarheid* ('quality of life') and *kleine ergernissen* ('minor annoyances'), or *veiligheid* ('public safety') and *boeven vangen* ('catching crooks') might function primarily as occupational projections onto reality, reflecting the urge of professionals to carve out their own work domain (see further section 4).

2.2   *Citizens' concerns at a central position?*

From the outset citizens' concerns have been at the core of municipal efforts to fight disorder. Early city wardens focused on civic fear and discontent caused by an abundance of petty crimes (chapter 5). Later on, the emphasis shifted to minor annoyances. Thereby the needs, demands and fears of citizens *directly* informed the work of these officers. As stated before, this was increased by the growing use of new means of measurement, giving municipalities more information about what bothered residents the most. In addition, terms that captured civic concerns – such as *leefbaarheid* ('quality of life') or of *schoon, heel en veilig* ('clean, intact and safe') – started to dominate municipal policies during the 1990s.

More recent policies are also imbued with citizens' concerns. Municipal policies prioritise common annoyances and residents are sometimes given the opportunity to define directly which disorder problems should be dealt with. As such, municipal disorder policing is reminiscent of forms of community policing that involve citizens in defining problems, or that expand the responsibilities of officers (chapter 3; Herbert, 2001; Skogan, 2006). In specific local projects residents are involved in identifying problems and agenda setting, such as the citizen participation project in Eindhoven, described in chapter 6, or similar projects such as the *Buurt bestuurt* (the neighbourhood governs) in several other cities. However, these forms of citizen participation are used mostly to collect reports and to stimulate the 'eyes and ears'-function of the citizenry, not to bolster informal social control.

In this respect, not the reinvestment in citizenship or social cohesion, but residents' concerns are given prominence. That is, *without* a necessary relation to 'collective efficacy' (Sampson, Raudenbusch & Earls, 1997; Taylor, 2006). Dutch munic-

---

2.   Although some would also see the execution of assignments as a trademark of professionalism.

ipal disorder policing is often informed by fairly straightforward ideas of serving residents' needs, leaving out *why* it might be important to address minor rule infringements. Moreover, this focus on citizens' concerns in many cases is particularly framed in the new public management discourse that depicts the citizen as a 'customer'. Although individual officers might criticize managerial tools, (pre-)performance management and New Public Management-style analyses appear to be important. Apparently, the objectification of disorder in managerial instruments provides strong and convincing proof of what matters the most.

A direct consequence of this way of dealing with citizens' concerns is that 'policing the figures' becomes a goal in itself. This is a typical example of goal displacement (Merton, 1968): quality of life indicators and report figures are administrative abstractions of neighbourhood (dis)order, but quite often disorder policing itself becomes defined by these abstractions. Hence individual contacts with citizens reporting issues matter less than aggregated patterns of complaints and disorder policing becomes synonymous with responding to citizens' reports on an aggregated and abstract level. As a result, many respondents claim that city surveillance agencies are becoming alienated from the very same citizen they regard so highly.

2.3   *Pragmatic management of disorderly behaviour*

Although municipal officers have largely changed from city wardens to professional enforcement officers, the basic assumptions of their preventive approaches have not. The idea that disorder is the result of situational opportunities and lack of control remains highly influential. It is assumed that people behave in a disorderly fashion, ranging from putting their household waste outside too early, to street youth hanging around and causing noise, because nobody effectively watches them and there is nothing or nobody to prevent them from acting in a disorderly manner.

What did change is the way that situational interventions are framed. Chapter 5 described how departments for surveillance now aim for behavioural compliance. A term that says it all – rule infringements are seen as behavioural deviations that can be prevented by influencing the choices of those who commit them. In their own accounts of their work municipal officers also emphasise that it is important to respond properly to non-compliant citizens, stimulating behaviour in various ways and regulating behaviour by 'decent treatment' (chapter 7). This suggests that the management of disorderly behaviour is generally deemed more important than only giving fines to citizens.

However, municipal disorder policing is largely devoid of ambitions about structurally altering the views of non-compliant citizens. Hence merely the situational opportunities and temptations, not the beliefs of non-compliant citizens are targeted. In yet other words, and adding to the previous section, neither informal social control, nor the beliefs of those that break the rules appear to play a prominent role in municipal disorder policing (save the ideas of some individual officers). What is left is a pragmatic and precautionary focus on a range of behavioural interventions, depending on the situational circumstances on the spot. Often this implies officers aim at 'solving problems by talking'.

On the surface, this image seems to be at odds with trends of strict law enforcement that have been discussed throughout this study. As noted, these trends can often be related to a turn in Dutch national policy in the beginning of the 2000s (Ministry of the Interior and Ministry of Justice, 2002; cf. chapters 2 and 5). At that time the idea of setting clear limits and being harsh on minor rule infringements – in a zero tolerance style – became fashionable, but as noted above the urge for strict enforcement was also stimulated by the rising professionalism of a new occupational group that feels it has to prove itself. Recent varieties of strict enforcement – as discussed in chapter 8 – are often focused on particular localities and target groups. However, on closer inspection these varieties of strict enforcement do not differ qualitatively from the approaches of behavioural management discussed above, although these interventions are mainly confined to deterrent options. Moreover, these varieties can be seen as extreme examples of service provision in which municipalities respond to continued reporting by a group of residents, often encouraged by the attention paid to them by political players.

2.4   Hotspot policing

The prominence of service provision and a down to earth situational approach might also explain the popularity of hotspot policing. The (rhetorical) claims that disorder policing is meant to close the gap between local government and neighbourhood residents, have meant that in practice those areas where people report the most complaints enjoy priority. Even the participation projects are less about building trust between officers and residents than they are about instrumentally collecting more reports (cf. Terpstra, 2016). Hotspot policing basically enables providing service to those areas with most demands. Moreover, hotspot policing provides an opportunity to adapt flexibly the investment of policing capacity based on what might work best in each situation. By sheer uniformed presence, by fining as a means of deterrence or by warning as another tactic to prevent disorderly behaviour, the hotspot policing discussed here appears devoid of ambitions to structurally change citizens' behaviour for the better. Likewise, harsher approaches to rule infringements are merely meant as disincentives.

This hotspot approach is further encouraged by the prominence of managerial logic described above. Those aspects of disorder that can be counted (literally) are given prominence over less measurable aspects (cf. Pollitt, 1993). Moreover, hotspot thinking is strengthened by political logic in focusing on the grievances of residents, directing attention to places with the highest incidences of burglaries, youths hanging around or junkies.[3] Although these views have found their way straight into the views of a sizeable share of the municipal officers (chapter 7), this confinement of frontline work to strict requests and targets calls into question whether municipal officers have sufficient room to shape their work according to their personal (frontline) views and experiences. In section 4 this issue will be addressed more extensively.

In summary, Dutch municipal disorder policing for the greater part defies categorisation in the policing strategies discussed in chapter 2. Although some characteristics of the broken windows theory and community policing can be noted in the policies and practices of city surveillance agencies, strengthening informal social control, nor zero tolerance style policing as done in Giuliani's New York are relevant in the context of Dutch municipal disorder policing. Dutch municipalities appear to give disorder policing their own particular twist. If there is one strategy that does appear to have a strong influence however, it is situational crime prevention. Theories and assumptions of opportunity reduction have been of constant relevance for the practice of municipal disorder policing, be it in terms of situational disincentives to prevent pretty crimes, or more elaborate strategies of behavioural compliance.

3   INTERPRETING MUNICIPAL DISORDER POLICING

After having discussed municipal disorder policing as a new profession with specific strategies and goals, this section interprets these developments against the background of social, political and cultural changes. It does so by referring to the four sociological interpretations discussed in chapter 3. The first interpretation presented here is a benevolent reading, seeing municipal disorder policing as a response to the general disappearance of informal social control and rooted in concerns about 'The Citizen' *in general*. In contrast to this, the second, sceptical interpretation links municipal disorder policing to the interests of a specific group of complaining citizens who know how to influence the local government. The other two interpretations discuss municipal disorder policing as rooted in governmental concerns (instead of those of citizens). The third interpretation claims that disorder policing should be seen as a state attempt at regaining symbolic authority, whereas

---

3.   In some cases, frontline logic appears to be claimed as part of a political endeavor, such as in Rotterdam's regime change in public safety policy (Tops, 2007; see also chapter 2). The difference here seems to lie in the political prioritising (and even marketing) of frontline action in Rotterdam, often based on temporal or confined integral projects and meant to address notorious hotspots, versus frontline *logic* described here, that seems to be characterised by a more spontaneous dynamic between various professionals that 'find each other' in their common concerns, that 'speak the same language' and address issues through 'short lines'.

the fourth interpretation claims that disorder policing is part of a governmental focus on control and risk reduction.

3.1   *Bolstering informal social control?*

The descriptions above conjure up a rather pragmatic image of municipalities' involvement with residents, as their interaction with citizens appears to boil down to responding to reports and investing in behavioural regulation. Yet there might be more behind this seemingly shallow focus on citizens' reports – a concern about neighbourhood decline and a common diagnosis of its root causes.

Firstly, some municipal politicians and managers appear to worry about profound problems beneath citizens' concerns. In Nijmegen for instance, respondents refer to worried citizens who felt abandoned by the police and the local government. In The Hague municipal policy for the new city surveillance agency is informed by concerns about neighbourhood decline. Feelings of security among citizens also played (and still play) an important role. Increased monitoring and measuring residents' concerns and their feelings of insecurity result in a claim that addressing antisocial behaviour and related annoyances is of importance to keep public places 'liveable' and inviting, making sure that the streets are safe enough to attract visitors and customers. Secondly, municipalities agree in their diagnosis of the causes for neighbourhood decline – the disappearance of informal social control and the general erosion of social cohesion. This brings to mind Jane Jacobs' work about the decline of social interaction in urban landscapes and the absence of 'eyes on the streets' (although she blames urban planning for it; cf. Jacobs, 1962).

Hence early forms of municipal disorder policing by city wardens were part of the answer to these urban and social changes. These officers were meant to be new 'eyes on the streets', informed by worries about the decline in public spaces. In addition, in a few specific, emblematic cases, problems, for instance with drug dealers and users contributed to the idea that norms were eroding and the 'publicness' of public spaces was lost (cf. Lyes, 2015). Thus, comparable to Jacobs' seemingly regretful analysis of urban change, some respondents bring to mind 'the good old days' in which people used to correct each other (Zukin, 2010; cf. Ranasinghe, 2012). Likewise, recent policies in cities like Nijmegen and Rotterdam aim at officers who 'know and are known' locally, not only to collect more reports, but ideally to get a better understanding of the neighbourhoods they patrol, at times even suggesting stimulating informal social control by using 'familiar faces'.

In general however, such ideas about bolstering social cohesion or informal social control appear to be more of a rhetorical exception in Dutch municipal disorder policing. Although these ideas might have an impact on public safety policies of some municipalities (Van Houdt & Schinkel, 2014), citizens' concerns mostly appear to matter in themselves, and not because communities need to be strengthened or residents are expected to take social control into their own hands.[4] The reasons for this prominence of citizens' concerns are varied and rather hard to discern in a discourse that merely states that 'the citizen should be listened to'. These may be related to consumerist ideas of serving citizens' needs, to democratic beliefs that citizens must be given the opportunity to partake in local decision making, or to a sheer urge for measurability. In any case, municipal officers and managers accept the erosion of collective norms, sometimes resignedly, and conclude that informal order is something from the past. Officers do not have the ambition to restore that order, they merely 'fill the vacancy' and their interventions in public spaces are a long shot from providing the opportunity for 'strangers to meet' or for a 'sidewalk ballet' (Jacobs, 1962).[5]

3.2   *Reclaiming public spaces as exclusivist practice?*

Other findings in this study oppose a benevolent interpretation altogether and point to the more exclusivist tendencies in disorder policing. This particularly applies to forms of law enforcement that deal with specific 'target groups'. The policing of street youth or homeless people for instance, is generally not accompanied by punitive or disciplinary intentions, or by attempts at correcting behaviour. These practices can be simply considered as an 'aesthetic removal'.[6] The creative and expansive application of powers by municipal officers further supports such exclusivist tendencies. In this respect, denouncing hanging around in doorways and 'fixing target groups up with a fine' bring to mind what has been said about 'defining deviancy up' and the 'anti-social behaviour agenda' in chapter 3. In addition to such target group policing, more general questions can be raised about municipalities' relations with citizens. The reports and quality of life scans mentioned as important managerial instruments restrict neighbourhood order and disorder to a narrow interpretation as only those familiar with the process of reporting are heard. This emphasis on reporting strips disorder of a context that might provide more understanding of the causes of disruptive conduct, such as underlying conflicts, intolerance or bad-temperedness of those who complain (see also section 4).

---

4.   This in fact is a stance that is reminiscent of Dutch varieties of community policing (Terpstra, 2008b, cf. chapter 2). As such, these findings contradict the advent of a 'participation society' or a 'do-it-yourself democracy' (Van de Wijdeven, 2012).

5.   If there is any indication of municipal officers acting as officers that provide opportunities for carefree interaction – as Jacobs would have it – it would be in the notion of being a host in public spaces. However, this idea of 'hosting' is under pressure in times when municipal officers are keen to assert themselves as proper policing officers and are eager for new and more tasks that are allegedly more serious (chapter 9).

6.   See also Walby & Lippert (2011) on the dispersal of homeless people by conservation officers in Ottawa, Canada (cf. Allen & Crookes, 2009; Becket & Herbert, 2010; Millie, 2008).

Such findings raise the question how such a parochial vision of neighbourhood order must be understood. Interpreted sceptically, these practices could be seen as the result of revanchist tendencies of middle class citizens. These citizens want to cleanse their environment of those that tarnish the reputation of their neighbourhood and have a negative influence on their quality of life (cf. Smith, 1996). However, in the cases discussed here there is but little evidence for such class-based revanchism. First of all, residents' frustrations do not appear to be rooted in a specific class-based urge to drive out marginal people. Rather, complaining residents feel threatened by drug dealers and drug users or they claim they are tired of street youth disturbing their sleep. Moreover, neo-liberalism has but little explanatory value here (unlike Smith's analyses of revanchism), especially since municipal officers predominantly patrol neighbourhoods and parks where notions of 'keeping the city free for consumption' hardly applies (Sleiman & Lippert, 2010). If there is any indication for exclusivist law enforcement in these terms this is limited to specific urban areas and times (cf. Hae, 2011; Hobbs et al., 2000; Van Aalst & Van Liempt, 2012). In addition, in the Netherlands municipal disorder policing by and large is still done by public providers and paid for by public resources, unlike elsewhere, where for instance, some public areas are incorporated in business development districts and the policing of disorder seems to be part of a further neo-liberal privatisation of public places (Beckett & Herbert, 2008; Mitchell & Staeheli, 2006; Smith, 2002; Terpstra et al., 2013). Lastly, even the toughest approaches described here show that the deterrent approach by municipal officers is often but one of many strategies and rationalities in play. Numerous other partners and organisations deal with these 'target groups', ranging from health care and psychiatric aid, to youth work and social work (see also Baillergeau, 2014; Deverteuil, May & von Mahs, 2009).

Instead of an intended exclusion of marginal groups, 'sweeping the streets' often seems to be more related to the managerial ambitions and the evolving professional identity of municipal officers described above. As such, municipalities do not opt for an open war on deviancy, but want measurable results in streets and areas with recurring problems. Hotspots are expected to be downscaled, the number of residents' reports is meant to drop and their evaluation of the district to go up. These measurable goals can allegedly be achieved most easily if the persons who cause trouble in these hotspots are simply deterred. By predominantly listening to a group of citizens and prioritising their annoyances, municipalities define disorder as merely that which irritates citizens the most.

3.3   *Symbolic politics: acting decisively and regaining authority?*

Hence municipal disorder policing is but seldom meant as a downright exclusion of marginal groups. Often it is the combination of different interests and 'logics' defining its practice as such. In other words, instead of seeing these practices as the conscious defence of middle class status, a variety of interests determines relatively strict enforcement approaches – those of managers, officers and – last but not least – politicians.

This points to a third way of interpreting seemingly exclusivist policies – looking at what politicians and local government actors would have to gain from such policies. Here David Garland's theory of a culture of control could be of help. As discussed in chapter 3, Garland (2001) refers to a policy predicament of high crime (and disorder) and insufficient state capacity to deal with it. Policies of strict law enforcement by municipalities might be seen as a way to deny this predicament. In fact, by emotionalised reactions, vocal 'acting out', and a 'turn to the people' who have to be protected against the "fearsome stranger", local governments might well attempt to regain authority over issues of crime and disorder (2001: 137).[7]

Many findings support this view. Disorder policy in some cases can be interpreted as a governmental desire to regain an authoritative reputation, as interventions with strong symbolic characteristics. Rotterdam's efforts to reclaim the streets for instance (chapter 5), or – again – the vocal and tough responses to target groups in the cases of chapter 8 can all be seen as examples of 'acting out', responding to the demands of a frustrated citizenry meant to reinvest in the idea that the local government is in control. Moreover, as these local policies were stirred into action by the pressure applied by small groups of residents, they are adjusted to the interests of the victims of disorder. In other words, neighbourhood residents' fears and frustrations define municipal policies.[8] This is underscored by officers when they state they are obliged to keep on patrolling in empty hotspots and when they resignedly observe there is a lack of structural solutions for disorder. Sometimes they state that their work consists of removing the source of citizens' annoyances and acknowledging their feelings of insecurity by reassuring them through physical presence. In this respect, 'reassurance policing' appears to play a somewhat ambivalent role. Neither in the policies as described in chapter 5 nor in the views of municipal officers this concept is highly regarded. However, when political logic dominates decision making, as described in chapter 8, reassurance by uniformed municipal workers does appear to play an important role.

In these cases politicians and local government actors such as mayors and aldermen interfere more directly with their own forces of municipal surveillance, transmitting citizens' wishes directly to 'their' municipal officers. Nevertheless, it might not be these citizens' interests that are decisive here. Quite a few respond-

---

7. The policy predicament on which Garland's rests his theories in the Netherlands can be recognised most clearly in the 1980s when the Roethof committee was launched. One of the reasons why the Roethof committee was established in the first place was because police and justice did not seem to be capable of addressing the abundance of petty crimes. Other partners had to be involved. Municipalities and their early city wardens were among the first to deal with the large number of petty crimes.
8. As such, municipal disorder policing might be devoid of considerations about how to enhance trust between citizens, but it might still enhance the trust of citizens in government agencies.

ents are candid about the eagerness of council members to pay attention to residents' whims from electoral motivations (cf. Garland, 2001: 131). Municipal officers' own views and judgments are overruled in these cases, and their discretionary autonomy is smothered in political demands. They become 'civil servants' in the most literal meaning of that term: servants of citizens.

3.4   *Managing risks and controlling deviancy?*

This focus on governmental interests also provides an opportunity to understand other aspects of disorder policing discussed here. As said, municipalities seem mostly interested in managing the risks of (numerous) rule infringements by influencing the behaviour of non-compliant citizens in certain situations. This could be seen as representing another characteristic of Garland's notion of a culture of control. In their *adaptive* response to high crime (and disorder), governments invest in behavioural management, initially through opportunity reduction, later through problem oriented strategies (see section 2). Such strategies reflect the dominance of a risk reduction paradigm, as order is upheld by a basic controlling of opportunities and thus reducing the risk that rule infringements occur in the first place.[9]

The notion of a culture of control highlights deviancy as part of everyday life: crime and disorder are seen as arbitrary, quotidian events, and it is plausible that any individual will take advantage of opportunities (Felson, 1998; Garland, 1999). This seems to apply to how city surveillance agencies approach littering and parking a car in the wrong spot. In the municipal response to such infringements the malleability of situations plays a key role. Thus through the emphasis on situational crime prevention non-compliant citizens are expected to be sensitive to disincentives. Policing disorder in these cases does not lead to excluding the disorderly or re-conquering lost neighbourhoods but is tailored to minor interventions in opportunity structures. Such ideas are also expressed by municipal officers described in chapter 7. Officers' cynical view that most or perhaps even all people are incorrigible and that normative standards have declined in general, logically leads to a preference for dealing with disorder by controlling it. Even the administering of fines is often considered to be a behavioural intervention that is meant to have a preventative effect on other citizens, as a strategy that in some cases might work best to control widespread misbehaviour. The growing tendency to use municipal officers for surveillance in hotspots, during night times and for areas

---

9.   As discussed in chapter 3, Garland notes how state actors also adapt to the predicament of high crime and low capacity by filtering cases out of the criminal justice system. By 'defining deviancy down', the amount of behaviour that will become penalised is lowered, thus demanding less capacity. However, the developments in Dutch municipal disorder policing appear to be indications of the opposite. Although some maintain the invention of administrative fines and penal orders could be seen as support for 'defining deviancy down' as a large amount of incivilities are kept out of the criminal justice system (see for instance Devroe, 2012), these new forms of law enforcement show in fact *more* instead of *less* forms of behaviour are subject to fines.

where the police claim to lack capacity also points to the dominance of a risk man-agement paradigm. These officers are deemed to be most suitable for controlling anti-social behaviour in specific areas with a high incidence of incivilities (see also Van Stokkom & Foekens, 2015).

Furthermore, the idea of behavioural control can be recognised in the 'network approaches' of some municipal departments. In effect, not only municipal officers deal with rule infringements, but other responsible municipal parties are also involved in helping to manage disorderly behaviour. These departments, such as Public Maintenance or Urban Planning, share in the responsibility for behavioural management. These networks may be called examples of 'preventative partner-ships' in a Garlandian fashion. Through a more tight-knit network of partners – involving those originally outside public safety, such as youth work or healthcare (see chapter 8) – the control of deviancy has certainly expanded.

This section reflected on the findings from four different angles. The first two of these sociological interpretations are useful to explain some specific policies. The benevolent reading that sees disorder policing as rooted in concerns about the loss of informal social control for instance, seems apt to interpret some of the initial impetuses to city surveillance agencies. Viewing disorder policing as an exclusivist practice might have relevance for specific cases in which 'target groups' are scared off.

However, municipal disorder policing is not only about residents' wishes to get rid of deviant groups. Garland's theory of a culture of control shows that new forms of municipal disorder policing provide politicians, managers and officers alike with the opportunity to show force and decisive action, thus hoping to regain authority. Hence, residents' wishes are also encapsulated and appropriated by managers and politicians to meet their own interests. This study is rich in examples that support that view. At the same time city surveillance agencies appear predom-inantly concerned with containing and controlling a set of disorder issues. As a result, municipalities have embraced various risk management strategies to pre-vent rule infringements.

4   Discussion

This book dealt with a new response to concerns about incivilities and anti-social behaviour – municipal disorder policing. It portrayed a profession that at times might be searching for its occupational identity, but that also claims to know how to deal with disorder effectively.

This pragmatic focus on the effects of situational prevention leaves other, more fundamental approaches to disorder aside. In this respect, the earlier debates between proponents of a 'root causes' approach to crime and disorder and those supporting situational crime prevention have clearly been concluded in favour of the latter. In a classical article on situational crime prevention, Clarke made a point for a more "realistic approach" to crime prevention by emphasizing "choices and decisions made by the offender" (Clarke, 1980: 136). Clarke targeted the dominance of the root causes theory: an overt stress on 'dispositions' of offenders makes it "difficult to achieve any effects, i.e. in relation to the psychological events or the social and economic conditions that are supposed to generate criminal dispositions" (*ibid.*: 137). By contrast, Dutch municipal disorder policing is connected with Clarke's pragmatic 'alternative': situational interventions only aim to influence people's choices. As such, this profession does not pretend to provide answers to citizens' deeper concerns about disorder and does not deal with what could be behind incivilities, littered streets, non-compliance or a general feeling of insecurity.

This choice invites various reflections. On the one hand, these officers cannot be expected to deal with fundamental, social problems and a radical approach to disorder can hardly be demanded from them. On the other hand, however, by dismissing the root causes of (complaints about) disorder, municipal disorder policing is for its part severely limited. In this final section I reflect upon these limitations and its consequences.

4.1   *The complacency of a pragmatic profession*

This study showed that municipal disorder policing, for an important part, is the result of increased attention to citizens' feelings of insecurity and concerns about incivilities. More specifically, municipal officers are one of the means to address sentiments of unease, annoyance and fear.

This municipal attention is often applauded. Many respondents claim we should be content that something is done about residents' basic annoyances and fears. Whereas the police are seen as withdrawing from such issues (see chapter 1), at least these officers are willing to 'listen to the citizens' and to acknowledge their concerns. Municipal officers appear to do what the police have left aside (see also chapter 9). This seems to imply that municipal officers' tasks are so self-evident that any debate can be ruled out in advance. Rules stating that you should not let your dog litter public places, that you should not cycle in pedestrian zones, park on the pavement, throw your rubbish out too early or hang around in doorways are seen as defending basic forms of public order with which anybody agrees.

However, disorder issues and incivilities are not of themselves demanding to be policed. In fact, civic annoyances and feelings of insecurity might only be on the surface of more profound societal changes; they represent the tip of the iceberg, so to say. Lists of top annoyances do not reveal a great deal about how residents see their living environments, nor do they address the potential deeper causes of dissatisfaction and insecurity. In this respect, feelings of insecurity might be related to issues as diverse as a moral unease about societal changes (Spithoven et al., 2012), images of threatening outsiders, frustrations about immigrants or tensions between different groups of residents.

These underlying feelings and considerations appear to play a minor role in the policy and practice of municipal disorder policing and perhaps not surprisingly so. These pragmatic officers focus on what can be achieved through short term interventions aimed at behavioural change – interventions at which they have become increasingly proficient. Thus, new forms of Dutch disorder policing are quite shallow in their problem definitions: agencies for city surveillance address citizens' complaints without much interest in what causes them.

Moreover, in their eagerness for pragmatic and effective interventions, actors in municipal disorder policing create their own definitions of what is disorder and what is not. They do so by focussing on those issues that are highest in the quality of life monitors or those that are reported most frequently. Hence, only specific citizens' reports are eligible for policing, as noted in chapter 6. As these reports appear to form the most important relation municipal officers have with the neighbourhoods that they are policing, they limit disorder to a specific set of annoyances and strip it of its context. Instead of getting in touch with complainants to make sense of what problems are bothering them and why, the complaining citizen is regarded as always being right. Meanwhile, practices and policies of disorder policing that complacently proclaim they are 'listening to the citizen' in fact might cloak the fact that municipalities do not have the answer to complex urban problems, of which complaints about disorder in public places is merely one of the symptoms (cf. Wacquant, 2008). 'The Citizen' here appears as a rhetorical device, writ large in these monitors and lists, while tensions between different groups of residents or between residents and authorities themselves are ignored.

In this respect, municipal officers are like well-skilled craftsmen, plumbers who know technically how to deal with the leakage, but overlook fundamental changes of the piping. Even more, it might be in their own interest to advertise their pragmatic and effective, but temporary solutions to such local leakages: it is what grants them legitimacy as a profession. Hence disorder policing is not only about defending norms, it also *creates* these norms (Harcourt, 2001). By focusing exclusively on a limited set of disorder issues "the category of the disorderly is the product, in part, of the quality-of-life initiative itself" (*ibid.*: 162).

4.2   *Interpreting disorder*

A second possible explanation for municipalities' pragmatic approach to issues of disorder, takes the interpretation of disorder *itself* into account. As such, municipal officers' approach cannot be wholly reduced to a new profession's adherence to its own disorder definitions.

Beneath municipal officers' pragmatic focus seems to linger another assumption: disorder is conceived as unambiguously signalling decline and aloofness and should therefore be dealt with quickly and effectively (see also chapter 5). Put simply, disorder needs to be removed from sight. In this respect, the same assumption that informs broken windows policies informs municipal disorder policing: a disorderly neighbourhood communicates to residents and visitors 'it does not care' (Herbert & Brown, 2006; Harcourt 2001). A logical inference in terms of disorder policing therefore seems to be that improving neighbourhoods might succeed by focusing exclusively on signals of disorder (cf. Bottoms, 2006). It explains the stress on pragmatic interventions that claim to derive their success from banishing deviancy from public spaces, be it physical or social (cf. Becket & Herbert, 2010).

However, just as complaints or figures in quality of life monitors 'say' little about the neighbourhoods whence they come, the appearance of disorder might 'say' various things. Obviously nobody likes to see litter, but can it be assumed that litter symbolises that "nobody cares", or that people do not take care of norms of citizenship? Rubbish, dog litter or vandalised property could be inconvenient, annoying or even induce fear, and therefore deserve to be dealt with, but can they be interpreted simply as signalling people do not care? It might just as well indicate that people care about *other* things, have other things on their minds, are simply unaware of the rules or consider disorderly signals as a proof of a vital city.

Without wanting to deny the relevance of dealing with these signals of disorder, it could be relevant to consider various forms of disorder more thoroughly. This applies specifically to 'disorderly persons'. Throughout this study, it seemed that 'target groups', such as loitering youth or homeless people seem to be interpreted in similar ways as litter or wrongly parked cars, as unsettling other neighbourhood residents, and as "unsightly trash to be removed, objects with limited aesthetic value" (Walby & Lippert, 2012: 1029; see further chapter 8). Such framing of disorder caused by homeless people or street youth overlooks the fact that these people might well have a lack of space at home, lack a home at all, have a troubled relation with their parents, deal with addictions, or they might simply be looking for diversion.

Although this book did not discuss alternative solutions to problems of disorder, it could be worthwhile to pause briefly at solutions that are side-lined through the specific choices made in municipal disorder policing. Early Dutch attention to disorder by the Roethof committee for instance, encompassed a wider range of solutions to the problem of what was then called 'petty crime'. The early solutions proposed by this committee were more than mere pragmatic options to diminish the opportunities for disorder, but also involved investment in the sources of disorder, for instance by 'social bonding' of juvenile offenders to society. It appears that with the introduction of Dutch administrative prevention, the establishment of local 'integrated public safety policy', but also a general preference for quick pragmatic approaches and the rejection of 'patronising' social interventions, these solutions have been moved to the background (cf. Garland, 2001; Van Swaaningen, 1995). More specifically, this study showed that through a mutually reinforcing process of political preferences, a managerial urge to control, eagerness of municipal officers to prove themselves and the withdrawal of the police, pragmatic approaches became the key solution to the problem of disorder. Although some local policies propose alternative solutions to disorder, knowledge about the effects of minor rule infringements, the context of disorder issues and how it relates to other, social problems in neighbourhoods is generally taken into account only to a limited extent.

4.3   Some consequences

Hence Dutch municipal disorder policing has developed into pragmatic approaches to issues of disorder, but limits its solutions to addressing the symptoms. This has important consequences. Although irritation and unease might be diminished to a certain extent by the presence of more uniformed officers who know how to deal with incivilities, such solutions are hardly sustainable. It might be impossible to relieve feelings of insecurity with more uniforms and more reassuring surveillance for the simple reason that these feelings and the need for reassurance to an important extent are irrational and ineradicable (Boutellier, 2004). As such, they may even be part of a 'culture of fear', a trait deeply rooted in late modern culture that is entwined with a permanent distrust in mankind (Furedi, 2007).

In addition, there are certain risks to the uncritical embrace of complaints. As said, this overlooks possible tensions between groups of residents and between residents and the local government. If these tensions and issues are solved by issuing more fines for incivilities, by more hotspot policing, by merely responding to the complaints of a limited group of residents, this new form of municipal policing could lose credibility among other groups of residents. Instead of a new police force that 'listens to the citizen', they will be perceived as the instrument of an assertive ever-complaining minority that has the skills and power to influence municipal authorities. In this respect, sending municipal officers or police officers to 'disorderly neighbourhoods' might not only be a poor approach to solving issues of disorder, it might also exacerbate tensions, especially in those neighbourhoods where residents are suspicious of state agencies, or even oppose them. Moreover, by uncritically answering to the demands of these assertive residents and banishing all forms of disorder from public spaces, the resilience of big city residents might be further eroded, further feeding their fear for deviancy and hampering interaction between different users of public spaces (cf. Crawford, 2009; Van Stokkom, 2013a). A more thorough understanding of what causes complaints and unease about disorderly behaviour might be needed before establishing new hotspots and jumping to pragmatic interventions.

Of course these considerations imply too great demands on a policing profession. Municipal officers cannot be blamed for not being embedded in their neighbourhoods when they are sent to ever new hotspots. They lack time and capacity to investigate the backgrounds of complaints and of disorder, or to approach issues of disorder from multiple angles, when it is merely demanded of them that they enforce the rules. Perhaps they cannot be blamed either for not knowing how to make an estimation of various forms of disorder, other than 'not to ignore litter when you're out for parking tickets', when they do not have sufficient possibilities to develop a holistic image of the neighbourhood (cf. chapter 6).

As such, the critique that this holistic image is lacking among municipal officers might better be directed at how approaches to anti-social behaviour are distributed over various professions. Youth work for instance, is expected to deal with issues of social assistance, such as education and employment, health care with mental health problems. However, this study suggests that there is a fair chance that the knowledge and insights of these professionals do not reach municipal officers. Due to the lack of communication between various professions and the 'compartmentalisation' (*verkokering*, see chapter 6) of their respective tasks, every profession might well work in its own 'bubble'. The work of municipal officers is thus limited to the basic approach of situational prevention of disorder described here.

Whereas agencies for city surveillance have developed notably in a relatively short time, the issues considered here pose challenges that are too great. Although municipal officers themselves sometimes have relatively nuanced views about the causes of disorder (see chapter 8), they are evidently hampered by the limitations of their assignments and the municipal and political context in which they have to do their work. They are expected to get rid of disorder, whether it is physical or social, without having the position, power or capability to re-examine the very norms they are supposed to uphold.

Samenvatting

In de afgelopen dertig jaar zijn in Nederland zorgen over overlast in de publieke ruimte sterk toegenomen. Meer dan voorheen krijgen ergernissen over bijvoorbeeld illegaal geplaatst huisvuil, foutparkeren of op de stoep fietsen de aandacht.

De bestrijding van deze overlast is meer en meer de verantwoordelijkheid van gemeenten geworden. Die rol van lokale overheden vindt zijn oorsprong in de vaststelling van de commissie Roethof in 1984 dat de toename van (toen nog) 'kleine criminaliteit' meer aandacht verdiende en dat dat niet van politie en justitie verwacht kon worden. In de loop van de jaren '90 is de betrokkenheid van gemeenten bij overlastbestrijding verder toegenomen, terwijl de Nederlandse politie zich in de afgelopen twintig a dertig jaar steeds meer op haar 'kerntaken' is gaan richten. Haar aanwezigheid in de publieke ruimte en aandacht voor verondersteld kleinere overlastfeiten is daardoor juist afgenomen.

Samen hebben deze ontwikkelingen geleid tot de opkomst van een nieuwe beroepsgroep: gemeentelijk toezichthouders en handhavers. In dit boek staat deze beroepsgroep centraal.

Hoofdvraag en opbouw studie

Deze studie richt zich op de historische, maatschappelijke en organisatorische context waarin deze nieuwe toezichthouders en handhavers hun werk doen. De hoofdvraag luidt: **Vanuit welke factoren en perspectieven kunnen het beleid en de praktijk van het Nederlandse gemeentelijke toezicht & handhaving begrepen worden?**

Het eerste, theoretische gedeelte van deze studie behandelt vormen van toezicht & handhaving aan de hand van een drietal politiestrategieën uit internationale literatuur. Om een vergelijking met die strategieën mogelijk te maken wordt gemeentelijk toezicht & handhaving opgevat als *municipal disorder policing*. Ook wordt een drietal sociologische interpretaties besproken. Daarnaast wordt de methodologie uiteengezet. Er is vooral gebruik gemaakt van case studies en etnografisch onderzoek.

In het tweede, meest omvangrijke gedeelte van deze studie wordt in vijf empirische hoofdstukken toezicht & handhaving in zes grote steden besproken. Achtereenvolgens worden het dominante beleid en de veranderingen daarin bestudeerd, de wijze waarop lokale besluiten tot stand komen en de opvattingen van individuele toezichthouders. Daarna wordt door middel van twee case studies besproken hoe toezicht in 'hotspots' tot stand komt en wordt vorm gegeven. Tot slot staat de verhouding tussen het werk van toezichthouders en handhavers enerzijds en politiewerk anderzijds centraal.

Gemeentelijk toezicht: beleid door de jaren heen

De eerste vormen van gemeentelijk toezicht & handhaving volgden direct op de zogeheten Roethof projecten. In navolging van de gelijknamige commissie trachten deze projecten nieuwe oplossingen aan te reiken voor het probleem van veelvoorkomende kleine criminaliteit: door veranderingen in de bebouwde omgeving, door 'binding' van jongeren aan de samenleving en door extra functioneel toezicht. De eerste Nederlandse stadswachten sloten aan bij het laatste type oplossing. Dit nieuwe geüniformeerde personeel was daarmee vooral bedoeld om de gelegenheid voor kleine criminaliteit te helpen inperken.

Toch werden de eerste stadswachten niet alleen als succesvol gezien vanwege het effect dat zij hadden op kleine criminaliteit. Stadswachten werden namelijk vooral ook als oplossing gezien voor hoge werkloosheid en veel gemeenten zetten stadswachtprojecten op via subsidies voor langdurig werklozen. Het gevolg was dat stadswachten weliswaar een rol vervulden in de preventie van kleine criminaliteit en overlast, maar dat de ontwikkeling van een eigenstandige professie gehinderd werd door re-integratiedoelstellingen en de ondergeschiktheid aan de politie.

De eerste grote wijziging in gemeentelijk toezicht & handhaving vond plaats in de jaren tussen 2002 en 2007. Zowel op nationaal als lokaal niveau klonk een roep om meer toezicht en strengere handhaving van overtredingen en overlast. Op lokaal niveau speelden daarbij nieuwe leefbaarheidsmonitoren en veiligheidsindexen en de vaak geringe aandacht van de politie voor betrekkelijk kleine overtredingen een belangrijke rol. Tegelijkertijd zagen ambtenaren en bestuurders de bestaande stadswachten als incapabel. Deze 'Melketiers' zouden te weinig in huis hebben om 'het verschil te maken' en er was behoefte aan *handhavend* personeel dat kon bekeuren voor de overtredingen die behoorden tot de belangrijkste ergernissen van grootstedelingen. Deze veranderingen leidden tot de oprichting van nieuwe gemeentelijke diensten toezicht & handhaving. Deze afdelingen zouden gaandeweg volledig moeten bestaan uit 'BOA's' (buitengewoon opsporingsambtenaren), een type functionaris dat gemeenten al sinds de afschaffing van de gemeentepolitie in 1993 de gelegenheid bood om eigen ambtenaren actief te laten bekeuren voor specifieke overtredingen. De neiging tot strenger optreden werd versterkt door het verlangen naar een duidelijker beroepsidentiteit en de ontluikende beroepseer van deze nieuwe beroepsgroep.

De meest recente fase wordt gekenmerkt door een heroriëntatie bij de jonge diensten toezicht & handhaving. Beleid richt zich de laatste jaren minder op handhaving en meer op alternatieve manieren om 'nalevingsgedrag' te bevorderen. Ook beteugelen sommige diensten hun ambities. Ze beperken zich tot het toezien op een welomschreven aantal vormen van overlast, zoals verkeerd aangeboden huisvuil, parkeerproblemen en hondenpoep. Tot slot zeggen alle diensten zich nadrukkelijker op burgers te willen richten, bijvoorbeeld door hen actiever te laten meebeslissen over prioriteiten van de diensten toezicht & handhaving.

Lokale besluitvorming

Toch bepaalt dit beleid maar tot op beperkte hoogte de feitelijke inzet van toezichthouders en handhavers. Veeleer hangen besluiten over inzet samen met verschillende, meer informele beleidsnetwerken en vormen van besluitvorming die niet in beleid vastgelegd zijn. In hoofdstuk 6 worden die verschillende wijzen van besluitvorming besproken aan de hand van een drietal 'logica's': een politieke, een management en een frontlijn logica.

Een eerste, politieke logica heeft betrekking op hoe politieke besluitvorming over toezicht en handhaving plaatsvindt. Hoewel een gedeelte van die besluiten op een 'klassieke' manier genomen wordt – via raadsdebatten – werkt deze logica ook op andere wijzen. Zo spelen incidenten een grote rol, zoals bijvoorbeeld in het geval van ernstige overlast veroorzaakt door jongeren, daklozen of cafébezoekers. Burgemeesters en wethouders zien in zulke gevallen toezichthouders en handhavers vaak als een snelle oplossing voor acute kwesties die onder de aandacht gebracht zijn door een groep bewoners en/of lokale media. Deze manier van besluiten wordt verder versterkt door de terugtred van de politie en door het gegeven dat veel coördinatoren en BOA's zich graag willen bewijzen als professioneel en 'politie-achtig'.

In het geval van een 'management logica' draait het om het objectiveren en meten van overlast. 'New public management'-taalgebruik speelt daarbij vaak een grote rol: inzet van toezichthouders wordt bepaald op basis van 'contracten', 'prestatiemanagement' en de neiging om te sturen op de 'productie' van gemeentelijk toezicht en handhaving. Een drietal verschillende middelen wordt gebruikt voor het sturen van toezichthouders en handhavers: leefbaarheidsmonitoren, meldingen van bewoners en bonnenquota. In de praktijk worden er zelden harde conclusies aan de uitkomsten van dit soort instrumenten verbonden. Ze worden vooral gebruikt om *vooraf* een beeld te ontwikkelen van de plekken waar toezichthouders het meest van nut zouden moeten zijn. Evenwel betekent de inzet op 'hotspots' met de meeste meldingen en de laagste beoordelingen door burgers dat minder meetbare werkvormen – zoals preventieve surveillance of contacten met wijkbewoners – het onderspit dreigen te delven.

Een laatste logica hangt nauw samen met de observaties van toezichthouders zelf en hun ervaringen in de alledaagse samenwerking met partners, zoals wijk-management en politieagenten. In deze 'frontlijnlogica' spelen metingen en mel-dingen maar een beperkte rol en gaat het er vooral om actief te kunnen inspelen op overlastsituaties zoals deze geobserveerd worden door professionals op straat. Deze laatste logica lijkt daarom ook niet zozeer te draaien om hogere of abstracte doelen, maar om 'dingen voor elkaar krijgen' en 'dezelfde taal spreken'.

Deze verschillende 'logica's' botsen vaak. Zo hebben lokale frontlijnpartners soms kritiek op de bureaucratische houding van toezichthouders en handhavers. Volgens hen denken zij teveel in termen van managementopdrachten en abstracte doelen. Daarnaast ontregelt de dominantie van een politieke logica de voorkeuren van uitvoerders. Doordat bestuurders en politici inzet van BOA's eisen op nieuwe en acute hotspots, wordt het in sommige gevallen moeilijk om een structurele vorm van toezicht en handhaving te ontwikkelen, zo menen sommige uitvoerders en coördinatoren.

Opvattingen van toezichthouders en handhavers

In hoofdstuk 7 worden de ideeën van toezichthouders en handhavers zelf geanaly-seerd.

Ten eerste hebben deze professionals vaak uitgesproken opvattingen over hun verantwoordelijkheden. Zo zeggen veel BOA's zich in hun werk nadrukkelijk op burgers te richten, al verschilt de manier waarop sterk. Sommigen menen dat in direct contact met burgers uitgezocht dient te worden wat deze burgers het meest dwars zit. Anderen vinden dat opdrachten en meldingen genoeg inzicht bieden. Toch zijn er ook uitvoerders die een bredere opvatting van hun taken huldigen. Ze bekritiseren de neiging van sommige wijkbewoners om voor iedere kleinigheid de gemeente te bellen. Liever treden ze in contact met andere professionals of gaan ze uit van eigen observaties om te bepalen wat er moet gebeuren.

Daarnaast hebben BOA's ogenschijnlijk sterk uiteenlopende opvattingen over overtreders. Veel van hen benadrukken het belang van 'bejegening' en beklemto-nen dat overtredingen met een goed gesprek opgelost kunnen worden. Sterker nog, een goede bejegening vergroot de kans op structureel 'nalevingsgedrag'. Anderen leggen vooral de nadruk op de context waarin een overtreding plaats-vindt: iedere situatie verdient een andere benadering. Opnieuw lijkt het streven naar 'nalevingsgedrag' hier de drijvende kracht. Tot slot ziet een aantal uitvoerders meer heil in een stringente aanpak. Ook in dit geval wordt het regulerende effect van bekeuren als een van de belangrijkste motivaties opgevoerd.

Al met al lopen opvattingen van toezichthouders en handhavers sterk uiteen. Die variatie staat niet op zichzelf. Zo kunnen deze professionals gezien worden als typische *street level bureaucrats* en zouden hun opvattingen begrepen kunnen wor-den als een wijze om hun 'routines' uit te leggen en te legitimeren. Ook doen de opvattingen van deze uitvoerders denken aan sommige opvattingen onder politie agenten, al benadrukken veel toezichthouders en handhavers dat er een groot verschil is tussen de 'typische politiecultuur' en hun eigen beroepsgroep. Bovendien zijn bepaalde spanningen wel degelijk uniek voor deze professionals. Vooral de spanning tussen 'dienstverlening' en 'handhaving' valt op, temeer omdat 'dienstverlening' bij toezichthouders meer voorop staat dan bij de politie en er redenen zijn om streng te handhaven die voor de politie minder van belang zijn.

Handhaving in 'hotspots'

In hoofdstuk 8 worden twee casestudies besproken. In deze casestudies gaat het om de omgang met overlast van specifieke 'doelgroepen': jongeren in Rotterdam en een gemengde groep van drugdealers, druggebruikers en daklozen in Utrecht.

In beide gevallen begint nieuw beleid voor een doortastende aanpak met bestuurlijke aandacht voor ernstige overlast, mede als gevolg van aanhoudende klachten van wijkbewoners. Veranderingen in beleid worden vervolgens vooral mogelijk gemaakt door de ambities en inzet van managers die politieke aandacht zien als een goede gelegenheid om meer grip te krijgen op de aanpak van overlast. Zo werd in Rotterdam de politieke druk om iets aan jongerenoverlast te doen door managers vertaald in meer top-down controle van de aanpak van jongerenoverlast en jongerenbeleid. In Utrecht grepen managers de politieke aandacht aan als gelegenheid om gemeentelijk toezicht en handhaving nadrukkelijker op de kaart te zetten als oplossing voor de problemen in het centrumgebied.

Deze ontwikkelingen leiden er enerzijds toe dat de rol van toezichthouders en handhavers nauwer omschreven wordt en dat ze zich doorgaans moeten beperken tot strikte handhaving, het verzamelen van informatie om de 'doelgroepleden' beter te kunnen reguleren en (vaak) te verjagen van vooraf bepaalde 'hotspots'. Anderzijds blijkt tijdens diensten en interviews dat er ook ongemak en onvrede leeft onder uitvoerders. Zo is er lang niet altijd genoeg te doen, ervaren sommige BOA's ongemak bij de stringente aanpak, worden sommige opdrachten gehekeld als wereldvreemd en zoeken zij naar nieuwe taken.

Werkdeling tussen toezichthouders en politie agenten.

In het laatste empirische hoofdstuk wordt uiteengezet hoe verschillende respondenten het onderscheid tussen gemeentelijk toezicht & handhaving en de politie zien. Toezichthouders, agenten en andere respondenten bepalen (en betwisten) actief en op uiteenlopende wijzen de werkverdeling tussen beide beroepsgroepen. Er zijn daarin vier verschillende posities te onderscheiden.

Twee daarvan hebben een 'defensief' karakter en benadrukken de uniciteit van beide beroepsgroepen. Zo menen veel respondenten dat de politie wezenlijk verschilt van andere handhavende beroepsgroepen. Ze stellen dat politiewerk om een aantal specifieke kerntaken draait en dat dit werk ontdaan moet worden van taken die afleiden van 'boeven vangen'. Daarentegen benadrukken anderen juist dat gemeentelijk toezichthouders en handhavers zich uitsluitend zouden moeten richten op 'leefbaarheid'. Deze positie lijkt op haar beurt bedoeld om te vermijden dat de politie al te veel taken naar gemeenten afschuift.

Tegenover deze defensieve posities staan twee 'expansieve' posities, zienswijzen die gestoeld zijn op bereidwilligheid meer taken op zich te nemen. Zo menen sommigen dat er veel meer politietaken uitbesteed kunnen worden aan gemeenten. Politiewerk is een 'markt', zo wordt gezegd, waarin gemeenten een grotere rol kunnen spelen. De laatste positie stelt juist dat niet BOA's meer taken op moeten pakken, maar dat de politie terug moet naar toezicht in de openbare ruimte. Zij menen weliswaar dat toezichthouders en handhavers wezenlijk werk verrichten, maar hadden liever gezien dat de politie dit was blijven doen.

Conclusies

In het laatste hoofdstuk wordt een aantal conclusies getrokken over de veranderingen en perspectieven binnen deze zich snel ontwikkelende beroepsgroep.

Allereerst blijkt het om een nieuwe beroepsgroep te gaan die zijn plaats aan het ontdekken en (soms) bevechten is. Wijzigingen in beleid, maar ook opvattingen van individuele BOA's zijn vaak het resultaat van een zoektocht naar een eigenstandige positie en de afbakening tot politiewerk. In die zin kan de komst en ontwikkeling van gemeentelijk toezicht & handhaving mede gezien worden als de professionaliseringsstrijd van een nieuwe beroepsgroep.

Een tweede belangrijke conclusie is dat gemeentelijk toezicht & handhaving zich sterk richt op de zorgen van burgers, al is het beleidsdiscours in de loop der tijd wel verschoven. Zo ging het aanvankelijk om de zorgen om 'kleine criminaliteit', maar draaide beleid later vooral om 'kleine ergernissen' en deden termen als 'leefbaarheid' en 'schoon, heel en veilig' hun intrede. De gemeentelijke diensten toezicht & handhaving lijken hiermee verder weinig pretenties te koesteren. In tegenstelling tot sommige vormen van *community policing* gaat het hier niet om het verstevigen van informele sociale controle of sociale cohesie, maar vooral om dienstverlening, om het simpelweg aanpakken van die overtredingen waar de meeste meldingen over binnenkomen. Daarbij worden zorgen vaak ook verwoord in een typisch *New Public Management* discours, waarbij burgers als klanten worden gezien en meetinstrumenten – zoals leefbaarheidsmonitoren en aantallen meldingen – een belangrijke rol spelen.

Ten derde valt op dat gemeentelijke diensten toezicht & handhaving de nadruk leggen op een pragmatische benadering van overlast. De gedachte dat overtredingen het resultaat zijn van gelegenheden waarbij overtreders een rationele afweging maken beheerst het gemeentelijk toezicht al vanaf het moment van oprichting, zij het dat die benadering gaandeweg een wat andere formulering heeft gekregen.

Waar stadswachten aanvankelijk een rol werd toebedeeld in termen van 'situatio-nele preventie', werd later de nadruk gelegd op nalevingsgedrag; hoe kunnen de afwegingen van mogelijke overtreders zo beïnvloed worden dat ze de regels na-leven? Als zodanig draait toezicht & handhaving vooral om het beïnvloeden van gelegenheden en niet om de overtuigingen van mensen die regels schenden. Zelfs de voorbeelden van stringente handhaving die hier zijn besproken draaien vaak om dergelijke pragmatische overwegingen.

Deze twee elementen – een nadruk op de zorgen van burgers *en* op een pragma-tische benadering van overtredingen – lijken mede ten grondslag te liggen aan de populariteit van de hotspot benadering. Simpel gezegd biedt die benadering zowel de gelegenheid om het aanbod toe te snijden op de plekken met de meeste meldin-gen, als om capaciteit flexibel aan te passen aan wat nodig is om het aantal overtre-dingen effectief terug te brengen. Als zodanig lijken Nederlandse gemeenten welis-waar geïnspireerd door politiestrategieën uit het buitenland (en dan vooral door ideeën over gelegenheidsreductie), maar hebben zij toch een typisch, eigen variant van toezicht & handhaving ontwikkeld.

Gemeentelijk toezicht & handhaving kan daarom begrepen worden als een vorm van pragmatische formele sociale controle, zonder verdere pretenties dat dit zou helpen om sociale cohesie of informele sociale controle te verstevigen. Ook al spe-len zorgen om verloedering en buurtverval een rol bij de oprichting van een aantal diensten toezicht & handhaving, in hedendaagse praktijken lijken managers en uit-voerders zich vooral te richten op de meldingen van wijkbewoners. Daarbij moet vermeld worden dat slechts een kleine groep wijkbewoners zijn zorgen over over-last gevende groepen op de agenda weet te krijgen, maar dat het zelden gaat om een bewuste uitsluiting van specifieke groepen. Eerder hangt een stringente aan-pak van bijvoorbeeld jongeren op straat of daklozen samen met een streven naar meetbare resultaten en de geldingsdrang van sommige uitvoerders of managers.

Ook in andere opzichten blijkt dat niet zozeer de belangen van burgers de door-slag geven, maar die van overheidsactoren zelf. Zo wordt toezicht & handhaving door lokale bestuurders enerzijds soms gezien als een middel om gezag terug te winnen. Krachtdadige pogingen om de straat te 'heroveren' op de asociale jeugd of op drugsdealers en -gebruikers lijken niet zelden ingegeven te worden door een verlangen een signaal af te geven dat de lokale overheid grip op ernstige overlast heeft. Anderzijds lijkt veel van de bovengenoemde pragmatiek terug te voeren op de wens om overlast vooral beheersbaar te houden.

Diensten toezicht & handhaving zijn dus weinig geïnteresseerd in factoren die achter angst, ergernissen en ongenoegen kunnen schuilen. Dat kan van hen ook niet verwacht worden; het past simpelweg niet bij een professie die draait om toe-zicht en handhaving. Mede om die reden overheerst een benadering van situatio-nele preventie van overlast en antisociaal gedrag, vooral op hotspots. Die aanpak gaat er echter wel aan voorbij dat ongenoegen en angst wel eens structureel en de behoefte aan meer toezicht onbevredigbaar zouden kunnen zijn. Bovendien lopen gemeenten met een dergelijke aanpak het risico spanningen tussen groepen bewoners en tussen burgers en de overheid te veronachtzamen.

BIBLIOGRAPHY

Aalst, I. van, & Liempt, I. (2012). Urban surveillance and the struggle between safe and exciting nightlife districts. *Surveillance & Society, 9*(3), 280-292.

Abbott, A. (1988). *The System Of Professions: An Essay On The Division Of Expert Labor*. Chicago: University Of Chicago Press.

Agar, M.H. (2008). *The professional stranger: An informal introduction to ethnography*. Bingley: Emerald.

Allen, C., & Crookes, L. (2008). Fables of the reconstruction: A phenomenology of 'place shaping' in the north of England. *Town planning review, 80*(4/5), 455-480.

Andel, van H. (1989). Crime prevention that works: the care of public transport in the Netherlands. *The British Journal of Criminology, 29*(1), 47-56.

Ashworth, A., & Zedner, L. (2014). *Preventive justice*. Oxford: Oxford University Press.

Atkinson, R. (2003). Domestication by cappuccino or a revenge on urban space? Control and empowerment in the management of public spaces. *Urban Studies, 40*(9), 1829-1843.

Atkinson, R., & Flint, J. (2004). Order born of chaos? The capacity for informal social control in disempowered and 'disorganised' neighborhoods. *Policy and Politics, 32*(3), 333-350.

Baillergeau, E. (2014). Governing public nuisance: Collaboration and conflict regarding the presence of homeless people in public spaces of Montreal. *Critical Social Policy, 34*(3), 354-373.

Bannister, J., Fyfe, N., & Kearns, A. (2006). Respectable or respectful. (In)civility and the city. *Urban Studies, 43*(5-6), 919-937.

BeBOA (2010). *Visiedocument BOA: De buitengewoon opsporingsambtenaar in ontwikkeling*. Gorinchem: BeBOA.

Beckett, K., & Herbert, S. (2008). Dealing with disorder. *Theoretical Criminology, 12*(1), 5-30.

Beckett, K., & Herbert, S. (2010). *Banished: the new social control in urban America*. Oxford: Oxford University Press.

Bernard, H.R. (2006). *Research methods in anthropology: Qualitative and quantitative approaches* (4th ed.). Lanham, MD: AltaMira Press.

Bervoets, E. (2013). *Gemeentelijk blauw*. Apeldoorn, Netherlands: Politie & Wetenschap.

Bervoets, E., & Rovers, B. (2016). *Wat vindt het publiek van gemeentelijke handhavers? Onderzoek naar het imago van gemeentelijke handhavers in vijf gemeenten*. Retrieved from http://www.btvo.nl/wordpress/wp-content/uploads/2016/06/Imago-onderzoek-Gemeentelijke-Handhavers.pdf.

Bittner, E. (1970). *The functions of the police in modern society: A review of background factors, current practices, and possible role models*. Chevy Chase, MD: National Institute of Mental Health, Center for Studies of Crime and Delinquency.

Blokland, T. (2009). *Oog voor elkaar: Veiligheidsbeleving en sociale controle in de grote stad*. Amsterdam: Amsterdam University Press.

Boeije, H. (2010). *Analysis in qualitative research*. Los Angeles: SAGE.

Bottoms, A.E. (2006). Incivilities, offence, and social order in residential communities. In A.P. Simester, & A. Von Hirsch (Eds.), *Incivilities: Regulating offensive behaviour*. Oxford, England: Hart.

Boutellier, H. (2004). *The safety utopia: Contemporary discontent and desire as to crime and punishment*. Dordrecht: Kluwer Academic Publishers.

Boutellier, H. (2008). *Solidariteit en slachtofferschap: De morele betekenis van criminaliteit in een postmoderne cultuur*. Amsterdam: Amsterdam University Press.

Bouziane, M., & El Hadioui, I. (2011). *Straatcoach 2.0. Een empirisch-sociologisch onderzoek naar het functioneren van de Rotterdamse straatcoach in het Nieuwe Westen.* Rotterdam: EUR.

Braga, A.A., & Bond, B.J. (2008). Policing crime and disorder hot spots: A randomized controlled trial. *Criminology, 46*(3), 577-607.

Brink, G. van den (2004). *Schets van een beschavingsoffensief: Over normen, normaliteit en normalisatie in Nederland.* Amsterdam: Amsterdam University Press.

Brouwer, D.V.A., & van Rest, P.H.S. (1996). Van bijzonder naar buitengewoon? Vragen rond het nieuwe artikel 142 Sv. *Delikt en Delinquent, 26*(4), 327-349.

Bruinsma, G.J.N., Bernasco, W., & Elffers, H. (2004). *De stad en sociale onveiligheid: Een state-of-the-art van wetenschappelijke kennis in Nederland.* Leiden: Nederlands Studiecentrum Criminaliteit en Rechtshandhaving.

Bunt, H.G. van de, & Swaaningen, R. van (2012). Van criminaliteitsbestrijding naar angstmanagement en van preventie naar verbanning. In E.R. Muller (Ed.) *Veiligheid: Veiligheid en veiligheidsbeleid in Nederland.* Deventer, Netherlands: Kluwer.

Burke, K. (1984) [1935]. *Permanence and Change.* Berkeley: California University Press.

Button, M. (2002). *Private policing.* Cullompton: Willan.

Cachet, L., & Ringeling, A. (2004). Integraal veiligheidsbeleid: Goede bedoelingen en wat er van terecht kwam. In E.R. Muller (Ed.) *Veiligheid: Veiligheid en veiligheidsbeleid in Nederland.* Deventer, Netherlands: Kluwer.

Christensen, T. (2006). Smart policy? In M. Moran, M. Rein, & R.E. Goodin (Eds.) *The Oxford handbook of public policy.* Oxford, England: Oxford University Press.

Clarke, R.V. (1980). "Situational" crime prevention: Theory and practice. *British journal of criminology, 20*(2), 136-147.

Clarke, R.V. (1997). *Situational crime prevention: Successful case studies.* Guilderland, N.Y.: Harrow and Heston.

Cohen, S. (1979). The punitive city: Notes on the dispersal of social control. *Contemporary Crises, 3*(4), 339-363.

Cohen, March, & Olsen (1972). A garbage can model of organizational choice. *Administrative science quarterly, 17*(1), 1-25.

Colder, J.C., & Nuijten-Edelbroek, E.G.M. (1988). *Het winkelcentraproject: Preventie van kleine criminaliteit.* Den Haag: SDU.

Commissie Roethof (1984). *Interimrapport van de Commissie Kleine Criminaliteit.* Den Haag: Staatsuitgeverij.

Compston, H. (2009). *Policy networks and policy change: Putting policy network theory to the test.* Houndmills, Basingstoke, Hampshire: Palgrave Macmillan.

Cosgrove, F., & Ramshaw, P. (2013). It is what you do as well as the way you do it: The value and deployment of PCSOs in achieving public engagement. *Policing and Society, 25*(1), 77-96.

Cook, I.R., & Whowell, M. (2011). Visibility and the policing of public space. *Geography Compass, 5*(8), 610-622.

Crawford, A. (2006). 'Fixing broken promises?': Neighbourhood wardens and social capital. *Urban Studies, 43*(5/6), 957-976.

Crawford, A. (2009). Governing through anti-social behaviour. *The British Journal of Criminology, 49*(6), 810-831.

Crawford, A., & Lister, S. (2006). Additional security patrols in residential areas: Notes from the marketplace. *Policing and Society, 16*(2), 164-188.

Creswell, J.W. (1998). *Qualitative inquiry and research design: Choosing among five traditions.* Thousand Oaks, CA etc.: SAGE.

Crijns, J.H. (2010). Een terugtocht van de politie uit de openbare ruimte? Over de consequenties van de bestuurlijke strafbeschikking en de bestuurlijke boete overlast in de openbare ruimte voor de taak en de positie van de politie. *Strafblad* (5), 376-386.

Decorte, T. (2010). Kwalitatieve data-analyse in het criminologisch onderzoek. In T. Decorte, & D. Zaitch (Eds.) *Kwalitatieve methoden en technieken in de criminologie.* Leuven, Belgium: Acco.

DeVerteuil, G., May, J., & Mahs, J. von (2009). Complexity not collapse: Recasting the geographies of homelessness in a 'punitive' age. *Progress in Human Geography, 33*(5), 646-666.

Devroe, E. (2012). *A swelling culture of control?: De genese en toepassing van de wet op de gemeentelijke administratieve sancties in België*. Antwerpen, Belgium: Maklu.

Dijk, J.J.M. van (2012). Deuren op slot. *Justitiële verkenningen*.

Dijk, J.J.M. van, & Waard, J. de (1991). A two-dimensional typology of crime prevention projects. *Criminal Justice Abstracts, 23*(3), 483-503.

Dijk, T. van, Flight, S., & Oppenhuis, E. (2000). *Voor het Beleid, achter de cijfers: De uitkomsten van de GSB-monitor veiligheid en leefbaarheid nader geanalyseerd*. Hilversum, Netherlands: Intomart.

Eijk, G. van (2010). Exclusionary policies are not just about the 'Neoliberal city': A critique of theories of urban revanchism and the case of Rotterdam. *International Journal of Urban and Regional Research, 34*(4), 820-834.

Eikenaar, T., & Van Stokkom, B. (2014). *Van stadswacht naar nieuwe gemeentepolitie?: Gemeentelijk toezicht en handhaving in de openbare ruimte*. Apeldoorn, Netherlands: Politie & Wetenschap.

Engbersen, G., Snel, E., & Weltevrede, A. (2005). *Sociale herovering in Amsterdam en Rotterdam: Eén verhaal over twee wijken*. Amsterdam: Amsterdam University Press.

Eterno, J.A., & Silverman, E.B. (2012). *The crime numbers game: Management by manipulation*. Boca Raton, FL: CRC Press.

Felson, M. (1998). *Crime and everyday life*. Thousand Oaks, CA: Pine Forge Press.

Fijnaut, C., Boutellier, H., Riessen, J. van, & Bos, M. van den (2008). *Veel te winnen! Eindrapport visitatie-commissie veiligheid Eindhoven*. Retrieved from http://www.verwey-jonker.nl/doc/vitaliteit/ Eindrapport_Visitatiecommissie_Veiligheid_Eindhoven_1390.pdf.

Flight, S. (2012). Vooral honden en huisvuil. *Secondant* (5), 42-47.

Flight, S., Hartmann, A., Nauta, O., Hulshof, P., & Terpstra, J. (2012). *Bestuurlijke strafbeschikking en bestuurlijke boete overlast: Evaluatie na drie jaar*. Amsterdam, Netherlands: DSP-groep.

Freidson, E. (2001). *Professionalism: The third logic*. Cambridge: Polity press.

Furedi, F. (1997). *The culture of fear: Risk taking and the morality of low expectations*. Cassell: London.

Garland, D. (1999). The Commonplace and the Catastrophic: Interpretations of Crime in Late Modernity. *Theoretical Criminology, 3*(3), 353-364.

Garland, D. (2001). *The culture of control: Crime and social order in contemporary society*. Oxford: Oxford University Press.

Geertz, C. (1973). *The interpretation of cultures: Selected essays*. New York: Basic Books.

Gemeentelijk ombudsman Amsterdam (2013). *Zeer divers toezicht in de openbare ruimte*. Retrieved from https://www.ombudsmanmetropool.nl/uploaded_files/researchdocument/RA130604.pdf.

Glaser, B.G., & Strauss, A.L. (2012). *The discovery of grounded theory: Strategies for qualitative research*. New Brunswick: Aldine Transaction.

Goldstein, H. (1979). Improving policing: A problem oriented approach. *Crime and Delinquency, 25*(2), 236-258.

Haagsma, J.H., Smits, I., Waarsing, H., & Wiebrens, C.J. (2012). *De Sterkte van de Arm: feiten en mythes*. Apeldoorn: Politie & Wetenschap.

Haan, de W. (2001). Sociaal-ecologische benaderingen. In E. Lissenberg, S. van Ruller, & R. van Swaaningen (Eds.) *Tegen de regels IV: Een inleiding in de criminologie*. Nijmegen, Netherlands: Ars Aeqi Libri.

Hae, L. (2011). Dilemmas of the nightlife fix: Post-industrialisation and the gentrification of nightlife in New York City. *Urban Studies, 48*(16), 3449-3465.

Harcourt, B.E. (2001). *Illusion of order: The false promise of broken windows policing*. Cambridge, MA: Harvard University Press.

Harcourt, B.E., & Ludwig, J. (2006). *Broken windows: New evidence from New York city and a five-city social experiment*. Chicago, IL: University of Chicago.

Hart, J. de (2002). Theoretische uitgangspunten, conceptualisering en doelstellingen. In J. de Hart (Ed.) *Zekere banden: Sociale cohesie, leefbaarheid en veiligheid*. Den Haag, Netherlands: Sociaal en Cultureel Planbureau.

Hartman, C., & Tops, P. (2005). *Frontlijnsturing: Uitvoering op de publieke werkvloer van de stad*. Den Haag: Kenniscentrum grote steden.

Hauber, A. (1994). *Stadswachten. Effectiviteit, draagvlak en organisatorische aspecten*. Den Haag, Netherlands: Ministerie van Justitie, Directie Criminaliteitspreventie.

Hauber, A., Hofstra, B., Toornvliet, L., & Zandbergen, A. (1996). Some new forms of functional social control in the Netherlands and their effects. *British journal of criminology, 36*(2), 199-219.

Herbert, S. (2001). Policing the contemporary city: Fixing broken windows or shoring up neo-liberalism? *Theoretical Criminology, 5*(4), 445-466.

Herbert, S. (2006). *Citizens, cops and power: recognizing the limits of community.* Chicago, IL: University of Chicago Press.

Herbert, S., & Brown, E. (2006). Conceptions of space and crime in the punitive neoliberal city. *Antipode, 38*(4), 755-777.

Hirschi, T. (1969). *The causes of delinquency.* New Brunswick, NJ: Transaction Publishers.

Hobbs, D., Lister, S., Hadfield, P., Winlow, S., & Hall, S. (2000). Receiving shadows: governance and liminality in the night-time economy. *British Journal of Sociology, 51*(4), 701-717.

Hollis-Peel, M.E., Reynald, D.M., Bavel, M. van, Elffers, H., & Welsh, B.C. (2011). Guardianship for crime prevention: A critical review of the literature. *Crime, law and social change, 56*(1), 53-70.

Hoogewoning, F. (2004). Tegenhouden nader verkend. *Tijdschrift voor de politie, 66*(3), 4-8.

Houdt, F. van, & Schinkel, W. (2014). Crime, citizenship and community: Neoliberal communitarian images of governmentality. *Sociological Review, 62*(1), 47-67.

Innes, M. (2004). Signal crimes and signal disorders: notes on deviance as communicative action. *British journal of sociology, 55*(3), 335-355.

Jacobs, J. (1962). *The death and life of great American cities.* London, England: Cape.

Johnston, L. (2003). From 'pluralisation' to 'the police extended family': Discourses on the governance of community policing in Britain. *International Journal of the Sociology of Law, 31*(3), 185-204.

Jones, T., Steden, R. van, & Boutellier, H. (2009). Pluralisation of policing in England & Wales and the Netherlands: Exploring similarity and difference. *Policing and Society, 19*(3), 282-299.

Jones, T., & Newburn, T. (1999). Urban change and policing: Mass private property re-considered. *European Journal on Criminal Policy and Research, 7*(2), 225-244.

Jones, T., & Newburn, T. (2007). *Policy transfer and criminal justice: Exploring US influence over British crime control policy.* Maidenhead, England: Open University Press.

Kelling, G.L., & Coles, C.M. (1996). *Fixing broken windows: Restoring order and reducing crime in our communities.* New York, NY: Simon & Schuster.

Kickert, W.J.M., Klijn, E.-H., & Koppenjan, J.F.M. (1997). *Managing complex networks: Strategies for the public sector.* London, England: Sage.

Kingdon, J.W. (2014). *Agendas, alternatives, and public policies.* Harlow, England: Pearson Education Limited.

Koch, R., & Latham, A. (2012). On the hard work of domesticating a public space. *Urban Studies, 50*(1), 6-21.

Koemans, M. (2011). *The war on antisocial behaviour: Rationales underlying antisocial behaviour policies. Comparing British and Dutch discourse analyses* (Doctoral dissertation). Retrieved from https://openaccess.leidenuniv.nl/handle/1887/18125.

Krauthammer, C. (1993). Defining deviancy up. *The new republic, 209*(21), 20-25.

Krogt, T.P.W.M. van der (1981). *Professionalisering en collectieve macht: Een conceptueel kader.* 's-Gravenhage: Vuga.

Land, M. van der, Stokkom, B. van, & Boutellier, H. (2014). *Burgers in veiligheid: Een inventarisatie van burgerparticipatie op het domein van de sociale veiligheid.* Den Haag, Netherlands: WODC.

Larson, M.S. (1977). *The rise of professionalism: A sociological analysis.* Berkeley: University of California Press.

Laws, D., & Hajer, M. (2006). Policy and practice. In M. Moran, M. Rein, & R.E. Goodin (Eds.) *The Oxford handbook of public policy.* Oxford, England: Oxford University Press.

LeCompte, M.D., & Goetz, J.P. (1982). Problems of Reliability and Validity in Ethnographic Research. *Review Of Educational Research, 52*(1), 31-60.

Leidelmeijer, K., & Kamp, L. van (2003). *Kwaliteit van de leefomgeving en leefbaarheid: Naar een begrippenkader en conceptuele inkadering.* Amsterdam, Netherlands: RIGO research en Advies.

Leeuw, T. de, & Swaaningen, R. van (2011). Veiligheid in veelvoud: Beeld, beleid en realiteit in Rotterdams Oude Westen. *Tijdschrift voor Veiligheid, 10*(1), 26-42.

Leys, M., Zaitch, D., & Decorte, T. (2010). De gevalstudie. In T. Decorte, & D. Zaitch (Eds.) *Kwalitatieve methoden en technieken in de criminologie.* Leuven, Belgium: Acco.

Lipsky, M. (2010). *Street level bureaucracy: Dilemmas of the individual in public services*. New York, NY: Russell Sage Foundation.

Loader, I. (2000). Plural policing and democratic governance. *Social and Legal studies, 9*(3), 323-345.

Loef, L., Schaafsma, K., & Hilhorst, N. (2012) *Aanspreken op straat. Het werk van de straatcoach in al zijn verschijningsvormen*. Apeldoorn/Amsterdam: Politie & Wetenschap/DSP-groep.

Lofland, L.H. (1973). *A world of strangers: Order and action in urban public space*. Prospect Heights, IL: Waveland Press.

Lub, V. (2013). *Schoon, heel en werkzaam?* Den Haag: Boom/Lemma.

Lyes, M. (2015). Jane Jacobs and Sharon Zuking: Gentrification and the Jacobs Legacy. In D. Schubert (Ed.) *Contemporary perspectives on Jane Jacobs: Reassessing the impacts of an urban visionary*. Farnham, England: Ashgate.

Maas-de Waal, C., & Wittebrood, K. (2002). Sociale cohesie, fysieke buurtkenmerken en onveiligheid in de grotere steden. In J. de Hart (Ed.) *Zekere banden: Sociale cohesie, leefbaarheid en veiligheid*. Den Haag, Netherlands: Sociaal en Cultureel Planbureau.

Macdonald, K.M. (1995). *The sociology of the professions*. London, England: Sage.

Macdonald, S. (2006). A suicidal woman, roaming pigs and a noisy trampolinist: Refining the ASBO's definition of 'Anti-social behaviour'. *Modern Law Review, 69*(2), 183-213.

MacLeod, G., & Johnstone, C. (2012). Stretching urban renaissance: Privatizing space, civilizing place, summoning 'community'. *International Journal of Urban and Regional Research, 36*(1), 1-28.

Maesschalck, J. (2010). Methodologische kwaliteit in het kwantitatief criminologisch onderzoek. In: T. Decorte, & D. Zaitch (Eds.) *Kwalitatieve methoden en technieken in de criminologie*. Leuven, Belgium: Acco.

Marshall, C., & Rosmann, G.B. (2006). *Designing qualitative research*. London: Sage.

Martineau, E.M. (2006). *'Too much tolerance': Hang-around youth, public space, and the problem of freedom in the Netherlands*. New York, NY: City University of New York.

Matthews, R. (1992). Replacing 'Broken windows': Crime, incivilities, and urban change. In R. Matthews, & J. Young (Eds.) *Issues in realist criminology*. London, England: Sage.

Mein, A.G., & Hartman, A.R. (2013). *De stand van het boa-bestel: Eindrapport over het stelsel waarbinnen buitengewoon opsporingsambtenaren functioneren*. Utrecht: Verwey-Jonker Instituut.

Millie, A. (2008). Anti-social behaviour, behavioural expectations and an urban aesthetic. *British Journal of Criminology, 48*(3), 379-394.

Ministry of Justice (1985). *Samenleving en Criminaliteit: een Beleidsplan voor de Komende Jaren*. Den Haag, Netherlands: Ministry of Justice.

Ministry of Justice (1990). *Recht in Beweging: een Beleidsplan voor Justitie in de Komende Jaren*. Den Haag, Netherlands: Ministry of Justice.

Ministry of Justice (1994). *Besluit buitengewoon opsporingsambtenaar*. Den Haag: Ministry of Justice.

Ministry of Justice (2015). *Beleidsregels Buitengewoon opsporingsambtenaar*. Den Haag: Staatscourant, nr. 33381.

Ministry of the Interior (1993). *Integrale veiligheidsrapportage*. Den Haag, Netherlands: Ministry of the Interior.

Ministry of the Interior (2008). *Actieplan Overlast en Verloedering: maatregelen ter intensivering van de lokale aanpak*. Den Haag, Netherlands: Ministry of the Interior.

Ministry of the Interior and Ministry of Justice (1996). *Uitgangpunten toezicht in de openbare ruimte*. Den Haag, Netherlands: Ministry of the Interior and Ministry of Justice (Brief van de ministers van BiZa en Justitie aan de Voorzitter van de Tweede Kamer der Staten-Generaal, 4 november 1996, kenmerk: 588772/596/GB).

Ministry of the Interior and Ministry of Justice (2002). *Naar een Veiliger Samenleving*. Den Haag: Ministry of the Interior and Ministry of Justice.

Misztal, B.A. (2001). Normality and Trust in Goffman's theory of interaction order. *Sociological Theory, 19*, 312-324.

Mitchell, D. (2003). *The right to the city: Social justice and the fight for public space*. New York, NY: Guilford Press.

Mitchell, D., & Staeheli, L.A. (2005). Clean and safe? Property redevelopment, public space, and homelessness in downtown San Diego. In S.M. Low, & N. Smith (Eds.) *The politics of public space*. London, England: Routledge.

Mooney, J., & Young, J. (2006). The decline in crime and the rise of anti-social behaviour. *Probation Journal*, *53*(4), 397-407.

Moors, H., & Bervoets, E. (2013). *Frontlijnwerkers in de veiligheidszorg*. Den Haag, Netherlands: Boom Lemma.

Mortelmans, D. (2010). Het kwalitatief onderzoeksdesign. In T. Decorte, & D. Zaitch (Eds.) *Kwalitatieve methoden en technieken in de criminologie*. Leuven, Belgium: Acco.

Mucciaroni, G. (1992). The Garbage Can Model & the Study of Policy Making: A Critique. *Polity, 24*(3), 459-482.

Muir, W.K. (1977). *Police: Streetcorner politicians*. Chicago, IL: University of Chicago Press.

Nap, J., & Os, P. van (2006). *Referentiekader gebiedsgebonden politie*. Apeldoorn: Politieacademie.

Newburn, T. (2001). The commodification of policing: security networks in the late modern city. *Urban studies, 38*(5-6), 829-848.

Newburn, T. (2007). *Criminology*. Cullompton: Willan.

Newburn, T., & Jones, T. (2007). Symbolizing crime control. *Theoretical Criminology, 11*(2): 221-143.

Newman, O. (1972). *Defensible space: Crime prevention through urban design*. New York, NY: MacMillan.

Noordegraaf, M. (2008). Meanings of measurement. *Public Management Review, 10*(2), 221-239.

Noordegraaf, M., & Geuijen, K. (2011). *Handboek publiek management*. Den Haag, Netherlands: Boom Lemma.

Onrust, S., & L. Voorham (2013). *Vier politiestrategieën tegen veel voorkomende criminaliteit: Effectiviteit en werkzame strategieën*. Den Haag, Netherlands: WODC.

O'Malley, P. (2010). *Crime and risk*. Los Angeles, CA: Sage.

Ostaaijen, J. van (2013). Afrekenen met de deelgemeenten: Het functioneren van binnengemeentelijke decentralisatie in Rotterdam en Antwerpen en een vergelijking met dorps- en wijkraden. *Bestuurswetenschappen, 5*, 94-114.

Paskell, C. (2007). 'Plastic police' or 'community support'?: the role of Police Community Support Officers within low-income neighborhoods. *European Urban and Regional Studies, 14*(4), 349-361.

Pleysier, S. (2008). 'Integrale veiligheid' als dogma? Grenzen aan het heersende veiligheidsdiscours. *Tijdschrift voor veiligheid, 7*(1), 34-46.

Polder, W., & Vlaardingen, F.J.C. (1992). *Preventiestrategieën in de praktijk: Een meta-evaluatie van criminaliteitspreventieprojecten*. Arnhem: Gouda Quint.

Pollitt, C. (1993). *Managerialism and the public services*. Oxford, England: Blackwell.

Projectgroep Organisatie Structuren (1978). *Politie in verandering: Een voorlopig theoretisch model*. Den Haag: Staatsuitgeverij.

Projectgroep Visie op de Politiefunctie (2005). *Politie in ontwikkeling*. Den Haag: NPI.

Punch, M. (2006). *Van 'alles mag' naar 'zero tolerance': Policy transfer en de Nederlandse politie*. Apeldoorn: Politie en Wetenschap.

Punch, M., Hoogenboom, B., & Williamson, T. (2005). Paradigm lost: the Dutch dilemma. *The Australian & New Zealand journal of criminology, 38*(2), 268-281.

Punch, M., Vijver, K. van der, & Zoomer, O. (2002). Dutch "COP". Developing community policing in The Netherlands. *Policing: An International Journal of Police Strategies and Management, 25*(1), 60-79.

Ranasinghe, P. (2012). Jane Jacobs' framing of public disorder and its relation to the 'broken windows' theory. *Theoretical Criminology, 16*(1), 63-84.

Reijndorp, A. (2004). *Stadswijk: Stedenbouw en dagelijks leven*. Rotterdam: NAi.

Reiner, R. (2010). *The politics of the police*. Oxford: Oxford University Press.

Rekenkamer Rotterdam (2012). *Horen, zien en schrijven: Optreden van stadswachten in de openbare ruimte*. Retrieved from https://rekenkamer.rotterdam.nl/onderzoeken/horen-zien-en-schrijven/.

Rekenkamercommissie Schiedam-Vlaardingen (2012). *Code Lichtblauw: OK*. Vlaardingen: Rekenkamercommissie Schiedam-Vlaardingen. Retrieved from https://www.dsp-groep.nl/wp-content/uploads/Handhaving-en-toezicht-in-Schiedam.pdf.

Rhodes, R.A.W. (1997). *Understanding governance: Policy networks, governance, reflexivity and accountability*. Buckingham, England: Open University Press.

Rhodes, R.A.W. (2006). Policy network analysis. In M. Moran, M. Rein, & R.E. Goodin (Eds.) *The Oxford handbook of public policy*. Oxford, England: Oxford University Press.

RMO (2004). *Sociale veiligheid organiseren: Naar herkenbaarheid in de publieke ruimte*. Den Haag: Sdu.

Rosenbaum, D.P. (2008). The limits of hot spots policing. In D. Weisburd, & A.A. Braga (Eds.) *Police innovations: Contrasting perspectives*. Cambridge, England: Cambridge University Press.

Rosenthal, U. (1996). *Openbaar bestuur: Beleid, organisatie en politiek*. Alphen aan den Rijn: Samsom H.D. Tjeenk Willink.

Roodzant, R., Oosterhout, A.H.C. van, & Bouwmeister, H.F.M. (1994). Buitengewoon opsporingsambtenaar in wording. *Algemeen Politieblad 23*, 12-14.

Sackers, H.J.B. (2010). De burgemeester als veiligheidsbaas. *Justitiële verkenningen, 36*(3), 86-98.

Sampson, R.J., & Raudenbush, S.W. (1999). Systematic social observation of public spaces: A new look at disorder in urban neighborhoods. *American Journal of Sociology, 105*(3), 603-651.

Sampson, R.J., Raudenbush, S.W., & Earls, F. (1997). Neighborhoods and violent crime: A multilevel study of collective efficacy. *Science, 277*(5328), 918-924.

Savage, S. (2007). *Police reform. Forces for change*. Oxford: Oxford University Press.

Schuilenburg, M.B. (2013). De criminaliteitsdaling in New York. Over de zin en onzin van veiligheidsbeleid. *Justitiële Verkenningen, 39*(8), 9-22.

Schuilenburg, M.B. (2016). Overheidsparticipatie in burgerprojecten. *Justitiële verkenningen, 42*(5), 11-26.

Seale, C. (1999). *The quality of qualitative research*. London: Sage Publications.

Sennett, R. (1971). *The uses of disorder: Personal identity and city life*. London, England: Lane the Penguin Press.

Silverman, D. (2011). *Interpreting qualitative data: A guide to the principles of qualitative research*. London, England: Sage.

Simester, A.P., & Von Hirsch, A. (2006). Regulating offensive conduct through two-step prohibitions. In A.P. Simester, & A. Von Hirsch (Eds.), *Incivilities: Regulating offensive behaviour*. Oxford, England: Hart.

Simons, H. (2009). *Case study research in practice*. Los Angeles: Sage.

Skogan, W.G. (1990). *Disorder and decline: Crime and the spiral of decay in American neighborhoods*. New York, NY: Free Press.

Skogan, W.G. (2006a). *Police and Community in Chicago: A tale of three cities*. Oxford, England: Oxford University Press.

Skogan, W.G. (2006b). The promise of community policing. In D. Weisburd, & A.A. Braga (Eds.) *Police innovations: Contrasting perspectives*. Cambridge, England: Cambridge University Press.

Sleiman, M., & Lippert, R. (2010). Downtown ambassadors, police relations and 'clean and safe' security. *Policing and Society, 20*(3), 316-335.

Sluis, A. van, Cachet, L., Jong, L. de, Nieuwenhuyzen, C., & Ringeling, A. (2006). *Cijfers en stakeholders: Prestatiesturing en de gevolgen voor de maatschappelijke en politiekbestuurlijke relaties van de politie*. Apeldoorn: Politie en Wetenschap.

Smith, N. (1996). *The new urban frontier: Gentrification and the revanchist city*. London, England: Routledge.

Smith, N. (2002). New globalism, new urbanism: Gentrification as global urban strategy. *Antipode, 34*(3), 427-450.

SMV (2013). *Burgers over politie en buitengewoon opsporingsambtenaren*. Den Haag: SMV.

Spithoven, R., Graaf, G. de, & Boutellier, H. (2012). Geen angst maar onbehagen: resultaten van een Q-studie naar subjectieve sociale onveiligheid. *Tijdschrift voor veiligheid, 11*(3), 38-56.

Spradley, J.P. (1980). *Participant Observation*. New York, NY: Holt, Rinehart and Winston.

Steden, R. van (2007). *Privatizing policing. Describing and explaining the growth of private security*. Den Haag, Netherlands: BJu legal.

Steden, R. van (2011). Sturing van lokale veiligheid: een achtergrondstudie. In R. van Steden (Ed.) *Strategieën van lokale veiligheid: Een achtergrondstudie en drie reflecties*. Den Haag: Nicis.

Steden, R. van (2012). *Veelvormig en versnipperd: gemeentelijk toezichthouders en handhavers in het publieke domein*. Amsterdam/Den Haag: Vrije Universiteit/SMVP.

Steden, R. van (2017). Municipal law enforcement officers: Towards a new system of local policing in the Netherlands? *Policing and society, 27*(1), 40-53.

Steden, R. van, & Roelofs, M. (2010). Hoeders van de hygiënische stad. *Beleid en maatschappij, 36*(3), 157-169.

Steden, R. van, & Groot, I. de (2011). *De praktijk van vliegende brigades*. Den Haag, Netherlands: Nicis.

Steden, R. van, & Bron, E. (2012). *Gemeentelijk handhavers in Amsterdam: Een onderzoek naar hun werk op straat.* Den Haag: Boom Lemma.

Stokkom, B. van (2005). Zero tolerance in de praktijk. *Justitiële Verkenningen, 31*(6), 44-59.

Stokkom, B. van (2007). Omstreden orde: Naar een gepolitiseerde lokale veiligheidszorg. In P. Ponsaers, & L. Gunther Moor (Eds.) *Reassurance policing: Concepten en receptie.* Brussel: Politeia.

Stokkom, B. van (2008). *Symbolen van orde en wanorde.* Apeldoorn: Politie & Wetenschap.

Stokkom, B. van (2010). Orde handhaven en vrede bewaren: Waarom de omvangrijkste politietaak weinig prestige heeft. In B. van Stokkom, J. Terpstra, & L. Gunther Moor (Eds.) *De politie en haar opdracht: De kerntakendiscussie voorbij.* Apeldoorn: Maklu.

Stokkom, B. van (2013a). Onveiligheid als stedelijkheidsfobie: Angst en onmacht in de hygiënische stad. *Tijdschrift over Cultuur & Criminaliteit, 3*(2), 137-154.

Stokkom, B. van (2013b). *Frontlijnwerk met potentie: Buurtveiligheidsteams in Amsterdam.* Den Haag: Boom Lemma.

Stokkom, B. van (2016). Overlastbestrijding in Amsterdam: Samenwerking bij handhaven in de openbare ruimte. In H. Boutellier, R. van Steden, & B. van Stokkom (Eds.) *Perspectieven op veiligheid: Van burgerschap tot veerkracht.* Amsterdam: Vrije Universiteit.

Stokkom, B. van, & Toenders, N. (2010). *De sociale cohesie voorbij: Actieve burgers in achterstandswijken.* Amsterdam: Pallas.

Stokkom, B. van, & Foekens, P. (2015). *Stadshandhavers: Bouwstenen voor de inrichting van handhaving in de openbare ruimte.* Den Haag: WODC.

Straver, M.A. (2006). Onveiligheid en de legitimiteit van de politie. In K. van der Vijver, & F. Vlek (Eds.) *De legitimiteit van de politie onder druk?* Apeldoorn: Politie & Wetenschap.

Straver, M.A. (2008). Van 'nothing works' naar 'innovation helps'; voortschrijdend inzicht uit de USA. *Tijdschrift voor de Politie, 70*(9), 12-16.

Swaaningen, R. van (1995). Sociale controle met een structureel tekort: Pleidooi voor een sociaal rechtvaardig veiligheidsbeleid. *Justitiële verkenningen, 21*(3), 63-87.

Swaaningen, R. van (2005). Public safety and the management of fear. *Theoretical criminology, 9*(3), 289-305.

Swanborn, P.G. (2010). *Case study research: What, why and how?* Los Angeles: Sage.

Taylor, R.B. (2001). *Breaking away from broken windows: Baltimore neighborhoods and the nationwide fight against crime, grime, fear, and decline.* Boulder, CO: Westview Press.

Taylor, R.B. (2006). Incivilities reduction policing, zero tolerance, and the retreat from coproduction: Weak foundations and strong pressures. In D. Weisburd, & A.A. Braga (Eds.) *Police innovations: Contrasting perspectives.* Cambridge, England: Cambridge University Press.

Terpstra, J. (2008a). New security patrols in public spaces: Reassurance, fragmentation, and marketization. In M. Easton, L. Gunther Moor, B. Hoogenboom, P. Ponsaers, & B. van Stokkom (Eds.) *Reflections on reassurance policing in the low countries.* Den Haag: Boom.

Terpstra, J. (2008b). *Wijkagenten en hun dagelijks werk.* Apeldoorn: Politie & Wetenschap.

Terpstra, J. (2009). *Very irritating policing*: Overlast, *zero tolerance* en wijkpolitie. In H. Boutellier, N. Boonstra, & M. Ham (Eds.) *Omstreden ruimte: Over de organisatie van spontaniteit en veiligheid.* Amsterdam: Van Gennep.

Terpstra (2010a). Community policing in practice: ambitions and realization. *Policing, 4*(1), 64-72.

Terpstra, J. (2010b). *Het veiligheidscomplex: Ontwikkelingen, strategieën en verantwoordelijkheden in de veiligheidszorg.* Den Haag: BJu.

Terpstra, J. (2010c). Inleiding. In W. Duijst, J. Terpstra, D. van Toor, & L. Gunther Moor (Eds.) *Aanpakken van overlast.* Dordrecht: SMVP.

Terpstra, J. (2012). Particuliere beveiligers als publieke handhavers: De inzet van private BOA's door gemeenten. *Justitiële Verkenningen, 38*(8), 35-50.

Terpstra, J. (2016). Tussen Heumensoord en Winschoten. Over de tegenstrijdige betekenis van burgerparticipatie in de veiligheidszorg. *Justitiële verkenningen, 42*(5), 80-88.

Terpstra, J., & Kouwenhoven, R. (2004). *Samenwerking en netwerken in de lokale veiligheidszorg.* Zeist: Kerckebosch.

Terpstra, J., & Havinga, T. (2005). Gemeenten, boetes en kleine ergernissen. *Justitiële Verkenningen, 31*(6), 10-22.

Terpstra, J., & Trommel, W. (2006). *Het nieuwe bedrijfsmatige denken bij de politie: Analyse van een culturele formatie in ontwikkeling.* Apeldoorn: Politie en Wetenschap.

Terpstra, J., Gunther Moor, L., & Stokkom, B. van (2010). De kerntakendiscussie in Nederland. Retoriek en realiteit. In B. van Stokkom, J. Terpstra, & L. Gunther Moor (Eds.) *De politie en haar opdracht: de kerntakendiscussie voorbij.* Apeldoorn: Maklu.

Terpstra, J., & Schaap, D. (2013). Police culture, stress conditions and working styles. *European Journal of Criminology, 10*(1), 59-73.

Terpstra, J., Van Stokkom, B., & Spreeuwers, R. (2013). *Who patrols the streets?* Den Haag: Eleven.

Terpstra, J., Foekens, P., & Stokkom, B. van (2015). *Burgemeesters over hun nationale politie.* Den Haag: Stichting Maatschappij en Veiligheid.

Terpstra, J., Duijneveldt, I. van, Eikenaar, T., Havinga, T., & Stokkom, B. van (2016). *Basisteams in de nationale politie: Organisatie, taakuitvoering en gebiedsgebonden werk.* Apeldoorn: Politie & Wetenschap.

Thumala, A., Goold, B., & Loader, I. (2011). A tainted trade? Moral ambivalence and legitimation work in the private security industry. *British Journal of Sociology, 62*(2), 283-303.

Tops, P.W. (2007). *Regimeverandering in Rotterdam.* Amsterdam: Atlas.

Uitermark, J., Duyvendak, J.W., & Kleinhans, R. (2007). Gentrification as governmental strategy: Social control and social cohesion in Hoogvliet, Rotterdam. *Environment and Planning, 39*, 125-141.

Uitermark, J., & Duyvendak, J.W. (2008). Civilizing the city: Populism and revanchist urbanism in Rotterdam. *Urban Studies, 45*(7), 1485-1503.

Versteegh, P., Plas, T. van der, & Nieuwstraten, H. (2011). *The best of three worlds. Effectiever politiewerk door een probleemgerichte aanpak van hot crimes, hot spots, hot shots en hot groups.* Apeldoorn: Politieacademie.

Vijver, K. van der (2004). Public safety and the role of the police: Some theoretical considerations. In K. van der Vijver, & J. Terpstra (Eds.) *Urban safety: Problems, governance and strategies.* Enschede: IPIT.

VROM (2004). *Leefbaarheid van wijken.* Den Haag: VROM.

Vuijsje, H. (1989). *Lof der dwang.* Amsterdam: Ambo.

Wacquant, L. (2008). *Urban outcasts: A comparative sociology of advanced marginality.* Cambridge: Polity.

Walby, K., & Lippert, R. (2011). Spatial regulation, dispersal, and the aesthetics of the city: Conservation officer policing of homeless people in Ottawa, Canada. *Antipode, 44*(3), 1015-1033.

Weisburd, D., & Braga, A.A. (2008). Hot spots policing as a model for police innovation. In D. Weisburd, & A.A. Braga (Eds.) *Police innovations: Contrasting perspectives.* Cambridge, England: Cambridge University Press.

Wijdeven, T.M.F. van de (2012). *Doe democratie: Over actief burgerschap in stadswijken.* Delft: Eburon.

Wilson, J.Q. (1969). The urban unease: Community vs city. In H.J. Schmandt, & W. Bloomberg (Eds.) *The quality of urban life.* Beverly Hills, CA: Sage.

Wilson, J.Q., & Kelling, G.L. (1982). Broken Windows: The police and neighborhood safety. *Atlantic Monthly, 249*(3), 29-36.

Wittebrood, K., & Nieuwbeerta, P. (2006). Een kwart eeuw stijging in geregistreerde criminaliteit. Vooral meer registratie, nauwelijks meer criminaliteit. *Tijdschrift voor criminologie, 48*(3), 227-242.

WRR (2003). *Waarden, normen en de last van het gedrag.* Amsterdam, Netherlands: Amsterdam University Press.

WRR (2005). *Vertrouwen in de buurt.* Amsterdam, Netherlands: Amsterdam University Press.

WRR (2012). *Vertrouwen in burgers.* Amsterdam: Amsterdam University Press.

Yin, R.K. (1984). *Case study research: Design and methods.* Beverly Hills, Calif.: Sage.

Young, J. (2003). Searching for a new criminology of everyday life: A review of 'The culture of control' by David Garland. *British journal of criminology, 3*, 228-242.

Zukin, S. (2010). *Naked city: The death and life of authentic urban places.* Oxford: Oxford University Press.

Appendix – Six city surveillance agencies

In addition to the similarities in policy goals and tasks described in chapter 5, the city surveillance agencies in this study can be distinguished by their own particular approaches. These differences are caused, for instance by the available human resources. In Tilburg and The Hague especially, a 'Melkert-heritage' brought along limitations as a relatively large number of officers in these agencies originally were part of work reintegration projects. In addition, various political preferences and differences in administrative culture have an impact on local disorder policy. Likewise, collaboration with the police (or the efforts to improve it) might be of influence on their orientation. Here each city surveillance agency is briefly characterised.[1]

Rotterdam's city surveillance agency has three sub units – Surveillance, Law Enforcement and Parking. The unit for Law Enforcement is the most relevant here. With about 370 employees spread over three geographical clusters and one sub team for flexible use of municipal officers, this is the prime responsible organisation for municipal surveillance in Rotterdam's public spaces.

The municipal officers in Rotterdam are part of a tradition of 'firmness' and ambitious public safety goals, but were reprimanded by their Audit Office. At the time of writing, this agency seemed caught between two tendencies. On the one hand, municipal officers were expected to focus on residents' annoyances and develop a more locally embedded form of neighbourhood surveillance through locally well-known municipal officers. On the other hand several 'central teams' clearly have a more repressive approach, such as environmental officers, 'intervention teams' (investigating the causes of residential disturbances), youth enforcement officers and a central team of bikers.

The Hague's city surveillance agency, called *Leefbaarheid en Toezicht* ('Quality of life and surveillance'), is spread over The Hague's eight boroughs. These teams contain between ten and twenty employees. In addition, these teams supply a total of

---

1. This characterisation is based on findings that were reported in 2014. By the time this study is published, these numbers and organisational circumstances will probably have been changed.

16 bikers to a central team for flexible use, for instance to patrol big events and special actions.

The Hague's city surveillance agency has been preoccupied with concerns about professionalisation and the relation with the police. Not only did policy plan *Handhaven op Haagse hoogte* lead to a stricter definition of tasks, it also paved the way for a thorough reorganisation of its employees by placing The Hague's municipal officers in police stations and under the command of police constables. Although there was not enough space to investigate the impact of these changes, another study has shown this mainly improved information sharing and did not lead to other priorities for municipal officers (Van Stokkom & Foekens, 2015).

At the time of writing, Utrecht's city surveillance agency (*Toezicht en Handhaving Openbare Ruimte 'Surveillance and Law enforcement Public Space'*) had just centralised its five geographical teams into a more central team with opportunities for flexible use of municipal officers. *THOR* employs about 150-160 officers.

In Utrecht no recalibrations or revisions of policy goals can be noted. On the contrary, Utrecht's city surveillance agency seems willing to fulfil new tasks that are sometimes reminiscent of police work, such as surveillance in areas with a high incidence of burglaries, a special 'firework team' or nightshifts in the area of the city centre. Nevertheless, not all employees welcome these changes as they impact on the capacity on other terrains[2], and some of them express doubts as to whether the present workforce can manage all these extra, heavier duties.

The city surveillance agency in Eindhoven (*Stadstoezicht*) has about seventy fte in personnel, divided over several teams – citizen participation, enforcement of fiscal laws, a team for CCTV and citizens' reports, a team 'action plans public safety', a team special tasks and a team 'complex surveillance'.

In Eindhoven municipal officers also have a considerable amount of public safety related tasks. Eindhoven's city surveillance agency derived notable priorities from Eindhoven's public safety agenda[3], for instance to inform entrepreneurs on how to prevent robberies, or for surveillance to prevent theft from cars, anti-social behaviour caused by street youth, or bicycle theft. Collaboration with the police is also given considerable attention. At the same time, Eindhoven's city surveillance agency aims at improving the relation with citizens reporting disorder through the establishment of a project for citizen participation.

---

2.   Something also noted by Bureau Berenschot (2013). In their evaluation of the investment in the Breedstraat area by Utrecht's city surveillance agency, they noted prevention, general surveillance, and a 'neighbourhood approach' in other areas of Utrecht were under pressure due to such new tasks.

3.   Gemeente Eindhoven (2009) *Beleidskader Integrale Veiligheid 2010-2013*.

Stadstoezicht Tilburg is divided over two large geographical teams, comprising a total of 54 employees. A relatively large portion of these are surveillance employees without additional powers. An additional seven employees man the CCTV post and six more work in the special *Task Force Tilburg Safer* in which police officers and municipal officers closely collaborate to tackle several priorities indicated by Tilburg's city council (cf. Eikenaar & Van Stokkom, 2014).

In Tilburg issues of professionalisation played a large role, due to *Stadstoezicht's* relatively large share of employees with a background of long-term unemployment. Revisionary plan *Stadstoezicht 3.0*, in part, was meant to tackle the issues that resulted from this past. Nevertheless, the municipality of Tilburg cherished high ambitions at the time of writing, for instance to allow Tilburg's municipal officers play a role in fighting youth crime and collaborate more with the police.[4] A special project that might serve as a prediction of such ambitious collaboration is the *Taskforce Tilburg Safer*, in which police officers and municipal officers jointly address five public safety priorities (cf. Eikenaar & Van Stokkom, 2014). The involvement of these officers in citizen participation was one of other designated objectives, together with more neighbourhood specific surveillance.[5]

Finally, Nijmegen's *Bureau Toezicht* ('Bureau for surveillance') consists of sixty employees, divided over three teams – the 'Neighbourhood team', the 'Centre team' and 'Street coach team'. Added to this are six employees for flexible use.

On the one hand, Nijmegen's municipal officers are 'integral officers' with an all-round task description and designated for 'holistic policing' (see chapters 6 and 7). According to many, they function as 'hosts' in public space, and less so as law enforcement officers. Special 'network officers' in the city centre are in accordance with this approach. On the other hand, several managers highlight the importance of rule enforcement, especially since some expect the mayor to give these officers more tasks in response to the withdrawal of the police. As a result a debate on the extent to which municipal officers can be expected to replace the police is clearly notable in Nijmegen.

---

4.   Gemeente Tilburg (2012) *Definitief afdelingsplan Afdeling Veiligheid en Wijken*, Gemeente Tilburg (2011) *Kadernota Veiligheid. Samen voor meer veiligheid.*
5.   Gemeente Tilburg (2012) *Collegeadvies Doorontwikkeling professionalisering Stadstoezicht.*